FOURTH EDITION

AN

ACTOR'S GUIDE

Your First Year in Hollywood

FOURTH EDITION

AN
ACTOR'S
GUIDE

Your First Year in Hollywood

MICHAEL SAINT NICHOLAS & LISA MULCAHY

Allworth Press books may be purchased in bulk at special discounts for sales promotion, corporate gifts, fund-raising, or educational purposes. Special editions can also be created to specifications. For details, contact the Special Sales Department, Allworth Press, 307 West 36th Street, 11th Floor, New York, NY 10018 or info@skyhorsepublishing.com.

15 14 13 12 11   5 4 3 2 1

Published by Allworth Press, an imprint of Skyhorse Publishing, Inc.
307 West 36th Street, 11th Floor, New York, NY 10018.

Allworth Press® is a registered trademark of Skyhorse Publishing, Inc.®, a Delaware corporation.

www.allworth.com

Cover and interior design by Mary Belibasakis

Library of Congress Cataloging-in-Publication Data is available on file.

Print ISBN: 978-1-62153-466-2
Ebook ISBN: 978-1-62153-468-6

Printed in the United States of America.

TABLE OF CONTENTS

AUTHORS' ACKNOWLEDGMENTS

From Michael:

In writing this book, I was fortunate to receive inspiration and assistance from many talented people. Many thanks to:

Max Alexander, Irene Andersen, Jay Bernstein, Veanne Cox, Bill Dance, Mike Fenton, Andreas Glas R.N., Brad Greenquist, Buzz Halliday, Earl Hamner, Michael Harris, Mariette Hartley, Michael Levine, Sheila Manning, Mark Measures, William McNamara, Eric Morris, Chris Nassif, Julian Neil, John Oliver, Linda Poindexter, Kirk Schroder, Craig Tapscott, Mark Teschner, and Jimmy Wlcek.

From Lisa:

Additional appreciation to:

Tad Crawford, Kris Hutchinson, Deanna Meske, William and Joan Mulcahy, David Muller, Garry Purdy, Kyle Walters, Ben Whitehair, Zoe Wright.

To Michael Saint Nicholas, whose voice and vision fills this book; it is an honor to update your excellent and detailed work.

AN OVERVIEW OF LOS ANGELES

As an actor, even if you have never visited Los Angeles, you probably have already heard a lot about it. Think for a moment. What images pop into your mind? Besides earthquakes and an occasional riot, you are probably conjuring pictures of Hollywood, studios, bright lights, and movie stars. And let's not forget limousines, palm trees, Beverly Hills mansions, and paparazzi. What about movie premieres, Rodeo Drive, Rolls Royces, and the Sunset Strip? Yes, these are all valid images that have come to symbolize one aspect of Los Angeles, also known as the City of Angels, or simply, La La Land.

You'd have to be a hermit to miss them. Every day people around the globe see, hear, and read about life in L.A. Just turn on the news. Chances are, at some point, you will be treated to a small slice of juicy Hollywood gossip. If you're tuned into a tabloid TV show, then you'll probably get a whopping portion! Open a magazine or newspaper. Somewhere inside lurks a tell-all report on your favorite celebrity or the latest rundown of a high-profile court case. Or go to the movies. There's a strong probability that those palm trees, that street corner, or that sandy beach can be found somewhere in Los Angeles.

So whether you realize it or not, you have had more exposure to L.A. than probably any other city in the world. However, it is important to realize that much of the imagery—the famous people, the beautiful scenery, the extravagant life-styles, the glamour—while truthful, has been sensationalized to some degree. You will find that, like any other big city, Los Angeles has its own unique personality with both enjoyable and aggravating qualities, and actually many down-to-earth characteristics.

Being an actor, you will quickly notice that the greatest aspect of Los Angeles is that it's the mega-metropolis for work in the arts. It is here that all the major studios and independent production companies are busy churning out thousands of feature films, television programs, commercials, and music videos in Hollywood and its surrounding areas every year. In addition, tremendous opportunities exist in theater and dance throughout the vicinity. There are hundreds of performing arts theatres in Southern California alone! And if that's not enough, you will find a significant presence of the art, music, and modeling industries as well. So grab your paintbrush, string that guitar, and head on down the catwalk! No other place has so much to offer actors, artists, musicians, and models. Hollywood is truly a magnet for artists of all kinds!

You ought to know that "Hollywood" refers to both a general vicinity (although there are no defined boundaries, and it technically doesn't exist) in Los Angeles and to the entertainment industry as a whole. Around 1910, the motion picture business was born in what is now considered Hollywood, and for many decades it served as the center for all show business-related activities. Hence, Hollywood became synonymous with show business. Today studios and entertainment firms can still be found in the Hollywood area, but many have expanded into neighboring areas. Nevertheless, the term "Hollywood" is still used, mostly by the media, to refer to the industry, which in reality often has little to do with Hollywood, the area.

Besides Hollywood, there are many other well-known regions that make up Los Angeles. Some of these include the cities of Beverly Hills, Malibu, Santa Monica, Burbank, Studio City, and Pasadena—to name a few. In all, there are eighty-eight incorporated cities and approximately 140 unincorporated areas linked by more than a dozen freeways within the five districts that comprise L.A. County! It really is an enormous place! And most of its nearly ten million inhabitants find it extremely helpful—almost a necessity—to have an automobile (more on this in chapter 3). This inevitably leads to frequent traffic congestion, which has tested the patience of many. Fortunately for actors, the entertainment industry is somewhat localized in Hollywood, West Hollywood, the Westside, and the Eastern San Fernando Valley, though these areas are still hardly within walking distance of one another.

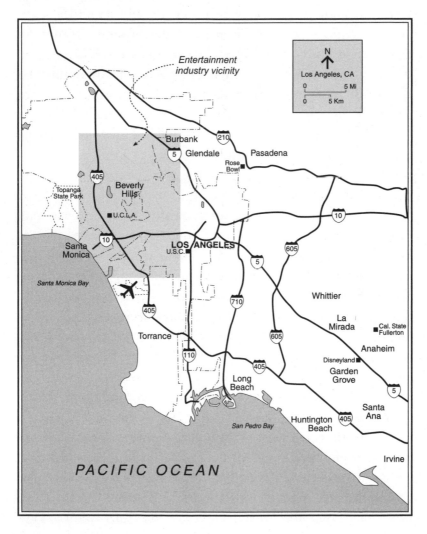

One interesting thing about Los Angeles is that it has many different telephone area codes, such as 213, 310, 323, 626, 818, and a few others! With the advent of fax machines, voice-mail, pagers, and especially cell phones, more telephone numbers were needed.

Undoubtedly, most would agree that one of the best features of Southern California, or the "Southland," is the superb weather. One can generally anticipate year-round comfortable temperatures. During summer, temperatures usually range between eighty and one hundred degrees, and the air is dry. During winter, temperatures drop to between fifty and seventy degrees. Thus, you will never have to shovel snow off of your driveway in Los Angeles. From late April through October, it virtually never rains, and only does so sporadically during the remainder of the year; so expect lots of California sunshine. The only time you might need your heavy-duty galoshes is from late December through March, when rainstorms historically can pummel the region. But be sure to bring your entire wardrobe anyway. You never know what you might need for an audition.

For many people, the usually incredible weather outweighs L.A.'s negative attributes, which include smog, crime, wild-fires, winter floods, and an occasional earthquake. Smog is a problem that has slowly been improving, though it still can be quite significant during the summer. Strict emissions regulations for automobiles were enacted in recent years, which have helped curb the problem; however, a majority of regions still succumb to moderate or poor air quality. One can literally see a brown cloud hovering in the sky from many locations. To avoid the smog, some seek out the coastal communities, which are bathed by cooler, cleaner ocean air year-round.

As in most major cities, another negative aspect of life in L.A. is crime. Back in the 1990s, car-jackings were on the rise, although they seem to have diminished significantly when such crimes became federal offenses and companies began selling increasingly popular tracking devices for automobiles. One simply has to use common sense when it comes to safety in L.A. for cars and all aspects of life (i.e., lock your doors, don't walk alone at night, be cautious of strangers). The same safety rules apply in L.A. as they would in any other major city.

While any large urban area can expect predictable problems, such as pollution and crime, no one can deny that in the past, L.A. had been hit harder with other difficulties than most cities. Terrible riots erupted in 1992, devastating floods and fires struck in 1993, a major earthquake shook in 1994, and even more floods rose in 1995. And of course, L.A. residents experience a few raging wildfires every couple of years in the mountainous areas.

On the positive side, these events tend to bring the people of Los Angeles together. They have shown that love, compassion, and a willingness to assist rests within the hearts of many. And despite these calamities, many Angelenos still count their blessings. Most are willing to cope with these disturbances in exchange for comfortable weather, close proximity to beaches, exciting city life, and, of course, show business.

In terms of human relations, Angelenos are perceived to have a more relaxed and liberal approach to life. In this transient town, acceptance and tolerance of others is more common than in other parts of the country, though it would be crazy to suggest that problems are nonexistent. Here you will find people from every imaginable background pursuing their own unique lifestyles. Nothing is too unusual for L.A.

This melting pot of many different people, including considerable Hispanic, Asian, and African-American populations, as well as many other subgroups, makes for a unique cultural and culinary experience that cannot be duplicated in many other cities. Here I bet you will find more Thai restaurants than McDonald's. Additionally, there is no shortage of Mexican, Japanese, Chinese, Indian, or American cuisine. Whatever your palette desires, the people of L.A. will provide.

Another nice quality of the residents, specifically the actors, is that many are big dreamers. They easily could have pursued careers in their hometowns or in smaller cities, but chose L.A. because they are dreamers. They are a particular breed of people, filled with optimism, spontaneity, and an ability to imagine greatness. They have somehow come to believe that in Los Angeles just about anything is possible. And they're right. If there is one truth about Los Angeles beyond all the hype and the hoopla, it is that anything and everything can happen, and does all the time.

But beware: Big dreamers also tend to have big egos. It has been said that some people in L.A. are plastic, superficial, and narcissistic. This, of course, can be said about people anywhere. But in Hollywood, the quest for fame and fortune can sometimes overtake the individual. For some, the car they drive or the clothes they wear become more important than the people in their lives and life itself! And while there's nothing wrong with driving a fancy car or wearing nice clothes, just be sure that your focus on "making it big" doesn't leave you dazed and confused about what really counts in life.

When you do make a ton of money, and hopefully are still a balanced person, there will be plenty of ways to spend it. By taking a drive around town, you'll notice that a tremendous amount of money is made in the entertainment industry not only by performers, but by agents, directors, writers, and producers as well. Go for a ride in Beverly Hills and Bel-Air. You'll see a multitude of luxury automobiles and elegant homes throughout. The same is true for the Hollywood Hills, Brentwood, Pasadena, and Malibu. Next, take a stroll down Rodeo Drive. All of the top fashion designers have storefronts with clothing and jewelry worth more than most people's cars. For trendier shopping, head on over to Melrose Avenue. You'll find a hipper crowd and a more eclectic environment. Finally, steer over to Malibu to see sprawling oceanview estates. You will realize that there is a large pie out there, and a piece of it may as well be yours.

To every newcomer, Los Angeles can seem like an intimidating place. It is easy to get lost in such a large and diverse city, not only physically but emotionally, so it will be important to get your feet on solid ground. Unfortunately, many people come to this town with unrealistic plans. They have little money saved, no understanding of how to proceed, and no strategy to survive. Desperation often follows when stardom doesn't happen in a few weeks or months. Many leave disappointed and feeling like a failure, others repeatedly call on friends and relatives to finance their venture, and still others join a small homeless population, sometimes standing at intersections begging for money. You don't want to do any of those things.

The following chapters will show you the best way to start an acting career in Los Angeles. They will show you how the business works and help you to develop a strategy that will allow you to play the game successfully.

For additional information on L.A.: The L.A. Chamber of Commerce (213-580-7500 or *www.lachamber.org*) sells relocation packages. Included are maps, a renter's guide, an apartment and home buyer's guide, job information, and a community choice book with information on schools, shopping, weather, and cost-of-living.

In addition to the L.A. Chamber of Commerce's vast resource of information, here are some more great websites that can answer virtually any question you can come up with about the basic mechanics of Los Angeles life:

Los Angeles County Government Website
www.lacounty.gov
This official government site provides vital details on everything from Los Angeles geography, to the way business is practiced in the city, to arts and recreation specifics, to social services, to the municipal transportation system—and that's just scratching the surface.

Los Angeles Almanac
www.laalmanac.com
A treasure trove of maps, crime stats, health essentials, and important info about environmental concerns like local

weather and earthquake preparedness. This site is also packed with fun facts and trivia, like its "Mysterious L.A." section. Here's the place to get the real skinny on the Curse of Griffith Park, Los Angeles Bigfoot sightings, and whether vampires really haunt Hollywood streets at night!

Los Angeles Tourist Info
www.latourist.com
OK, you're definitely not a tourist, but as an L.A newbie, you'll still appreciate the detailed info this site can provide you. Everything you need to know about hotels, attractions, shopping, and local bargains.

Los Angeles City Info
www.lacity.org
The city's well-organized municipal info site, featuring vital alerts and messages from the mayor, complete city calendars, and site-specific neighborhood resources.

Los Angeles Community Info
www.libertyhill.org
This terrific community service site can really help you get a true feel for L.A. culture and its most crucial issues. Focusing on "L.A. without the glitter," the Liberty Hill organization drives community leadership on issues such as the environment, LGBTQ equality, and poverty and economic justice. Important and illuminating!

A BASIC UNDERSTANDING OF HOW ACTORS GET WORK

Before you embark on an acting career in the entertainment industry, you first need to learn the nuts and bolts of the business.

This will help you in developing your strategy for survival, by giving you a concise understanding of what to anticipate along the way. There is much information to take in, but for now, a brief summary follows with more detailed information to come later in the book.

Most new actors arrive in Hollywood with little knowledge of how the system operates. They expect that getting cast on a show or movie will be as easy as it was in high school or college, where a handful of people showed up for open auditions, and one of them got the part on the spot. Others buy into the great myth that people are simply "discovered" off the street and made into mega-stars overnight. To these people, I lovingly say, "Wake up!" While stories of instant and seemingly easy stardom from Hollywood's early days have been told many times, it is extremely rare and unrealistic in today's world. Hollywood does not hire actors or create stars that way. Most successful actors in Hollywood have worked long and hard for years trying to establish themselves. Generally, they have followed certain steps and have understood how the game is played.

Aside from having friends and relatives who will hire you, which, by the way, happens frequently, as a new actor in town you will typically have to follow a standard cycle to gain professional, or paid, employment.

It All Starts with You, the Actor

Before you get the ball rolling, you'll need to examine your skills, talents, background, and credits. As with any profession you are seeking to enter, it helps to have experience and/or training. Maybe you've got experience from high school, community theatre, or college. Maybe you've been in a commercial in your hometown, you've won a beauty pageant, or you've been a model or dancer. Anything related to the field of acting or entertainment will help you.

If you have no credits, it will be a good idea to start with some training right away. This will not only help you develop your craft, but also show you are serious about it. It's true, some of today's stars haven't had one acting lesson in their lives, but the vast majority have. Even working actors study regularly. Therefore, consider studying regardless of your background.

Once you've determined you have some talent, and hopefully some experience, then it's time for professional assistance.

You'll Need an Agent or Manager

While it will be extremely important to pursue acting jobs on your own, you will need to have an agent or manager representing you if you want to have a professional acting career. I can't stress how important this is if you want to be taken seriously in Hollywood.

An agent acts on your behalf to arrange auditions and interviews with casting directors, and he or she then negotiates your contracts when you are hired. Agents do not actually get you the job; you have to do that with your talent. Some actors forget this. Powerful and respected agents can be persuasive and in some instances help to obtain work for their clients, but you realistically can't count on their influence alone, especially if you are a newcomer.

Regardless of how established you are, the standard agent fee is 10 percent of the money you earn from your acting work—a modest fee for all the work they do. Agents and ways to obtain them will be discussed in greater detail in chapter 10.

Managers assist in career planning, development, and strategy. They complement the efforts of an agent by arranging additional auditions and meetings with casting directors and producers. They are typically hired by established actors. However, some newcomers have had luck in securing a manager who believed in them when agents would not. Managers usually take 15 percent of your paycheck, sometimes even 20 percent.

In order to hook up with a legitimate agent or manager, you typically have to be a member of the Screen Actors Guild/American Federation of Television and Radio Artists—more commonly known as SAG-AFTRA. This formidable union, representing the interests of film, TV, and radio performers, were originally two unions founded back in the 1930s—they merged in recent years in order to provide even better services for actors in terms of negotiating wages, enforcing employment contracts, and ensuring proper working conditions, benefits, and professional protection. There are some agents and managers who take non-SAG clients, but the majority won't. If you are seriously considering a professional acting career, then you will need to become a member, since most paying jobs in this town are union. Unfortunately, getting into SAG is a little tricky. You can't just show up and slap down your initiation fee. You have to become eligible, and to do so is a Catch-22. To qualify, you must work a union job and be paid union wages; however, you are not supposed to work union jobs unless you already are in the union. It's seems rather crazy, but there are ways to sneak in, and they will be discussed later in the book in chapter 6.

Off to Auditions!

After securing representation with an agent or manager, hopefully he or she will be arranging auditions for you on a regular basis, as you continue to pursue auditions yourself. Some weeks you may have five or more auditions; others you may have none. It varies a lot.

Auditions can take place at any time during the day, though usually they transpire during business hours. They can be located anywhere in L.A, but typically they happen somewhere in Hollywood, the Westside, or the Valley. Usually you'll get a day's notice to prepare for an audition, but on occasion your agent will call and ask you to be ready in just a couple of hours. Therefore, you'll need tremendous flexibility in your schedule. (This is why so many actors historically have worked as waiters late at night.)

The Casting Director

Once you've driven across town to your audition, maintaining balance and composure amidst the traffic and heat of L.A., you'll swiftly go inside and wait to be seen by the casting director. Newcomers have all kinds of scary images of casting directors, but in reality, they are surprisingly normal people who are hired by producers to cast, or assemble, a particular project. Their job is to find the best actors for all the roles in the production (though the lead roles are usually pre-cast from lists). To accomplish this task, they do one of two things: They call on a pool of actors whom they already know, or, if they have time, they submit their casting needs to the Breakdown Services to get submissions from agents. The Breakdown Services are a daily rundown of what is currently being cast for television, films, commercials, and Equity theatre. Only agents and personal managers can receive the full list. (Currently, actors can go online at www.BreakdownServices.com and get a subscription; however, the listings are typically a very limited version of the entire list of opportunities available.) Everyday, the breakdowns are delivered via fax or email to agents, who in return submit headshots and videotapes, when available, of suitable actors for consideration.

The audition process is an art in itself, one that you will continually practice and improve upon. While many actors, given a few weeks, can deliver a superb reading of a script, fewer can do the same when given only twenty-four hours' notice. Therefore, ways to develop a more clear and confident approach to the audition process will be explained in great detail in chapter 13.

Once a casting director has auditioned a group of actors— anywhere from twenty-five to a hundred people, or up to a thousand or more for larger roles in movies—he or she selects the most appropriate and has them come back to read for further evaluation. This situation is termed a "callback." Most times a handful of actors are called back; other times ten or fifteen might be called back. Regardless, they all return and eventually meet the director and/or ad agency executives if it's for a commercial.

The Director

The director has the job of artistically navigating and conducting the course of the movie, television program, or commercial being made. Directors are considered the men or women with the "vision" for the project. They take a script and turn it into real life, taking responsibility for every shot in the final product. Through thousands of creative choices, they bring their own particular flavor and mark to the film. Once the casting process has reached its final stages, they have a strong influence as to who will be hired, especially if the project is a film.

The Producers

Producers are the people who manage the entire project from start to finish—creatively, logistically, and financially. There are many producers on any given project, with each having specifically defined responsibilities, some major and some minor. Of all the producers, executive producers have the most clout because they often have a significant financial interest in the project, representing a studio, network, or their own independent production company. They ultimately hire everyone—actors as well as the director—and usually have the power to make the final decision on everything, especially in television projects.

Getting the Part

Because you are talented, intelligent, charming, and confident, you will hopefully book a job soon. Some actors "get the part" on their first audition in Hollywood; others go to fifty or one hundred auditions before they finally land something. The key is persistence. Generally, as a new actor, you are doing extremely well if you book one out of every ten auditions you attend. Therefore, be prepared. Such odds make it a very challenging process.

Also, depending on the role, you might be called back several times before finally securing it. This can be very grueling, especially if the part ultimately goes to someone else. But you will know you are on the right track if you are consistently being called back on your auditions.

With each job you land, you try to build on that success and become more and more well-known. As this happens, it will become easier to gain entry into casting directors' offices for auditions. They will have seen your work and won't have to be persuaded to meet with you. Some directors or producers may also specifically request you for parts. This process of establishing yourself usually is a lengthy one though, and it may span many years. But don't be discouraged. Some young actors have made great strides during their first year by landing just one impressive role.

Other Ways In

You've just read the conventional way actors obtain work and you might be thinking that there has to be an easier way. A back-door entrance. A way to sneak in and avoid the system. Well, there is. Sort of. While you continue to pursue an acting career by auditioning, which is absolutely essential, there are several ways to increase your chances of success.

Over the years many actors have attracted the attention of agents and casting directors in a variety of unconventional ways, successfully and unsuccessfully. Some have placed ads for work in the trade papers or painted their cars as billboards; others have pretended to be agents or managers and submitted themselves for parts. A few actors have even posed as messengers and driven through security gates of the major studios undetected to make late-night deliveries of their own headshots to the offices of casting directors. Many more have schmoozed their way into the Hollywood elite, attending party after party, networking a chain of high-powered acquaintances.

I can't say that all of these unconventional methods are positively proven to be effective, but schmoozing and networking do seem to have a high success rate in terms of helping to land work. This is based on the simple truth that people tend to hire people they know and like, as opposed to strangers they don't know and might not like. People simply want to help and work with their friends. Therefore, the more of a friend you are to people in the industry, the greater your chances of success. But remember, I said "friend," not a "I'm just being nice to you so that you'll help my career" kind of person. People can spot those types a mile away.

Some actors today are taking the bull by the horns by selling themselves on film directly to casting directors (or in some cases, sending unsolicited video directly to a director or producer). This practice is known as "self-submission"—and interestingly, a growing number of casting directors actually prefer to evaluate actors through this method. Here are the basics: an actor puts him/herself on film, reading from sides of a film script they've been provided with, or in some cases doing a self-selected scene that they feel shows off their acting skills in a most favorable and more generalized way.

The great thing about a self-submission? You call all the shots—from the way you choose to interpret a character to the way you physically look on film. The tough thing about a self-submission? If you aren't exactly what the casting director or film entity is looking for, you'll be instantly dismissed, without an in-person chance to show you can make adjustments and take direction. Also, if the quality of your film is not great, it could reflect poorly on your true physical appearance (we've all taken atrocious photos, haven't we?), and you'll be misrepresenting yourself, without meaning to.

Still, you may be asked to do a self-submission, or you may feel very strongly that making one yourself will indeed prove you're perfect for a certain role. (This definitely can work—Hilary Swank was actually cast in her Oscar-winning role in the film *Boys Don't Cry* through a video submission to director Kimberley Pierce, FYI.) If so, keep your submission simple—use subtle indoor lighting, stand or sit against a blank background, and wear a flattering, contrasting color to that background. Ask a talented actor friend to do an off-camera read for you so your dialogue work really pops. You can also hire a professional to plan and film your self-submission from start to finish—these services are starting to appear on a pretty regular basis all over L.A., and can usually accomplish the whole thing for under a hundred bucks. However you choose to proceed, play to your strengths as a performer—it will give you the confidence you need to ace the job. (More on self-submissions in Chapter 13.)

Another wise way to get your foot in the door is by utilizing a good casting/employment website. We'll also go into further depth on the usefulness of these resources in Chapter 13, but to get you thinking, check out a few of these very solid options for job seekers:

Central Casting
www.centralcasting.com—Since 1925, the background performer's ace-in-the-hole when it comes to finding work that pays well.

Backstage
www.backstagewest.com
The show biz bible provides excellent job listings for actors of all experience levels.

The California Film Commission
www.film-ca.gov
This government resource lays out the ways the film business operates in the state of California in meticulous detail, and offers links to many good employment sites for actors, crew, and additional film professionals.

As for digital/professional resources? Social media's become a complete game changer, of course. Getting the word out with a tweet about your latest project might reach a very influential follower if you're savvy; networking with Facebook friends can put you in the know about that role nearly nobody knows about yet. Chapter 12 is devoted completely to selling yourself the right way in today's digital age, including ways you can utilize digital professional services if that route is right for you.

STARTING YOUR LIFE IN L.A.

Because Los Angeles is such a gigantic city, finding a place to call "home" can at first seem overwhelming, especially if you don't already have friends or relatives somewhere in town. There are literally hundreds of areas from which to choose, which makes throwing a dart at a map seem like an attractive solution! But don't get frustrated. Being an actor, you probably will want to live somewhere near the action of the entertainment industry. Though it's not essential, it's nice to be around other actors and industry players on a daily basis to keep your interest piqued and focused, and your desire alive. Therefore, this chapter aims to show you where the entertainment industry is located and why you might want to live within its domain. It also covers the basics of renting a space, and discusses the benefits and drawbacks of owning a car in L.A.

Where is the Entertainment Industry Located?

It's actually difficult to pinpoint exactly where the boundaries of the entertainment industry are. In the old days, Hollywood would have been the decisive answer. But with expansion of the industry, there are actually several major regions where actors and other industry people can be found buzzing around town.

There are basically three areas where the vast majority of studios, talent agencies, and casting directors are located: (1) Hollywood/West Hollywood; (2) the Westside, which includes Beverly Hills, Century City, Westwood, West L.A.,

Brentwood, Santa Monica, Culver City, Venice, and Marina del Rey; and (3) the East San Fernando Valley, specifically Burbank, Toluca Lake, Universal City, Studio City, Sherman Oaks, North Hollywood, and Van Nuys. While the Valley is clearly defined, the Westside merges with Hollywood and West Hollywood. For the sake of simplicity, I've tried to separate all locations into three basic regions, but understand that the boundaries are not and cannot be precisely defined.

The San Fernando Valley (more commonly known as "The Valley"—remember the '80s movie and song *Valley Girl*?) is separated from Hollywood and the Westside by the Santa Monica Mountains, which are commonly referred to as the Hollywood Hills, or simply the Hills. This mountainous region is speckled with beautiful homes in many sprawling canyons, including Beachwood Canyon, Laurel Canyon, Coldwater Canyon, Nichols Canyon, Benedict Canyon, and Topanga Canyon, to name a few. If you have the money, contact a broker and purchase your palace in one of these canyons; otherwise, plan to move into one of the other more economically feasible regions for now.

All of the regions have their own unique ambience, some more enticing than others. You ought to drive through each to determine which best suits your lifestyle. Once you find an area you like, be sure to check it out at night too, as some neighborhoods change for the worse at sundown. Also, be aware that even individual neighborhoods vary a lot from street to street. Often, a seemingly safe block can border an undesirable one. So make a thorough investigation into locating the safest, nicest, and most affordable housing available to you. A brief description of each of the regions follows.

Hollywood/West Hollywood

Mann's Chinese Theatre! The Hollywood Bowl! The Walk of Fame! Yes, Hollywood is indeed filled with all of these famous landmarks and more, not to mention multitudes of tourists. You've seen or heard about these famous structures often in the media, but rarely do you hear about the real Hollywood. Beyond its glamorous image, Hollywood has more commonly come to be associated with crime, drugs, prostitution, and transients. It's also known for some of the more eccentric types you'll find walking the streets in L.A. If you take a drive down Hollywood Boulevard, you could see a real-life cast of unusual characters. Hence, some have nicknamed it "Hollyweird."

For a real good peek at Hollywood, seek out the '90s movie *Jimmy Hollywood*, starring Joe Pesci and Christian Slater. It wasn't a box-office hit, and it's a little old school, but it gives a real good glimpse into life in Hollywood—the actual place—as much of it was filmed within its confines.

Despite its negative aspects, you will still find many talent agencies, theatres, acting schools, and nightclubs, along with myriad tourist attractions in Hollywood. There is a definite urban feel, though it's still a far stretch from New York City. Probably the best aspect is that the rent is lower on average than in most other locations. Because of it, Hollywood's countless apartments have become home for many, many actors. Studios in the area include Paramount, Sunset-Gower, CBS, and Prospect.

West Hollywood is filled with many popular nightclubs and fine restaurants, and has a trendy and hip feel to it. It's where the actual "Melrose Place" is located (though it's just a tiny street), with many unique clothing stores and artsy hang-outs dispersed along Melrose Avenue. There are also many fine bookstores and antique shops, in addition to the Beverly Center, a huge shopping mall on the corner of Beverly and La Cienega (See-EH-neh-ga). Many entertainment industry people, including casting directors, agents, and public relations folks, have offices scattered throughout the vicinity. There are also many theaters, and, of course, many actors to be found. In addition, West Hollywood is known for its gay community.

The Westside

The Westside has an air of wealth, activity, and sophistication. Many of its residents feel that it's the only place in L.A. where "life" happens. Heavily penetrated by the entertainment industry, it's a popular place for actors of all levels. Cities in the Westside include:

Beverly Hills. You'll find Beverly Hills to be one of the nicer areas in Los Angeles. In addition to the rich and famous, many top talent agencies and production companies have established themselves here. Tall office buildings and elegant hotels line Wilshire Boulevard, and just north lie the elegant shops of world-renowned Rodeo Drive. You won't have to look hard to see famous designers' boutiques, Rolls Royces, and even celebrities along Rodeo Drive and its surrounding streets. North of Santa Monica Boulevard are mostly elegant and quiet neighborhoods occupied by many people who have been successful at one time or another in the entertainment industry. Most new actors have a hard time finding affordable apartments in Beverly Hills, though plenty of apartments exist (mostly south of Santa Monica and especially Wilshire Boulevard). As a result, many more established actors and industry players dominate the scene in this posh community.

Century City. West of Beverly Hills, Century City essentially has an urban atmosphere because of a collection of some of the tallest buildings in L.A. (besides downtown L.A.). Located between Century Park East and Century Park West, they are home to a wide range of professional businesses, including numerous production companies and some leading talent agencies. Directly south, you'll find 20th Century Fox studios. Below Fox and to the West, you will find upscale apartments, condos, and houses. Lots of established actors live around here, too.

Westwood. Both a strong "city" ambience and a cozier collegiate atmosphere blend together in Westwood. A long string of luxury high-rise apartments line Wilshire Boulevard in this part of town, with the UCLA campus resting just north. In Westwood Village, you'll find many movie theaters, popular restaurants, and several square blocks of shopping. Obviously, a lot of UCLA students live in the area in many of the apartments, but you'll also find a fairly wealthy mix of retired and industry people living in condos, and, farther north, in the expensive homes of Bel-Air.

West L.A. You'll find a combination of old and new apartment buildings interspersed with businesses, warehouses, and a few high-rises. Bisected by the 405 Freeway, also known as the San Diego Freeway, it's a busy area with both urban stretches and others dominated by single-family homes. Many find its greatest asset to be its close proximity to the beaches, freeways, and the entertainment industry. A wide variety of professional people live in this area, along with many actors.

Brentwood. This classy neighborhood, made famous by O. J. Simpson back in the mid-1990s, is home to many celebrities as well as many lesser-known working actors. Located just west of the San Diego Freeway, it's lined with many upscale and trendy restaurants, fine shops, and elegant homes. The southern portion, between San Vicente and Wilshire, is filled with hundreds of higher-end apartments. Though not heavily dominated by entertainment companies, it's within close proximity to all the action, and therefore many actors live throughout the area.

Santa Monica. This beach community has an inviting, friendly atmosphere. Elegant hotels and condominiums line much of Ocean Avenue, which overlooks the Pacific Ocean, and many comfortable, yet expensive, homes lie nearby. Two of its most notable attractions are the Santa Monica Pier and the Third Street Promenade, a lengthy outdoor mall that attracts many talented street performers. You'll also find many, many restaurants and bars here. It's a great place for entertainment and becomes crowded on the weekends.

There are many nice apartment buildings in and around Santa Monica. Being a rent-control district, one would think great apartments could be acquired for cheap, cheap, cheap! Unfortunately, that's not the case. Overall, you can expect to pay higher than average rent. (You might be able to find a steal once in awhile, but such an apartment is usually on the lower end in terms of quality and location.) Even though it's a little out of the way from the heart of the entertainment industry, many actors prefer the area because of the cooler temperatures, the cleaner air, and the beach.

Culver City. A tremendous array of people, including actors, live together in Culver City, ethnically, spiritually, and economically. You'll find upscale neighborhoods, juxtaposed with average surroundings, and even seedier ones. It's really a tossed salad, but overall the rents are more affordable than in other places. Much work in the entertainment industry transpires here, with Sony Pictures and Culver Studios in the neighborhood.

Venice. A quaint and unusual beach community, it has attracted many actors and artists of all kinds. Densely packed, here you will find a wide range of residents, tourists, street performers, eccentrics, body builders, and rollerbladers on any given day strolling the boardwalk. In past years, several incidents of gang violence and crime have tarnished its image. But for the most part, it still flourishes with a diversified group of mostly artistic people, even though few entertainment firms are situated in the area. In terms of housing, you will find numerous apartment buildings, and, closer to the beach, a concentrated mix of houses, duplexes, and small apartments. Some of them are amazing!

Marina del Rey. Home of the Marina City Towers, a series of luxury high-rise condos built by Howard Hughes that surround L.A.'s largest marina, Marina del Rey is another wealthy part of L.A. You'll find plenty of expensive restaurants and popular nightclubs in this well-kept community. Many of the residents are retired or currently involved in the entertainment industry. You can be sure that most apartments or condos are fairly expensive here.

The San Fernando Valley
As a whole, the Valley is more of a family community and calmer than the Westside. However, it's certainly not dead;

parts of it are still bustling with activity. Ventura Boulevard, which runs the southern length of the Valley (about seventeen miles), is lined with hundreds of great restaurants, eclectic shops, bookstores, clothing outlets, and just about everything imaginable. The rest of the Valley is composed of thousands of apartment buildings, single-family dwellings, small office buildings, and shopping strips. High-rises are virtually non-existent, except for a few lining nearby Ventura Boulevard. There are many places within the Valley in which actors choose to live, but the most popular ones are listed in detail below.

Burbank. Many of the major entertainment firms (Disney, Warner Bros., NBC, and other smaller ones) can be found in Burbank. Surprisingly, it maintains a suburban feel. A fresh and clean place, it has both many single-family dwellings and apartment complexes. Besides the studios, its other major attraction is the Media Center, a large shopping mall just east of the Golden State Freeway, also known as the "5 Freeway." Burbank is filled with many people who work in the entertainment industry in varying capacities.

Toluca Lake/Universal City/Studio City/Sherman Oaks. Another mecca for industry people, this region contains many affordable apartment buildings and homes. In the hills south of Ventura Boulevard, more expensive houses and estates are tucked away. Overall, there is a cozy and charming ambience combined with fairly safe neighborhoods. Many entertainment people live here because it is close to studios and has easy freeway access. You'll find many smaller talent agencies and several important casting offices located here as well.

The major attraction is Universal Studios, which is both an actual studio lot where movies and television programs are taped, and a theme park that attracts thousands of tourists every year. For nighttime entertainment, many flock to Universal City Walk, which offers great restaurants, unique shops, and an enormous movie theatre complex, in a safe, sanitized, and extremely colorful environment.

North Hollywood. Lying just north of Studio City, it is home to many actors because of its very affordable rents. The southern part, which borders Studio City, is the nicest. The farther north you go, the more rundown it gets. In recent years an effort has been made to upgrade it and make it a friendlier place for artists and actors, and it is starting to look better. Its best quality is its close proximity to the major studios, agents, and casting offices in the Valley.

Van Nuys. Many single-family homes and apartment buildings make up this rather plain, and sometimes poor-looking area. Located in the middle of the Valley, Van Nuys is sought out by some because of its economical housing. Not much happens in this part of town with regard to the industry, so you'll find all professions of people living here. However, it's close to both the San Diego Freeway (405) and the Hollywood Freeway (101), which means it's not too far from all the action.

Renting an Apartment or House

Now that you are familiar with the areas often sought out by actors, you'll need to know what to expect when you try renting an apartment or house. Many of the questions newcomers frequently contemplate will be answered on the following pages.

Is it Hard to Find an Apartment in L.A.? No. In fact, most buildings have vacancies. People from New York City find this difficult to comprehend, since securing an apartment in the Big Apple can be a major undertaking. So don't worry! A buyer's market definitely exists. You literally will have tons of apartments to choose from. Even with the 6.8 earthquake in January 1994, when thousands of people were displaced and had to find temporary residences, there was still an abundance of vacant units.

What about Finding a House? You may have to search harder if you are on a budget and want to live in a house. Most houses—with two bedrooms and one bath, for example—start at about $1850 a month and can easily be $2000 or more. In the Hollywood Hills or Malibu where the houses are usually larger, you could easily pay $4,000 to over $10,000 a month! Needless to say, most new actors in Hollywood can't afford that.

Where Should I Stay Before I Am Able to Rent a Place? You've got several options. By far, the best thing you can do is stay with friends or relatives, if possible. Of course this will not apply to everyone; so if this isn't you, then skip this paragraph. If this is you, then it can be an ideal situation because you have someone to show you around town and hopefully direct you to specific buildings or homes in his or her neighborhood.

Another option is to stay at a hotel. Many offer special rates if you stay from a week to a month. Several apartment complexes, specifically "Oakwood" in Sherman Oaks, offer affordable monthly rentals in addition to long-term leases. Such places can be extremely beneficial, as it may take you more than a week to determine exactly where you want to live.

To find a hotel before you arrive, you should obtain a copy of the *L.A. Times* Sunday Edition from a major news-stand in your city or at your closest airport. If you cannot find a copy of the *L.A. Times* anywhere, then order a copy directly from them (1-800-LA-TIMES) or check out their Web site at *www.LAtimes.com*. Inside the Classifieds, you'll find the Residential Rentals section where several hotels usu-ally advertise. You should make a few calls to inquire about rates. Also, you can check with any major hotel in your home-town. They'll have a catalog listing all of their affiliated hotels nationwide. Find one in the L.A. area, preferably in one of the locales mentioned earlier, and then inquire about prices and availabilities.

Finally, some people opt to make a short trip to L.A. one to three weeks before they move here permanently to arrange an apartment lease. They stay at a hotel for a few days and sign a lease that starts at the beginning of the next month. They then return home, finish up their old life, pack up the car, and zoom into town to a new apartment that's ready and waiting!

How Much Will an Apartment Cost and What Can I Expect in Renting? Compared to other cities in the country, living in L.A. is very expensive! A one bedroom apartment on average rents for $1800 a month. A two bedroom rents on average for $2400 a month. In places like Beverly Hills or Brentwood, you'll probably have to pay several hundred dollars more.

On top of your first month's rent, you will often have to pay a security deposit (which will be refunded at the end of the lease, unless you decide to have a punching contest with a wall), which usually amounts to one-half or a full month's rent. So expect to pay a total of about one-and-a-half to two months rent (first month plus security) just to move into an apartment.

You will also probably have to pay a nonrefundable $25 to $30 fee for a credit check. If you have bad credit, then you will have some difficulty renting at many places. You may have to stay away from the bigger or corporate-owned apartment complexes, since their credit departments won't accept people with blemished records. Your best bet will be a smaller, independently-owned apartment complex, and you might have to beg.

It is important to note that some of the bigger apartment complexes also require a current pay stub or your previous year's tax returns to verify that your monthly income is approximately two-and-a-half times your monthly rent payment. If your tax forms show little or no income, then you will have to look for independently-owned buildings not requiring this. All of this may seem a bit overwhelming, but regardless of your circumstances, you will definitely be able to find a place to live in L.A.

Most buildings in L.A. offer six-month or one-year leases, and only a handful offer terms that are month-to-month. As an enticement, some will offer two weeks free on a six-month lease or one month free on a year's lease. You should always ask about this, even if the apartment manager fails to mention it while showing the apartment.

Also, a majority of apartments do not come with a refrigerator. Therefore, you will have to rent one from the landlord or an outside vendor, buy one, or bring one (which could be a difficult feat, unless you're arriving via U-Haul).

Finally, negotiate everything you can possibly think of, especially the price. Landlords are eager to fill vacancies, so you have an advantage. But before deciding to rent out any given apartment, you should visit at least five different ones. This will help you know whether you are getting a good deal. Many people have the tendency to become overly excited about the first apartment they see, not realizing that there might be better values out there. So don't be too quick to sign on the dotted line. No matter how good a deal sounds, it probably will not disappear overnight.

What If I Have Pets? Most apartments allow small pets like cats, but usually there is an extra security deposit of about two hundred dollars. Most do not allow dogs, so be up-front about this when looking at an apartment. You won't be able to hide your Chihuahua from your landlord, no matter how small it is. You may have to search longer if you're a dog owner, but there are thousands of buildings and eventually one will accept you and all of your animal companions.

What About Living with a Roommate? Many young actors live with roommates simply because it saves them money. Obviously, the cost of splitting a two-bedroom apartment is much less than living alone in a one-bedroom. Therefore, if you are on a budget, you might consider having a roommate.

If you don't already know someone with whom you would like to share an apartment, there are several roommate placement agencies that can help. Their fees vary, and they offer you unlimited leads on affordable apartments (you specify the price range) with compatible people (you specify the traits). These agencies can be found in the yellow pages and many advertise in newspaper classifieds—check the *L.A. Times*.

Also, you can often find individuals seeking roommates who have placed their own ads in these newspapers. Additionally, check the Internet. There are also many websites aimed specifically at bringing roommates together—people who have rooms to rent with those looking for a place to stay. You never know . . . your new roommate may be waiting for you in cyperspace!

No matter where you search, however, remember that your personal safety is paramount. It's perfectly OK, and in fact *very* advisable, to Google anyone you're considering rooming with to check for a criminal background; checking this person out on Facebook and Twitter is also a good idea to weed out general weirdness. You can also ask for references, from employers and family members, when evaluating a roommate, and be willing to offer your own references in return. This may sound like overkill, but unfortunately in a big city like Los Angeles, you just can't be too careful.

If you end up meeting your new roommate through one of those services or the classifieds, make sure he or she is someone you like. This sounds obvious, but you'd be surprised at the number of people who choose roommates that they come to dread. Use your gut instinct—if the snake crawling around her neck doesn't mix well with your fear of reptiles, then don't move in together.

Should I Search the Newspaper to Find an Apartment? This is not necessary and can actually be rather disappointing. Many times an ad in the paper sounds fabulous, but in reality the apartment is the pits. It's not always the case though, so if you feel inclined, you should try it a couple of times. Maybe you'll get lucky and find your dream apartment.

One of the easiest things to do is drive around a neighborhood that you prefer and investigate buildings that appeal to you. Usually a sign will be posted outside, often with a phone number and specific information about the available unit(s). Many times a manager lives on the premises, so an apartment can be inspected immediately with a quick cell phone call. Even if no sign is apparent, it is still wise to stop and ask because some owners never bother to advertise publicly.

What About the Safety of Buildings? Many apartments offer gated parking, which is an excellent option to have in L.A. Thousands of cars are snatched up every year! A gated parking facility helps keep your car safer, though not completely secure, as criminals can get into any parking lot they want to. A gate is just a good deterrent.

In terms of the safety of your apartment, you should ask the manager about any crimes that have occurred in the building or on the premises. If you sense any hesitation or vagueness in the response, ask again and be very specific. If you feel uncomfortable with the answer, it's probably best to look elsewhere.

When choosing an apartment, it's always a plus if it comes with an alarm. If not, you can easily install a magnetic alarm yourself in five minutes to any door or window, and they cost only about $5 to $10 a piece. Such alarms can be found at hardware stores everywhere. The nominal price is worth it if you have any concerns about safety.

A Review of Good Questions to Ask Your Potential Landlord:
- What's the rent?
- Is the rent negotiable?
- Is the lease for one year, six months, or month-to-month?
- Is there a month's free rent on a year's lease?
- What, if any, utilities are paid?
- How many parking spots do I get? (In case you have a roommate who also has a car)
- Has there been any crime in the building or parking garage?
- Does a refrigerator come with the unit?
- What about washer/dryer facilities?

What About Earthquake Safety in L.A.? Some feel it's wise to choose a building that appears to be newer, because it will probably be more structurally sound. In 1971, and again in the 1980s, stricter earthquake building codes were established;

therefore, buildings built after these dates are going to be safer during a major earthquake. Most buildings that suffered structural damage in the January 1994 quake were built before 1971.

Newer buildings are built on rollers, which allow them to rock back and forth during a quake, much like a raft on the ocean. Rollers are supposed to make buildings safer and less prone to structural damage. Thus, it might be wise to inquire about the age of a building and its seismic, or earthquake, safety while an apartment manager is showing you a unit.

An apartment on the top floor might be the safest, not only because it's guarded from prowlers, but because most apartment buildings in the 1994 earthquake suffered the worst damage on the first floor. This is because the building is anchored to the ground level, and that area experiences the most pressure when the building shakes.

Should I Really Be Concerned About Earthquakes? Earthquakes come with the territory in Southern California, as with many other places in the world. It is not suggested that you live in constant fear of them, as most earthquakes are very minor and can barely be felt. The worldwide publicity that is generated about them makes many people believe that the earth is shaking violently in L.A. on a regular basis. It isn't . . . just once in a while!

For example, an earthquake that measured 6.8 on the Richter scale shook for about thirty seconds on January 17, 1994, causing a major disturbance for the city. Nevertheless, the city recovered quickly, as it always seems to from any disaster, and life was back to normal in a few days. Just remember that environmental hazards exist wherever you live—snow and ice in the Northeast, hurricanes on the East Coast, and tornados in the Midwest. You should be aware of earthquakes, but don't let a fear of them stop you from pursuing your dream!

By the way, since you'll be living in earthquake country, you ought to know how the Richter scale works: A tremor that measures 4.0 on the scale is ten times stronger than a 3.0 (a 3.0 can barely be felt). A quake that registers 5.0 is ten times stronger than a 4.0. Thus, a 5.0 is one hundred times stronger than a 3.0! You get the idea.

Transportation in L.A.

In addition to addressing your living situation, you will have to face another important aspect of life in L.A.: Getting around town.

The Need for Reliable Transportation. Life in L.A. is much easier if you own some form of reliable transportation (i.e., a car or motorcycle). The reason is that the city is so vastly spread out, and as an actor you will have to be traveling to auditions all over town. One alternative is a bicycle, but unfortunately bikes are not permitted on the freeways or on the key links between Hollywood and the Valley. Another option is the bus system, but be prepared to tack considerable time onto your round trip (at least an hour or more) to compensate for waiting, bus changes, and the ride itself. Therefore, you probably should bring a car with you or buy one soon after your arrival.

Insurance and Registration. You should know that insurance rates are extremely high in Southern California. For example, just having the minimum state-required liability insurance for a male under twenty-five years of age starts at about $1,700 a year! (They are, however, statistically the most dangerous drivers.) But, overall, rates are still extremely high for good drivers of both sexes and all ages. If you want theft or comprehensive coverage, your rates skyrocket even higher. This can be quite a shock for people new to Southern California.

To avoid the higher rates, some actors keep their cars registered in their home state, but technically this is a "no-no." California law states that you must register your car here within twenty days of relocating. Therefore, actors who don't register their cars in California are always prepared to explain that they are "only visiting" in the event of an accident or being pulled over by the L.A.P.D.

If you do register your car with the state, there is an additional entrance fee (currently $300) to bring in a vehicle that is not up-to-par with California emissions standards. You won't have to pay for an inspection though, as California does not require vehicle inspections ever. Your only fees will be an emissions test every two years and an annual registration payment. The registration payment is equal to about 2 percent of the value of your car plus approximately $30 in fees. For more information on car regulations, licenses, and vehicle registration, check out the California DMV website at *www.dmv.ca.gov*.

Parking. You should pay close attention to parking signs. Abiding by them can be quite a challenge in L.A. It's not that parking spaces are scarce; rather, there are just so many signs with so many different restrictions. For example, one post might have as many as four signs with varying restrictions for different times of the day and/or days of the week! If you violate any of the posted restrictions, then usually one of an adept team of parking enforcement officers will happily ticket your vehicle—and they mean business! So please read all signs carefully and keep plenty of quarters, dimes, and nickels in your car to feed all those hungry parking meters.

Getting settled is an important step in beginning your career in Hollywood. You need to have stability in your life with regard to shelter and transportation if you hope to have any time to focus on your career. With these covered, your next task will be finding a way to support yourself financially.

Industry Interview: Perspective from Kyle Walters, an L.A. Actor, on Housing

How did you deal with housing when you first arrived in LA?

My first couple of weeks in LA were pretty overwhelming. I reached out to everyone I knew who was living here, and ended up staying with a friend from high school. He showed me the lay of the land. I also came from New York City, so I had the additional stress of buying a car. I think when it comes to housing, and the details of moving here in general, the best idea is to do as much research as you can before you get to LA. At the same time, though, you can't put too much pressure on yourself—don't feel you have to find the perfect first apartment. In the end, over your first year or two here, you'll learn what works for you, and you can make changes to your situation. Ultimately, you'll want to find a neighborhood you really like; auditions aren't centrally located, so you'll be driving distances anyway. It's more important to take your time to find that area you feel pretty good about living in.

FINDING WAYS TO SUPPORT YOURSELF

Supporting yourself financially will be one of the most important aspects of both keeping your acting career alive and maintaining a sense of peace. Simply put, you can't focus on acting if you're worried about paying the rent! To survive in L.A., you will need to have enough money to cover certain necessities, such as food, housing, utilities, and transportation. In addition, as an actor, you'll need money to pay for such essentials as photographer's fees, headshot duplication, résumés, acting classes, postage, and envelopes—to name a few.

If you've already got a bankroll stashed away, then you've got a head start. The more money you have saved, the better. It will give you a cushion, as you adjust to life in L.A. and begin pursuing your career in high gear. But regardless of your situation, you should still devise a plan to keep money flowing into your life, in the event that your well runs dry, whether it be in a month or even a year.

So how are you gonna make some dough? Well, in Los Angeles there are many different ways actors earn survival money. Actors are creative people, and when it comes to making money, we have to be. The reason is that we must keep our daytime hours free for auditions and interviews. This means that most nine-to-five jobs are out of the question. Thus, many actors choose to work for themselves independently, or they work a number of widely varied jobs in the evenings. The common thread that distinguishes most of the jobs is flexibility: flexibility to work odd hours of the day or flexibility to take time off during normal business hours. Many actors even have two or three jobs in the event that one dries up.

Common Jobs Actors Hold to Support Themselves

Following is a list of some of the common positions that actors hold. Keep in mind that these don't have to be considered second careers; rather, they are temporary jobs that actors take during lean times to pay the bills. Some actors get frustrated because they envision doing these jobs for decades! The key is to understand that such jobs simply help to pay the rent until acting does. Remember, many great actors have at one time or another labored at these less-than-glamorous positions.

Bartender/Waiter/Waitress. By far, this is the most common (and most stereotypical) job held by actors. Good cash income and flexibility make this an ideal position. Some actors have even caught the attention of agents and casting directors by waiting on them in popular restaurants near studios and agencies. This is rare though, so for the most part you'll just be earning some survival money and getting a few free meals.

Office Temp. Temping allows you to earn a livable income while maintaining tremendous flexibility. Though most of these jobs take place during the daytime, actors can usually get out of work when an audition comes up. The key is to be tactful and crafty. The best strategy for working consistently as a temp is to be signed up with several large agencies. The more agencies you're registered with, then the greater your chances of steady employment. If you are unfamiliar with word-processing or spreadsheet software, nearly all of the agencies allow you to learn them for free in their offices on their computers. Whether or not you plan to temp, it's still a good idea to know them anyway. If you have absolutely no desire to deal with computers, there are still many unrelated temp jobs, like reception and warehouse positions, which pay less but are just as prevalent.

Chauffeur. Many actors have made good part-time money driving high-powered people all around town. Usually working in the evenings for special events, parties, or dinners, many have found chauffeuring to be a flexible job that potentially can provide important connections with industry people; that is, if the partition in the limousine isn't closed. To be a chauffeur, you need a special license from the DMV.

Security Guard. Many private security companies and the major studios often hire young actors to be security guards. A relatively easy job, security patrol can be a regular gig or a temporary "on-call" type of position. You can work any time of the day, as most companies need guards around the clock. Positions vary in pay, depending on whether or not you are licensed to carry a gun. Some actors find it a nice way to practice monologues or memorize lines while on the job! Sometimes you won't have time for such rehearsal, but just being stationed on a major studio lot is a great opportunity—and that happens frequently. You'll have the chance to learn more about the business and possibly even meet some important people.

Gym Membership Salesperson/Personal Trainer. For those actors who are into health and fitness, earning an income at a gym might not be a bad idea. You can make good money selling memberships, and great money working as a personal trainer. Plus, you may even get some celebrity clients. If you have nutritional, exercise, and bodybuilding knowledge, you're a prime candidate for personal training, working through a gym or independently. Most personal trainers make anywhere from $40 to $100 an hour. Gyms are also great places to network, as many celebrities and other industry folks work out regularly in facilities near studios. Whether or not you decide to work at a gym, joining one still might be a good idea.

Usher at Tapings of Studio Shows. This is a good way to learn about the business and make new friends. You'll learn how television shows are taped, and you might even become acquainted with some of the cast, crew, or producers. Tapings are weekly and the wages aren't the greatest, so you might not be able to support yourself entirely with a job like this. However, you could make good connections.

Catering. Many actors have found this to be an excellent way to make money, maintain flexibility, and meet industry people. Most catering companies hire workers on an as-needed basis for movies, gala events, and parties, so you ought to hook up with a few of them to maintain steady work. Very often, you'll be serving celebrities and industry people, and while there's no guaranteed consistency in the work, you will definitely learn more about etiquette in the business. It's a very popular way for many actors to pay their rent.

Retail. L.A. is home to dozens of huge shopping malls with thousands of retail stores. It's also a mini-mall heaven! Many actors work in these retail shops during the evenings and weekends, selling everything from perfume to cosmetics to designer clothing. Because retail sales generally don't pay very much, most actors try to sell on a salary-plus-commission basis at the nicer upscale department stores, where they can earn bigger paychecks.

Massage Therapist/Healing Arts Practitioner. There is great flexibility in this field, as one can schedule clients at any time during the week, day, or night. To be certified in L.A., you must take a one-hundred-hour course given by one of several county-authorized schools. There are also some complicated regulations, which vary from city to city (and there are over eighty incorporated cities in L.A.!), which has caused some practitioners to simply bypass the whole system of certification. However, if you are seriously considering doing this, you should call the county to find out the details and the risks of working as an uncertified practitioner. If you are talented, then there is potential to make great income, from $50 to $100 an hour. You also could develop a client list of industry people with the right marketing, which could be extremely helpful to you in the future.

Aerobics/Yoga Instructor. If you are skilled in aerobics or yoga, you should strongly consider offering some classes. In L.A., there are hundreds of gyms where you could make an arrangement to teach your aerobics/dance classes on an ongoing basis. There are also a number of yoga centers that rent out space, for both classes and private instruction. This type of job offers great flexibility and can be very rewarding with the right advertising and commitment. While certification isn't technically required, most facilities only hire certified instructors.

Tennis/Golf Instructor. If you are talented in one of these sports, not only will you make a lot of money teaching others, but you'll befriend many entertainment industry people while doing it. Many top executives in the industry are always seeking to improve their game, and are willing to pay top dollar for your services. You should check out your options at all the country clubs and community facilities to find out where there's an opening or need. You might even advertise in the industry trade papers for private instruction.

Computer Software Tutor. Some actors who are also computer whizzes have placed small ads in the industry trade papers or have mailed flyers offering to tutor celebrities and industry people on how to use their computers at their own homes. You'd be surprised how many bigwigs aren't up-to-date with modern technology! If you know the common word-processing and spreadsheet software programs, then this might be a way to make good extra income while helping and schmoozing with high-powered people.

Studio Tour Guide. All of the major studios offer guided tours to the public, which flocks from around the world every day by the hundreds to get a closer glimpse at Hollywood. If you are charismatic and would enjoy speaking to groups of tourists, you should inquire at all of the studios. They usually have seasonal interviews and the competition is fierce for the moderately paying jobs, but the reward is learning about the business and making some good contacts.

Arts & Crafts Maker. Throughout L.A. county, indoor swap meets (flea markets) are held every weekend where entrepreneurs sell everything from luggage and clothing, to homemade arts and crafts. There are even a few stores around town that specialize in handmade crafts. If you've got a special talent for making unique objects or art, you could supplement your income by partaking in these extravaganzas. To understand what I'm talking about, look through the *L.A. Times* or *LAtimes.com* on Friday or Saturday, and you'll find advertisements for these weekly swap meets. You'll also see posters attached to telephone poles around the city. Attend a few swap meets and talk to the people. You might get some great ideas for your crafts.

Telemarketer. One of the most dreaded professions, telemarketing has been a great source of income to some actors who aren't concerned with rejection (as if actors don't get enough of that anyway!). Some have said that it teaches them how to really listen to other people and develop a stronger sense of confidence. If you think you can handle this type of work, selling everything from newspaper subscriptions to adjustable beds, you'll find plenty of opportunities advertised in the newspapers on a daily basis.

Salesperson. Salespeople are some of the highest paid people in the world. As in any major city, you'll find hundreds of opportunities to sell larger ticket items in L.A., including cars, electronic equipment, advertising, and business supplies. If you're good, you'll make a great income that will easily cover all of your basic necessities. As an actor, the key is finding a job that will allow you to work part-time or on weekends. Check out the *L.A. Times* for a smorgasbord of opportunities.

Construction Worker. Because of the sunny weather in Southern California, construction work happens virtually year-round. There is a lot of competition for a limited number of jobs, but if you should happen to land one, it generally pays very well. It is important to be in contact with as many contractors as possible.

Singing Telegram Performer/Stripper/Dancer. Some actors have supported themselves working only one or two days a week doing singing and/or stripping telegrams. If you've got a good voice and body, and know how to advertise, you might make some great money. Whatever you do, you'll have to be creative. You don't necessarily have to strip; you could be in a gorilla suit! It really doesn't matter as long as it's unique. These aren't particularly popular with industry folks—many are worried the gorilla might be an out-of-work actor who's just harassing them or trying to get their attention. But there is still a big market throughout L.A. for private parties, birthdays, and events. There are also many clubs that hire exotic dancers and strippers; however, working conditions might be degrading and possibly even dangerous.

Operator for Telephone Company or Answering Service. Some actors have made money answering phones because it's relatively easy, and it can be done in the evenings. Also, such a job sometimes allows for personal study or line/scene memorization while you're at work. This is best for those who don't like to be active while at work.

Cleaner. Though hardly a glamorous job, some actors have earned a livelihood by cleaning office buildings, studios, houses, and cars. This work, which usually occurs at night, can be permanent or temporary. Many cleaning people are hooked up with several agencies or companies that can place them on an as-needed basis.

Airline Employee. Airlines offer a variety of round-the-clock jobs. Whether working in reservations, loading, security, or administration, you will find jobs accommodating your schedule. You'll have your pick of airports, though you probably should stick with Los Angeles International Airport (LAX) and Burbank Airport, since they are the closest to where you'll probably be living.

Manufacturing/Warehouse Worker (Second- or Third-Shift Job). As in any large city, you'll find scores of manufacturing companies that stay open twenty-four hours a day, producing everything from apparel to vitamins. Though usually monotonous and not always the highest paying, such work could provide temporary stability if you have no other skills or income at the moment. Temp agencies can help place you in these types of jobs.

Owner of a Home-Based Business (Other Than Acting). Of all the jobs you might pursue, this can be one of the best or worst. When working for oneself, one has to be extremely motivated, especially when the television or refrigerator beckons from the other room. If you are a go-getter, have a good business idea, and hate to work for other people, this might be the best solution for you. If you find you can only produce when a boss is looking over your shoulder, this might not be a wise alternative.

Starting up a business requires a lot of effort and varying degrees of capital. Most actors who start a company begin on a small scale and develop their business if there is reasonable expectation of continued profit. Those who succeed are able not only to cover their basic necessities, but, sometimes, to live very comfortable lifestyles. Examples of home-based businesses include editing/typing/document preparation, mail-order, distributorships, gift baskets, commercial or graphic art, fine art, and website design. The possibilities are endless.

Entertainment Industry Employee. Though not usually flexible in terms of having daytime hours free, some newcomers in Hollywood opt for an industry job for a few months that will help them to understand the business and possibly offer some connections.

Industry-related jobs are advertised every day in the classifieds of the two main industry trade papers, *The Daily Variety* (*www.dailyvariety.com*) and *The Hollywood Reporter* (*www. hollywoodreporter.com*). Even if you aren't looking for a job, you ought to read these on a regular basis to find out what's happening in Tinseltown. Smart seekers also send cover letters and résumés to department heads of studios, talent agencies, casting companies, and production firms, as well as to directors, producers, and celebrities, asking them for jobs.

Many of the positions offered are for assistants, coordinators, receptionists, or production help. The greatest aspect of industry jobs is that you learn how the business works in a relatively short period of time. You also make contacts and connections that may prove to be valuable in the long run.

Think how great it might be to work as an assistant at a casting office and then sometime down the road return as an actor auditioning for a part!

You can also search for industry-related jobs by contacting the major studios via job hotlines or the Internet. They frequently list availabilities in a wide variety of categories: office-related, production, security, reception, kitchen, maintenance, and others. The job hotlines and websites for several studios are as follows:

MCA/Universal City Studios, Universal City
www.universalstudios.com

Warner Bros., Burbank
www.warnerbros.com

Sony Pictures Entertainment, Culver City
www.sonypictures.com

Walt Disney, Burbank
www.disney.com

Paramount Pictures, Hollywood
www.paramountstudios.com

20th Century Fox, Century City
www.fox.com

A Flexible and Industry-Related Option: Extra Performer (Also Known as a "Background Artist" or "Atmosphere"). Finally, another good source of income and education for the brand new actor in town is "Extra Work." The next chapter covers the ins and outs of extra work in great detail.

Whatever you choose to do, remember that having flexibility and enough income to survive should be your greatest concern (unless of course, you've decided to take three months to work an industry job as an assistant on a movie set). Having money to support your higher vision—your acting career—will make your journey much, much easier.

Keep in Mind, Though—Never Lose Sight of Your True Goal!

It's extremely important not to take a survival job that ends up eclipsing your acting career in terms of time and energy. Say you're a personal trainer whose initial intention is to make a nice cushion of cash while making your own hours—but you find you've taken on so many clients you start missing auditions (not to mention exhausting yourself). Or maybe word-of-mouth has really been great for your catering business, and you find yourself booking food service gigs every day of the week, instead just on weekends as you'd planned.

It's great to be successful (and, of course, make moolah) but you can only spread yourself so thin. Time to sit down and ask yourself a few hard questions: is my day job too demanding? If so, it may be time to start looking for an easier job. If I've started my own business and find I simply can't handle managing it *and* my acting career, can I delegate? (Partnering up with a friend who seeks a similarly flexible schedule may solve your problem.) And most importantly, am I still as focused on being an actor as I was before I started moonlighting? Only you know your true goals, and how hard you're willing to go after them. Don't let your dream get short shrift!

Time management and balance between your survival work and your acting opportunities is essential, will keep you living comfortably, and will allow you to make strides in your artistic life as well.

Industry Interviews—Moonlight (and Make It Work)

To sum up, let's get a bit of wise perspective from two actors who've learned the ropes when it comes to making a good living, AND propelling an acting career forward.

Deanna Meske's career spans many aspects of the industry, from her work on MTV, to an in-demand host, to internet productions, to films like *Elsa and Ed* with Shirley MacLaine. Deanna has developed her own production company for commercial and web-based projects, which is lucrative and allows her time to perform as well.

As I know you excel at other work, such as your filmmaking business, while pursuing your acting career, how do you so successfully balance and multitask? For other actors who are doing other work as well as acting, what would be your advice so that you don't become overwhelmed or exhausted, and can properly keep your eye on the creative goals that really matter to you?

Honestly, sometimes it manages me! Two years ago, I took a job as a presenter for Chevy on the autoshow circuit; while that was a great opportunity for me and I was able to travel and really work on my public speaking skills and improv skills, I missed a lot of major opportunities being on the road. My advice is to have your second job be something local, something that will let you get out to attend a casting or a callback. If you are filmmaking, realize that it has to take the back burner when auditions and booking come into play. Most of the productions I create are local, but there are some that take me on the road. But, since I set the production work up, I can change the dates and eat the costs on flights if an important casting comes up. For me, I don't produce any films or commercials that I am not in. I don't always have to be the lead, but I have to be in it so that I'm always on my acting path.

Kyle Walters has developed a strong fan base, thanks to his work on web series such as *Welcome to Sandition*, as well as his fine work onstage in L.A. and previously in New York City. He further flexes his creative muscles with a successful side business, as he explains:

You want to focus on finding a job that has flexibility. I do freelance web design and graphic design, so I can make my own hours to a certain extent, and it's pretty great to work from home most of the time. The biggest piece of financial advice I can give any actor, that I didn't follow myself? Stay out of debt. I'm working too many hours per week to pay my debt off. I heard being in debt described once as 'stealing from your future self', and I really believe that's true. Always remember you're in this business for the long haul. You're looking at thirty-forty years of being an actor if you work hard, and you've got to survive financially that entire time.

GETTING YOUR FEET WET WITH "EXTRA WORK"

The best way to learn about any business is through a "hands-on" approach. For new actors in the entertainment industry, that approach is "extra work," a great way to quickly learn more about the world of television and film.

What is "Extra Work"?

"Extra Work" refers to employment as a background performer in scenes for television or film. People who do this—"extras" or "atmosphere"—have no speaking lines and are barely ever recognizable; however, they are vitally important in creating realistic depictions of public places. Scenes in restaurants, courtrooms, hallways, and outdoors usually need to be filled with people who are walking, sitting, eating, or chatting. Just take a closer look at television one night. You'll see that there's a tremendous need for extras in Hollywood.

Extra work is not considered to be one of the most glamorous or financially rewarding aspects of show business. For that reason, some aspiring and working actors never even consider it. But before you dismiss it, as a newcomer to Hollywood you should read on to learn about the potential benefits of doing extra work for a short period of time.

There are several fantastic aspects you can look forward to. First, you'll have the opportunity to familiarize yourself with a real television or movie set. If you've never worked professionally before, it will help you immensely for your first principal acting job. Second, working as an extra is one of the ways a non-union person can become eligible to join the Screen Actors Guild /American Federation of Television and Radio Artists (SAG-AFTRA). Becoming a union member is one of the trickiest first hurdles for newcomers, and extra work is a great way to get your foot in the door. Third, while working, you'll be able to share and swap information with other extras about agents, casting directors, and all kinds of show-business related matters. Fourth, working as an extra on shows like soap operas can lead to "Under-Fives," which are speaking parts with five lines or less. The good thing is that under-fives pay *more* than regular extra work and they give you some great exposure. Finally, while working as an extra, you'll get to meet a lot of people and probably make a few good friends!

How Does One Become an Extra?

The nice thing about extra work is that you don't need to meet many qualifications or have any skills. You only need a body and an ability to follow directions. Therefore, chances are that you're probably well qualified. And the types they're looking for? Well, all kinds are desirable. That includes people who are tall, short, fat, skinny, young, old, and from all ethnic backgrounds. In fact, there is really no one who is unsuitable, although you'll probably have more opportunities to work if you're a clean-cut, mainstream type of person.

In L.A. there are many extras casting agencies. Some are legitimate and many are rip-offs. Only a few handle the bulk of the work in town. Some agencies are one- or two-person operations; others have up to twenty people or more. It really varies a lot from agency to agency.

So that you don't waste your time and money registering with a bunch of agencies that have little or no ability to get you extra work, I've made a list of several agencies that seem to have a consistent stream of work. Some may be casting extras for twenty television shows and movies at one time; others may only be handling a few feature films or commercials per month:

Central Casting (Union)/Cenex Casting (Non-Union)
220 South Flower Street, Burbank, CA 91502
(818) 562-2755
www.CentralCasting.org

Bill Dance Casting (Union & Non-Union)
4605 Lankershim Boulevard, Suite 401
North Hollywood, CA 91602
(818) 754-6634
www.BillDanceCasting.com

Jeff Olan Casting (Union & Non-Union)
14044 Ventura Boulevard, Suite 209
Sherman Oaks, CA 91423
www.JeffOlanCasting.com

To register with any of these agencies, you'll have to go to their offices during designated hours. Be sure to call first before showing up, or they probably won't see you.

Are There Fees When Registering?

Many casting agencies no longer charge registration fees; if they do, most agencies will charge you a one-time registration fee of $60 or under. (A lot of the illegitimate agencies sometimes want upwards of $300. Stay away from anyone who wants that kind of money!) This registration fee usually includes having your picture taken for their files, in their own format or style. Sometimes if you bring your own three-by-five color snapshot of yourself, your fee will be waived. A picture fee is sometimes charged of about $25.

In addition, some agencies withhold 5 percent of a non-union extra's paycheck, as a service fee. If you are non-union, you'll quickly see how non-union people always get the short end of the stick. This service fee is another type of inconvenience you will have to put up with until you're a union member. Chapter 6 will cover how to improve your status to "union."

If you are a union member, you can never be charged a registration fee, as mandated by the Screen Actors Guild. However some agencies avoid the rule by imposing a small "picture fee," which is usually $5 to $15, but no more. Often, though, there are no fees for union members.

It is best to call each agency ahead of time to obtain the specific details regarding what you must pay and what you must bring to registration. Usually you'll just need two forms of identification (a driver's license and Social Security card), and you'll be on your way to working as an extra. But always inquire ahead of time, so as not to waste your time or theirs.

What and How Are Extras Paid?

In Los Angeles, the pay rate for non-union extras is $64 a day, based on eight hours of work—a small pittance for work that can often be exhausting. Paradoxically, the exhaustion is frequently the result of sitting around all day doing nothing. SAG-AFTRA "general extra" wages, paid to extras who work on union films and television shows, are $148 per day (as of 2014), also based on eight hours.

Union wages are not tremendous salaries, but keep in mind that many shoots typically run longer than eight hours, usually ten or twelve hours, which will result in overtime. In the event that you go to work and are released after only one or two hours, you'll be pleased to know that you'll still get paid for a minimum of eight hours work! This happens a lot! It surprises some new people, but if you think about it, there would be no justice in scheduling someone for a whole day, and then only paying them for an hour or two of work and sending them home.

Overtime for Extras

Non-union overtime is paid at time-and-a-half for the first two hours after eight hours. After that, you'll receive twice your hourly rate until you've worked sixteen hours in one day. After sixteen hours, known as "golden time," you'll start earning your daily rate every hour. This happens rarely, but when it does you'll feel as if gold coins are falling from the sky.

Union overtime is paid at time-and-a-half for the first four hours of overtime, and twice your hourly rate from twelve to sixteen hours. At "golden time," you'll earn you're daily rate every hour, as do non-union extras. For both union and non-union, overtime is paid in increments of tenths of an hour.

Additionally, there are various pay supplements known as "bumps" that you may receive depending on the requirements of the day. For example, you'll be given additional pay if you wear your own formal clothes, change your own wardrobe several times (if required), use your car in a scene, perform hazardous duties, operate firearms, wear prosthetics, or you are used as a body double or stand-in. The amount of these bumps usually varies from $6.25 to $50.

Now That I'm Registered, How Do I Get Work?

Unfortunately, getting work or "getting booked" requires a continual effort on your part. Although you probably will have completed an extensive personal information form at each extras casting agency, most extras casting directors will never look at it. It's simply not worth their time.

Typically, extras casting directors book extras in one of several ways. The most common method is to have a message line, either voicemail or a continuously repeating loop, which is updated throughout the day with the specific types they are looking for. For example, a typical message might say "we need males, 5'8" to 5'10", ages forty to fifty, with short hair, any race, to play cops." Upon hearing this message, if you fit the description, then you would call the designated number and try to get booked. The extras casting director will either pull your image up on a computer, or pull your picture from a file and check to see if you are, in fact, right for the job. If you are, then you'll most likely get booked.

Another way casting directors fill their needs is by allowing extras to call them directly throughout the day to inquire about work. Some don't prefer unsolicited calls, but many don't mind once they get to know you. A good way to determine how extras casting directors feel about this is to first get booked by responding to a message line, and then ask if you can call them directly in the future for work. If they say it's okay, then be sure to check back with them in a day or two. Don't wait a couple of weeks because they will have forgotten you by then. Extras casting directors deal with hundreds of people every day and have a hard time remembering everyone, especially new people. Also, as a newcomer it's best not to engage these casting directors in long conversations. This is because they are frequently busy and under pressure, with phones ringing off the hook. Over time, progressively develop your relationship and it will become easier to chat and ask about work.

A third way agencies book extras is by having a general work line that actors can call, and if extras are needed, a casting director may pick up. Usually you'll supply three important bits of information: your name, age, and race. They are needed because the requirements for scenes are usually very specific. In no other profession would you be asked such personal questions, but in this line of work such personal data is essential. Think about it. Wouldn't a casting director need a predominance of Chinese people when casting a scene set in Chinatown?

Finally, the last way extras may be booked is through a "calling service." A calling service is a small company, usually one to four people, that has connections with most of the extras casting agencies. They call casting people directly to get you work, and frequently casting people call them to fill work when they are swamped. For instance, an extras casting director may have to book fifty extras for a show quickly. Rather than put this information on a message line and take calls from countless people who may or may not be right for the job, he or she will contact the calling service and tell them what types are needed. Calling services also usually supply books of their clients to agencies for quick reference. The calling service then does most of the work by gathering up and scheduling a list of people. Essentially, they book the show for the extras casting director. This whole process happens frequently in the world of extras casting.

Thus, calling services are like agents or brokers for extras who want to work regularly. They cannot guarantee employment, but usually can get an extra two to six days of work per week, depending on how much work is available and how good a calling service it is.

If you are planning on doing extra work on a regular basis, you might consider signing up with a service. The fee is usually about $50 to $70 a month. You should ask the extras casting agencies which calling services they recommend and prefer before picking one.

When You Are Booked

Once you've lined up an extra job, you'll be given a call time, a location address, an assistant director (A.D.) to check in with, and any wardrobe requirements. (Since you won't be getting paid very much, never go and buy clothes specifically for work. You will hardly be noticed working as an extra, and ninety-nine times out of one hundred, the wardrobe you currently own will be suitable.) All you need to concern yourself with is showing up on time, acting professionally, and doing what you're told. Every day will be different. Just have fun!

Getting Booked is a Part-Time Job Itself

Working regularly as an extra will only come with a lot of effort. If you don't have a calling service, then you will have to do a lot of calling on your own, anywhere from one to one hundred calls a day. Even if you do have a calling service, you'll still need to make some calls, since they can't ensure work for every day of the week. At first this process can be frustrating and annoying, but with time, the ritual of searching for work will become second nature to you.

Industry Interview: Advice from Bill Dance, Owner of Bill Dance Casting, on Extra Work

Could you tell me how you go about casting extras? What does your day consist of?

Well, a lot of it depends upon the films that we are doing and the types we need. We get full breakdowns from production companies with what the movie is about, the specific number of extras in every scene, and what the extras need to look like. Once we get these breakdowns after production meetings with the A.D.s and we get a shooting schedule, we then go through our files. We look at individual pictures and Polaroids, and we actually start picking people for various scenes. It's a very hands-on, very artistic kind of approach versus just putting bodies on a set. We actually sculpt what a scene looks like. Every single person is hand-picked. That's the difference in terms of what we do. So it's a one-on-one hand-picking, hand-sculpting of every person to be in a scene, whether it's a coffee shop, like a country western coffee shop where we pick the cronies at the counter or the waitress or the cowboys coming in. We get the layout and the vision of what the director has in mind, and they give us how many people they want, and then we sculpt what we feel realistically that scene calls for.

We also show pictures. Sometimes a director may want to see pictures of what a scene is going to be, so we'll show a number of pictures just to give him an idea of faces, and from there we start to sculpt.

So that's what we do. It's hand picking and laying out pictures like a painting, and then we actually start to call these people individually.

So the days can be pretty hectic?

Well, every day there is something to do. We are either prepping a show or currently casting a show or adapting to changes in a schedule. We also see new people every day, we register new people every day, and people come in to update their files. We also have interviews going on throughout the day, so it can be pretty hectic. It's a full day.

What advice would you give to somebody who wants to work regularly as an extra?

I think you have to be persistent. It's a matter of people getting to know you. It's about being responsible. It's about being positive. People sometimes are negative and we just don't want to have to deal with all of that. It's difficult enough, you know, putting stuff together. So I think being on time, being responsible, and showing up are all very important.

Your "type" does not matter. All types are needed. But you have to ask yourself, what type do you naturally fit into? Are you an upscale country club type or are you a biker type? Are you more of a street type, or a punky, funky type . . . like a rave type? I think people need to be truthful to themselves, in terms of the type that they are. Some people can stretch more than others, to play various roles.

But the key is to be very persistent, and very positive. Project a positive attitude and follow up a lot of times.

What advice would you give to a new person fresh off the bus in L.A.?

Well, there are different people with different aspirations. There are those who strictly want to be background people. They want to be background artists. There are people who want to be actors, and of course, doing the extra work is obviously a tremendous stepping stone. It's a stepping stone in terms of getting a SAG card. It's also a stepping stone of being on a set and learning the craft, and watching the technical people work. If you happen to be a "stand-in," that's a great opportunity too.

I'm a person who believes in training. I really do. I think people should take acting classes. I think they should take dance classes. Any kind of voice classes are great too. I mean, training is part of an old system they used to have years ago in the studios. It leads to a well-rounded individual versus someone coming out to L.A. and just relying strictly on a look. So I advise people to train. Universities are great. Get into a good acting class.

The thing I hear the most often is that people come out here for something like a six-month period and expect to make it overnight. It just doesn't happen that way. It takes time. So I think in stepping off that bus, you have to remember it's a matter of perseverance. It's a matter of great patience. It's a cultivating process where you have to learn the craft. It's about experience. And I think if you really want to do this passionately, you do it and you don't give yourself an allotted period of time. You say, "This is what I want to do."

For my whole life, I was a dancer. Since I was three years old, I studied dancing. Then I worked professionally as a dancer. And I've been in the industry my entire life. So I don't know any other world, but working in the industry. This is my commitment. It's tremendously hard work. It's very rejectionary, and there are a lot of people vying for certain jobs. So you have to really want to do this.

And again, there are different levels. Some people want to do the background work. If they want to do that, my suggestion is to get good pictures, be it 3x5s or 8x10s. Get pictures that are very natural, and then register with the various companies that are in town. Not one company does all the movies here. And just be very persistent, and have a cell phone or number where you can be accessible, where we can reach you.

If you want to be an actor, you definitely have to learn your craft. It's a matter of studying acting, knowing how to break a scene down, knowing how to cold read. You have to know how to audition. There are classes you can take that will help you.

The thing that I hear casting directors talk about quite a bit is that it's about a first impression. So if you want me to come see you in a play or a workshop, make sure it's good. Make sure that you are at a level where it is developed, versus showing something too soon, too fast. It doesn't happen overnight. It's going to take time. You'll kind of know it. It's a process that you go through.

It's all about training. It's about preparing yourself. It's like someone who is planning to run a mile-long race. Hopefully, you prepare to run three or four miles so that when you have to run one mile you are able to handle it. That's much wiser than training for only a quarter of a mile and when the day comes that you have to run the mile you are out of breath and aren't prepared. Preparing as an actor is the same.

Many times people are not prepared. You have to ask yourself, can you pick up a scene and read five pages of dialogue and create a character? When you are doing two to three lines on a film set, you are doing it for twelve hours that day. You're going to be doing it multiple, multiple times. Can you repeat the performance? Can you still stay in the character? Are you listening to the other actors? Many times it's not the dialogue that you are saying, it's the subtext—what's going on underneath you that you are not telling someone.

I think our industry is an illusion. Many times people sit at home and watch commercials on TV and they say, "Well, I can do that!" And, of course, the key is to make our work look effortless, as if anyone can do it. But as you know, there is so much more underneath. It's like an iceberg. There's the tip of the iceberg that you see, but there is like ten times more under the border that we are not seeing—what's going into what you're doing. And I think that's the secret. I think so many people feel that it's just a look. But it's not just a look. There's so much more. There is a human quality. There is an artistry. There is a passion, there is a training. And this is the big misconception of what we do.

It's all about preparing yourself. I always say that if you are an actor, you should have multiple monologues ready to go. What if you met a casting director like myself and I said to you, "Could you do a comedic monologue for me right now?" I mean, at that split second, are you prepared that well? Have you done it enough, to where, when I ask you to do it—and I'm a casting director watching your ability—you could turn it on? And could you do something tragic, something classical? It's about being prepared. And I think the true artist, the person who is passionately in our industry as an actor, is prepared. They don't talk about what they do. They just do it. You can always tell the one who is serious about what he is doing. You just look and tell. It's almost twenty-four hours a day. It's about going to museums, it's about looking at paintings, it's studying art, it's reading, reading plays, going to the theatre. You know, Shakespeare said, "All the world's a stage." Whatever is going on around you is what enhances your work as an artist. Ask yourself, "What are you bringing to the table?" It's life experience. And as a casting director, that is what I am looking for. We are looking for that human quality, that fragile human quality. You learn to stop the acting, and you allow the human quality to come through. That takes time to develop. It takes being comfortable. It takes relaxing. A lot of actors do all kinds of sensory exercises to relax their bodies, to block out the real world, the tensions and the anxieties so they can get in touch with themselves, so that they can release that truthfulness.

And in terms of the acting, it must be something you have to do. And if you want to do it, just plant your feet in the sand and pursue it. Be persistent. It's going to take time. But if it's something you really want to do and you love doing it, and you have to do it more than anything else, then stick with it and after a period of time things do start happening.

Industry Interview: Advice from Linda Poindexter, Associate Casting Director for *Days of Our Lives*, on Soap-Opera Extra Work and Under-Fives

Could you tell me how you go about casting extras and under-fives?

The most important tools I use are pictures and résumés. I need to have 8×10s from actors.

The atmosphere parts are filled according to the sets working in each episode. For instance, an upscale restaurant scene requires actors with elegant wardrobes, and the nightclub set calls for actors who are trendy and know how to dance. I look at hundreds of pictures and résumés each day and try to fill the roles with actors who are fitting for each story line and setting. If you are established as a nurse in the hospital, then I won't be calling you to be a cop in the police station.

The under-five roles are cast by having actors do cold readings in my office. A lot of times I know an actor's work from having hired him or her previously, but if not I have them come to the office and read for me. I try and have general interviews so I can get to know as many actors as possible.

In terms of both atmosphere and under-fives, there isn't a lot of time to wait for people to call back. I have to cast the show for the next day so production can do the preparation and paperwork. We also do contracts on a daily basis for each episode.

We have a call-in line where actors call and leave their availability. My assistant gives me the list of names every morning and I try to hire people on the list because it shows me that those actors are really interested in working.

What should someone do if he or she wants to be hired as an extra or an under-five on a soap?

They should have a professional picture and a résumé. That is a necessity. You need to present a professional image, composite, and everything. You can't just take a Polaroid or jot something down on binder paper and send it in.

You need flattering 8×10 headshots. However, there's nothing more disconcerting to a casting director when they meet someone and they look nothing like their picture. If you loose or gain a lot of weight, or dye your hair, you should send in new pictures.

Also, most soaps have call-in lines, so call the call-in line. Once a week is fine. A lot of actors send postcards and their effectiveness depends on the casting director. I look at them, and they do jog my memory. We time and date stamp every picture and résumé we get. Sometimes someone will send in a picture and I'll call them the next day because I need that type or look. Sometimes people say, "Well, I've been sending pictures for a year and haven't heard from you." It's nothing personal; it's just that we get hundreds and hundreds of pictures every week. So if you sent a picture a long time ago and haven't heard anything, I'd send a new picture and just be patient.

Some people have a misconception that you only need certain types on soap operas. But you actually cast a wide variety of people, don't you?

Yes. For instance, tomorrow there are some characters that are supposed to be in L.A. (Our story takes place in Salem, a fictional town in the Midwest.) For the L.A. scenes, we need trendy, hip looking people. And around the holidays we had a homeless story.

There's an image that everyone on soaps has to be beautiful, and to a point that's true, because a lot of viewers tune in to live this fantasy. So we can't have really "down" stories. There's a lot of tragedy, but it's tragedy with beautiful clothes and beautiful people. We try to be as real as we can. I cast actors from all age and minority groups, and utilize many different looks.

What should they know and understand as they pursue their careers?

People ask me all the time, "If I do extra work, am I ever going to be considered for a day-player or under-five part?"

The answer is it really depends on the show and on the casting director. On our show, if you do extra work, it doesn't mean that you'll never be considered for under-five and day-player parts.

I try to hire people for under-five roles who have done extra work, for a number of reasons. First, I think it's only fair to give actors a chance to move up, and if I know the actor and his or her work, why do I need to go outside looking for somebody who's never worked in daytime before? It is also very important because there could be somebody who is a wonderful actor who's done tons of theater, but has never been on a daytime set. We shoot an hour episode every day, so you really can't afford to hire somebody who doesn't understand how it works—somebody who doesn't know about blocking or cannot handle the fast-paced shooting schedule. Though you might be the best stage actor in the world, you have to really know the genre you're dealing with. So what I tell people is, "No, it will not hurt your career if you do extra work."

Plus, doing extra work in daytime is different than doing extra work on films. You are treated with a lot of respect, you learn a lot, and occasionally we upgrade people on the set. If people really have a hang-up about doing extra work, nobody's going to know anyway. You don't have to tell people if you think it's beneath you. But I really don't understand it because extra work pays well in daytime and it's a great experience.

There are several people who started as extras and now have contract parts, or have gone on to work in feature films. If you have a desire to move up, then just make that known. When you get the opportunity, just say you're studying here, or you're studying there, or you're in this showcase, or whatever it is you're doing to promote your acting career.

In terms of how Hollywood works, you hear those vignettes about somebody who was sitting around and they were discovered. That's an exception. You have to help yourself and talk to people. Make connections, and let yourself be known and seen, and do as many showcases as you can. And plays. And study. All that helps you get ahead.

If you had a sister, cousin, or some relative who wanted to start an acting career, what words of wisdom would you offer?

I'd tell them to be realistic. A lot of people come to town and they say, "I've been here three months and nothing has happened!" That's totally unrealistic.

I'd also tell them that it's hard work. You have to be persistent. It's hard work to find an agent. Everybody says, "I need an agent but I can't find an agent because I don't have any credits!" So it's a big circle.

I think the biggest mistake is when people say, "My agent tells me that I can't do extra work anymore. But I don't have a job, and I don't know what I'm going to do. Still I can only do under-fives." Well, does your agent pay your rent? If you can earn $148 a day working as an extra on the soaps, why put yourself under that kind of pressure? If your agent is sending you out and you're busy with auditions five days a week, then that's another thing. But if you never hear from him, and you were told you can't do extra work because it will ruin your career, you just have to keep a level head and do what you feel is best.

If you are just moving to town and you get an opportunity to work as an extra on a film or on any television show, then do it and see who you meet and what it's like! Send your picture and résumé out to agents and casting directors, and maybe you'll get extra work on the soaps, because there are five or six soaps in L.A. now. Also there are a lot of sitcoms, and they use extras as well. Overall, I would just say you have to do what's good for you.

The other thing that happens is that people I'll call to work will say, "I can't work because I have a bartending job at twelve noon." If you're trying to build a career as an actor you need to get a job where you are available during the day. Most shows shoot during the day—not to say that we don't have shoots that go until midnight. But if acting is your priority, you have to be available to work as an actor. If being a bartender is your priority or being a waiter is your priority, that's okay. But if you're here and you want to act, then try to get a job where you can be flexible with your hours.

When you get hired, the most important thing is to be professional. Be on time, bring the right wardrobe, know your lines, and just be professional. I have people who, amazingly enough, show up a half-hour late. I understand that there are emergencies, but being late for your call causes real problems.

And whether you're working as an extra, an under-five, or a day-player, you're important. If you're not there on time, it creates problems for the whole production. A lot of people take that really lightly. They'll be booked as an extra and then they'll leave the set because they get an audition. If you commit to work, then make that your first commitment. Make that your priority for the day. Don't spread yourself so thin that you're trying to work on three shows and you're buzzing all over town because you don't want to miss the next gig. And once you get your foot in the door, be professional and learn as much as you can while you're on the set.

BECOMING A UNION MEMBER

I f you want to play in the big leagues, then you've got to be in the unions.

The Screen Actors Guild/American Federation of Television and Radio Artists (SAG-AFTRA)

There is a long history regarding the development of the Screen Actors Guild, commonly known as SAG. Following in the footsteps of the Actors Equity Association (AEA), formed in 1913 for theatrical performers, a small group of actors in June of 1933 sought to gain protection from the Hollywood studios, which were increasingly taking advantage of film performers through unregulated hours, substandard working conditions, and terrible pay. Their efforts to form a union were fueled in March 1933 by a 50 percent decrease in salary for contract players. By June, eighteen founding members came together and officially birthed what we know to be the Screen Actors Guild.

The guild grew to approximately 120,000 members and continues to act in the interests of all professional actors through a process of collective bargaining with producers. Through years of continual negotiation, it has established detailed regulations governing all aspects of employment for union actors working in union projects. As a new actor in town, you should realize that many actors in the early days risked their careers so that the benefits many take for granted today could be realized. Some of these include high minimum-pay scales, overtime pay, meals and rest areas, and assured payment for services. On March 30, 2012, SAG merged with AFTRA (founded in 1952), which used to be an open union that represented the interests of TV and broadcast professionals. Now, SAG and AFTRA's admission standards are the same (read: tougher). The union currently represents the interests of over 160, 000 performers.

As an actor in Hollywood, it is highly recommended that you at some point seek membership in SAG-AFTRA; that is, if you want to have a career in television or film. Most feature films and television programs are union projects and can hire only SAG-AFTRA performers. (In truth, they can hire non-union performers for their first union job, but this happens rarely and will be discussed later.) Additionally, being a member of the union is important because it legitimizes you as an actor. It distinguishes you from the masses as a serious professional. Unfortunately for newcomers, getting into SAG-AFTRA is a difficult task, as certain requirements must be met.

For union theatre work, which is the only type of theatre work that pays, you'll need to be a member of the Actors Equity Association, commonly referred to as Equity. Though there is some Equity work in L.A., by far the vast majority of acting jobs are in television and film. Therefore, joining Equity isn't a top priority.

SAG's Eligibility Requirements

Becoming a member of SAG is one of the biggest hurdles many newcomers face. You can't just show up and join; you have to become eligible. Once you're eligible, you then have to pay a hefty initiation fee plus semi-annual dues.

Following are several ways a non-union person can beat the system and become eligible to join, as there is no standard route or typical path to follow.

1. Being Employed Under a SAG Contract. This is probably the fastest way to get into SAG. All you have to do is find a producer who will hire you for a principal or speaking part. Easy enough? That depends. It can be very easy if you know someone in the industry who has the power to hire you—anyone from your director uncle, to the best friend of your mother's brother who's a producer. On the contrary, it can be very difficult if you don't know anyone in town. This is because, to get a union role, you typically need to audition for it, and to audition for it you typically need an agent to arrange it. The catch is that many agents don't bother to represent non-union people or send them to auditions. Interestingly, most producers and directors don't care whether an actor is union or not. All that matters is that they like your acting. So the problem in getting hired really lies with agents—the intermediaries—who often won't look at non-union people or submit them for union parts.

In the event you are hired to work on a union project, then the Taft-Hartley Law will be applied to you. It states that a non-union performer can be hired to work as a union performer, and then work union for another thirty days, but after that time period that person must join the union if he or she wants to work "union" again. Thus, when you are Taft-Hartley'd you become eligible to join SAG. To join, you simply need to have a letter from a producer of a SAG-signatory project that states he or she plans to hire you for his or her particular production.

2. You've Worked a Principal Role in Another Union. If you have been a paid-up member of an affiliated performer's union for at least one year, and you have worked at least once as a principal performer in that union's jurisdiction, then you are eligible to join SAG. The affiliated performer's unions are: AFTRA (American Federation of Television & Radio Artists), AEA (Actors Equity Association), AGVA (American Guild of Variety Artists), AGMA (American Guild of Musical Artists), and ACTRA (Alliance of Canadian Cinema, T.V., and Radio

Artists). To join, you need to mail a copy of your principal performer's contract to the SAG membership office. Once your eligibility has been verified, you will be contacted to schedule an appointment.

3. You Have Worked as a SAG Extra Player for Three Days. As with being cast in a principal part, a Catch-22 exists when attempting to work as a union extra when you are non-union. The problem is that you're not supposed to do union extra work if you're non-union; but to be eligible to join SAG, non-union people have to do union extra work for three days. It sounds crazy and it is, but there are several ways to accomplish this. A surprising number of professional actors today were able to join SAG by working as a union extra for three days at some point early in their career.

Working "union" as an extra is simply a technicality, as both union and non-union folks show up to work together and perform the same duties. The difference is this: When extras come to work, they receive either a non-union or a union voucher, depending on their status, which serves as a time card and receipt for the day's work. If you are non-union, your mission is to get one of those union vouchers.

The number of people who work union and non-union on any given production varies by the type of project and the location. For the L.A. zone and most of the country, SAG rules state that on television shows, at least nineteen extras must be union members. All the rest, above and beyond nineteen, can be non-union. On films, the first fifty extras must be union. After fifty, all others can be non-union. Thus, on a call for three hundred people for a film, only fifty have to be union. By those numbers, one can see that union vouchers are scarce and a commodity valued by non-union performers.

The only exceptions to the above numbers are for the New York zone. In New York, the first twenty-five extras on television shows must be union, and the first eighty-five on films must be union.

Below are several methods crafty non-union people use to accomplish the challenging feat of obtaining union vouchers:

Method A: Utilizing Your Unique Skills. One way to work as a union extra (when you're not) is to always pay attention to the unusual needs of the extras agencies. Many have special union phone message lines that list the types of union people they need throughout the day. You should always listen to these, even though you may be non-union. Though generic types are often being sought, occasionally a more specific type is requested that is not so readily available. In such cases, non-union people are sometimes booked if appropriate union people cannot be found. For instance, out-of-the-ordinary requests include: surfers with specific haircuts and/or surfboards, jugglers, horseback riders, dancers with specialized skills, collegiate-level athletes, very short or tall people, amputees, and more. In addition, stand-ins are often needed who match exact sizes and have strong resemblances to principal actors. So tune in! If you have any specialized skills or look like a particular actor, you will be needed at some point in time. By paying attention to what is being cast every chance you get, you will be able to land some union extra work.

(Keep in mind that if an extras casting agency is simply looking for "union women in their mid-twenties with brown hair," you probably have little chance of being booked if you are non-union. You might even upset a casting director. The obvious reason is that there are plenty of union women who fit that category.)

Method B: Befriending the Second Assistant Director on the Set. When you arrive on a set as a non-union extra, there is still a possibility to work union. After you check in and receive your voucher from the second assistant director (or the second second assistant director or a production assistant), take note of whether there are any unclaimed union vouchers. This happens when union extras fail to arrive. If it's already twenty minutes past the check-in time and the assistant director is still clutching a union voucher, then tactfully inquire about it. You might be able to exchange your non-union voucher for a shiny new union one. (Be aware that some A.D.s hate to be asked for vouchers. Just be polite when asking and don't take it personally if their response is less than cordial.)

Smart extras even ask for union vouchers when they don't see any, because sometimes they are hidden or tucked away. The moral is: If you never ask, then you'll never receive anything. If you ask all of the time, then eventually you will get something. This not only applies to extra work but to every aspect of life as well. Little children are experts at this.

Method C: The Schmooze. Get to know people! Above all, this is the easiest way to get your vouchers. You might even make some new friends in the process.

Every extras casting agency has visiting hours once a week. If you're intelligent and really crave those union vouchers, you should go as often as you can. These informal sessions are great opportunities for casting people to get to know you and for you to express your interest in union work. They also give you a chance to practice your communication skills. Just be yourself, and always bring a headshot/résumé with you so they have something by which to remember you. Learning to deal with these casting people will only help you when the time comes to deal with those who cast principal parts on television and in films.

Industry Interview: Advice from Bill Dance, Owner of Bill Dance Casting, on Becoming SAG-Eligible

What would you say to newcomers who are trying to get into SAG by doing extra work? What are some ways to approach it and ways not to approach it?

I think it happens when it happens. I think if people become very aggressive and very demanding and say things like, "I won't do anything unless you give me a voucher," that doesn't help. It's a matter of doing the work. The law of averages says that you're going to get into SAG eventually by being persistent, by being on the sets. If union people don't show up on a set, those vouchers are handed out. So, more than likely, that's how you are going to get one. Sometimes if you are a "right" type, and we show pictures to a director and you are very unusual or someone we feel we want to show even though you are non-union, many times if he really likes you, per his discretion, we can put you on a union voucher. So it's about pursuing the work. It's about just doing it. Eventually it will happen. It will. And it always happens when you least expect it. If you try to force it, it's almost like you push it away from you.

What to Expect When You Join

The cost of joining SAG-AFTRA (*www.sagaftra.com*) is a one-time fee of $3,000 plus annual dues starting at $198 (based on your previous year's SAG-AFTRA earnings), paid on May 1 and November 1 every year. Work dues are 1.595% of covered earnings up to $500,000. These are hefty sums, but remember the union has a lot to offer. Day-performers (actors with speaking parts) earned a minimum of $880 per day in 2014. This rate is subject to occasional increases, so be sure to check with SAG-AFTRA for the latest rate. These minimums are known as "scale" for day-players. There are other minimums for working three and five days, and a huge set of tables that determine residual payments for movies, TV shows, and commercials that run more than once.

The Benefits of Being in the Unions

Being a member of the unions has many great benefits, in addition to the most important ones, like having minimum contract requirements negotiated in advance through collective bargaining, and having assistance in the event of an employer dispute. Some of these include free assistance with income tax preparation (SAG-AFTRA's VITA Program), a SAG-AFTRA credit union that also offers members low-interest credit cards, casting lines by SAG-AFTRA that list casting announcements, and bulletin boards in union offices with notices posted by other members regarding apartments or houses for rent, automobiles for sale, airline tickets, and a few other things from time to time.

Another important benefit of being a union member is health insurance for qualified performers. In SAG-AFTRA, a performer must earn a minimum of $10,000 (in reported earnings from SAG acting jobs) within four consecutive calendar quarters to qualify for free basic health insurance, which kicks in three months after the close of the qualifying quarter. Performers earning more than $23,000 in any four consecutive quarters qualify for additional benefits that include dental, mental health/chemical dependency, and life insurance coverage. AFTRA members must earn $15,100 in a calendar year to qualify themselves for coverage and earn $30,750 in a calendar year to qualify their dependents for coverage.

A Final Note about Gaining Union Status

It's important to remember that while becoming a union member is an important step on the road to being a successful actor in Hollywood, it by no means ensures that you'll suddenly become a hot commodity. Keep in mind that there are already approximately 160,000 members!

One of the drawbacks of joining the union is that, once you are a member, you are not supposed to perform non-union work anymore, excluding student and graduate films. Thus, some industry people suggest you at least get some experience under your belt before rushing to join the union, because a résumé with no credits doesn't mean much, regardless of union status. Your credits and experience will still be very important. And since we're on the topic of résumés, it's time to focus on how to put together a professional-looking résumé and how to get an outstanding picture of yourself that will hopefully bring you the attention you deserve.

SAG-AFTRA is located at 5757 Wilshire Boulevard, Los Angeles, CA 90036; (323) 954-1600. For online information, go to *www.sag-aftra*.

Industry Interview: Ben Whitehair, Actor, on Getting a Unioncard

What was getting your union card like?

I joined AFTRA before the unions merged. For new actors, I definitely think getting your union card is a milestone—it's the marker of being a pro. It was a special moment when I got the letter saying I was eligible, and then my card, in the mail. Being in the union says I take my career seriously as a professional, and being union makes it easier to work on many projects. After all, do I want to work for anyone who can't have food on set for me, can't pay me a fair wage, or can't keep me safe? No, and as a union member, I have that benefit of having that safety, of having the people I work for hold themselves to that higher standard.

It's OK to say no—whether you are union or non-union—to work that's not quality. Saying yes to an audition, for example, doesn't mean you have to say yes to the job.

YOU'LL NEED A GREAT HEADSHOT

As a new actor in Hollywood, you will definitely need fantastic pictures of yourself, at least until you're very well-established and your work remains firmly planted in the minds of casting directors, directors, and producers. These pictures, most often referred to as "headshots," are your calling cards and you will go through hundreds, if not thousands, of them while seeking opportunities to work. It will be important to have headshots that show you looking your best, while at the same time, still looking like you.

If you are moving to L.A. from another part of the country, then you might wait until you arrive to have new pictures taken. You will find a greater selection of talented photographers who know what is acceptable and stylish in terms of headshots. There will also be many more places where you can get quality reproductions at affordable prices.

How to Find a Photographer

Finding a good photographer is a relatively easy task. As with actors, L.A. seems to have a plethora of skilled photographers, and a few you'd probably want to avoid. Locating the right one for you will require some investigation on your part, but if you know where to look and what questions to ask, it won't be a difficult undertaking.

Probably the best way to find a good photographer is by referral. If you have a friend with a dynamite headshot, ask who photographed it. Perhaps you'll see some headshots of actors in an acting class or while at an audition. Be sure to ask them the photographer's name. Or if you have an agent or a friend in the industry, ask them too. They'll most likely be able to give you several names. This is the quickest, easiest way to find the photographer you're looking for. You won't have to be "sold." You'll already know that you or someone you respect likes the product.

When it comes to finding a terrific photographer, Google is of course a very effective tool. Just plug in "Los Angeles headshot photographers", then spend some quality time scrolling through the sample images on these shutterbugs' websites. You'll no doubt see some beautiful images that are evocative of the vibe you'll want to project in your own pictures.

Another source of photographers is *Back Stage*, a weekly magazine and website (*backstage.com*) for actors in L.A. In addition to articles, casting notices, and reviews, you can find numerous photographers' ads, usually displaying a sample or two of their work. It's not a foolproof method of finding the perfect photographer, but it helps in locating a photographer who might suit you. You should also check theatre bookstores, such as Samuel French (7623 Sunset Boulevard or 11963 Ventura Boulevard), where many photographers advertise in a variety of actors' monthly, quarterly, and annual resource guides.

Your next step will be to contact the photographer and find out what types of packages are offered. In L.A., the cost of hiring a photographer varies a lot, and the expensive ones aren't necessarily the best! So have a price range in mind, and if the photographer's quote falls within your budget, then make an appointment to review his or her book. The book, or portfolio, contains examples of the photographer's best work. All reputable photographers have one.

You ought to meet with several photographers before choosing one to take your pictures. Sometimes people get overly excited about the first person they meet. Just remember there is no hurry. Taking a week to check out different people will not be wasted time. In the long run, you'll be glad you did.

There are several important topics you should cover with every photographer you meet. I've listed below many common concerns that should be addressed during your initial visit.

What Will the Session Cost? The cost of headshots varies tremendously, typically ranging from $200 to $700. The more expensive photographers aren't always the best, so you really have to choose one based on quality, and not just price. Despite the big difference, the average cost usually runs between $300 and $400.

How Many Shots Are Included in the Session? This used to be a necessary question a decade ago. Most photographers offered package deals, where they would typically shoot two or three rolls of you. Other photographers simply shot on a "per-roll basis," from one to as many as you'd like. With the advent of digital photography, many photographers can shoot a hundred or more shots. A good digital photographer won't actually limit the number of shots, because he/she will be willing to explore with you different ways you might want to present yourself, over the course of about an hour of shooting in general. I recommend asking if the electronic photographs you receive will be ready for touch-ups or airbrushing.

How Many 810s Will I Get? With digital, the possibilities are endless. However, you won't need more than two or three pictures, because it gets extremely expensive to print multiple shots and it's usually unnecessary (unless you are a character actor with many distinct looks).

Will the Shoot Be Indoors or Outdoors? Some photographers only shoot one way or the other; others are well-equipped to do both. It's really a personal choice for the actor. Generally, people with more of a "street look" or an active, athletic image tend to get their pictures taken outdoors, to complement their personality. Those shots are softer, and more lightly textured. People who tend to be more upscale, conservative, or glamorous usually go for indoor lighting, which is sharper, crisper, and filled with more contrast. However, there is no firm rule on which types of photos you need to have. It's purely a personal choice.

Who Keeps the Images? About half of all the photographers in L.A. will give you the images right after your shoot. This is good because you can have headshots blown up rather easily, without having to ask the photographer to do it and then waiting several days. It's also advantageous because you have complete control over them. They become your property.

Of the photographers who choose to keep the images themselves, some will charge you their cost for blowing up shots, without making any money on them. Others tack on a few extra dollars to the cost of each print. Be sure to ask the cost so that you're not shocked when the time comes to order.

How Much Do Prints Cost? Typically, good quality prints in a quantity of 100 duplicates will run you $65-95 when reproduced on good paper at a quality lab. While you certainly could get it done for less, most photographers use quality photo labs that can create a superior original from which you'll make cheaper mass reproductions. If you still choose to make your own print, I highly recommend going to a photo lab as opposed to your local Walgreens.

How Many Different Looks Am I Allowed During the Shoot? This varies from photographer to photographer, but most suggest a couple of looks. (FYI, many photographers offer package pricing for a series of looks—say, three looks for $400, and another $75-100 for each additional look.) You won't want to change wardrobe every five pictures anyway. You'll want to have a large pool of shots to choose from, so just pick a couple of outfits that suit your personality. It's a good idea to know what specific type of wardrobe you want beforehand, rather than trying out many different looks during your shoot. Doing that will only make you more nervous and cause you to feel under pressure to present a perfect pose for every single shot.

Will the Actor Be Responsible for Hair and Make-up, or Will the Photographer or a Make-up Artist Take Care of It? Men generally wear little make-up during their photo shoots and their hair is usually low-maintenance, so this is not an issue for them—though it's still a good idea to cover up any dark circles under your eyes and get rid of any shine on your face with some powder, regardless of your gender. Usually the photographer will take care of this. However, women especially will want to clarify this issue with the photographer. Many photographers suggest that you come made-up beforehand, and they then add some finishing touches. In some instances, the photographer may recommend a make-up artist to assist, which can cost an additional $75 to $160.

Is There a Satisfaction Guarantee? Most photographers will reshoot your pictures in the event of a lighting or exposure problem, or if the style is not what you had specifically requested. But don't assume this; be sure to ask. However, poor facial expressions or postures are your responsibility. Therefore, you'll probably be at a loss if you try to get pictures retaken just because you didn't come across as charmingly as you would have liked.

Choosing the Right Photographer

Overall, there are really three factors you should weigh when selecting a photographer. One of the most important is cost. You have to go with someone you can afford. Don't spend $700 if you don't have it, because you will have duplication costs as well. Granted, you might get some great pictures with an experienced and expensive photographer, but if cash is limited, there are still many photographers in L.A. who can take excellent pictures for less.

Another important factor is quality. It's strongly recommended that you visit at least three or four photographers before choosing one. You'll be coming from a much more knowledgeable and informed viewpoint when interpreting the quality of any particular person's work. Don't choose someone just because his or her fee is dirt cheap—you'll probably have to have your pictures retaken again by someone else.

The third factor, often overlooked, is compatibility. Even if the cost of a photographer's services is within your range and the quality of work is exceptional, you'll be taking a risk by hiring him or her if you don't relate well. You must share the same vision and have a mutual understanding of how you want your pictures to come out, or it is pointless. If you don't feel comfortable or relaxed, the tension will inevitably come through in your pictures. Therefore, having some type of compatibility, whether on a friendly or professional level, will make all the difference in the world.

Appropriate Wardrobe for Pictures

Once you've decided on a photographer and have set up a time to shoot your pictures, choosing your wardrobe will be the next important decision. You'll have to ask yourself a few questions. What type of person are you? Are you a character actor or a leading man/woman? Are you a street type, or are you more refined-looking? Are you warm and fuzzy, or are you intense and commanding? You should think about these questions and take a few moments to think about the types of roles you are suited for. For now, forget about being able to play a wide spectrum of roles. Just think about how people will see you. Ask your friends for their honest opinions.

If you're more of a street type, you might wear a leather jacket, jeans, and a T-shirt. More conservative-looking people usually wear a dressier shirt, vest, sweater, or sport coat. Some go purely for a business look, with men wearing a coat and tie, and women wearing an elegant suit, dress, or sweater. By far, older actors tend to go for more conservative looks, while younger actors are more street-oriented. But don't feel as though the boundaries can't be crossed. Just go with what suits you.

Whatever you wear, make sure it has some style to it and be certain it makes you feel comfortable. That means no out-of-date ties, jackets that are too small, bell bottoms (unless you are extremely hip and trendy), or high-water pants. In terms of color, don't wear solid shirts that are similar in tone to your skin color. They blend too closely and get lost in one another. Don't wear any extremely busy patterns either, as they will detract too much from your face, which should be the main focus. It's better to wear textured clothing, or colors that offer a nice contrast to your complexion. Your photographer will probably offer you some suggestions before your shoot.

The Day of Your Shoot

Though you won't want to make a big production out of getting your pictures taken (because it only creates anxiety), you should do several things that will help make everything flow nicely. First, be sure to get a lot of rest the night before. Make-up covers a lot, but it can't replicate the unique glow that a well-rested, relaxed face gives off. Second, try to exercise a few hours before your shoot. This creates a radiant youthful look, from increased circulation and endorphins released throughout your body. Third, give yourself ample time to prepare your wardrobe (and make-up, if necessary), and enough time to get to your photographer's location. Many photographers book clients in one- or two-hour blocks, so you need to show up on time. Running late will only make you edgy. And finally, relax and enjoy your shoot. If it helps, bring some music that makes you feel good and play it during the session. Or even bring some personal belongings that evoke positive feelings within you. Do whatever it takes to feel comfortable.

The Best Pictures and Current Styles

If your photographer is working with film, you'll get proof sheets of the negatives within a few days. Hopefully you'll be pleased with them. From these you'll choose the best shots, and there will probably be several great shots on each roll. For digital photos, the photographer will probably burn a CD for you with all the photos taken during the shoot. Then you can take it and have all the shots. But it varies from person to person, so if you go with a digital photographer, be sure to ask about his or her particular process.

When making your selections, you should look for pictures that capture one of two things: either your true personality, or the personality you want to portray. The first is much easier to do for newcomers, and probably much safer. Look for shots with a natural expressiveness that isn't too posed. The second type, shots that reflect a certain image you want to portray (i.e., the hunk, the villain, the nerd), can be difficult to use as an actor if you don't really have a definite grasp on the types of parts you are well-suited for—and many newcomers don't. But if you're certain you're a villain or a demented scientist, then zero in on that particular niche.

It's always good to ask someone else for his or her opinion. Sometimes we're biased when it comes to judging ourselves. Therefore, consult a friend, preferably a working actor, as to which shots he or she likes. Your agent (if you have one) will probably advise you. Your photographer will more than likely point out his or her favorites, too.

In your decision-making process, don't worry too much about having the "perfect" picture, because they really don't exist. Headshots are photography, and photography is art, and evaluations of art will always be subjective. No matter how good a picture might be, there will always be someone who doesn't like it for some reason. So just pick the ones about which you and your advisers feel most passionate.

The key is to have pictures that look like you, while you're looking good—very, very good. If you are considering reproducing a photo that looks marvelous but distorts your image in a significant way, whether it be through heavy make-up, an unusual hair-style (one-of-a-kind or super-poofy), or an uncharacteristic expression, you will be wasting your money. The reason is that casting directors and agents will be expecting to see the look on your headshot, and not anything else. So make sure that the picture looks like you!

But don't misunderstand. Your picture shouldn't depict you as mediocre, average, or boring. It has to catch the attention of casting directors as they weed through stacks and stacks of other headshots. Make sure your photo gives off a positive, honest, and likeable image. It must stand out by conveying an intriguing yet approachable persona. It must have a feeling and a point of view, and look candid, too. The photo is not so much about what you look like; it's about what you are trying to capture. So when you are doing your shoot, remember to think of the feelings you are trying to express. You might be expressing something like, "My life is so incredible since meeting you" or "I just got named Salesman of the Year."

For theatrical roles, you will want to have a headshot that conveys a somewhat serious, dramatic look, but not too overdone or melodramatic. Pictures that can express vulnerability and strength at the same time are great. A few actors can get away with a pouty look too. For commercial roles, you will want more upbeat pictures that express warmth and enthusiasm. You'll want to show off your smile and your teeth, as a majority of commercials need happy people. (But if you don't think you're a commercial type, don't be discouraged. There are plenty of spots that also call for character types. The more unusual and funny-looking, the better.)

Three-Quarter Shots: A Recent Trend

In recent years, a growing number of actors have started using three-quarter shots in addition to traditional headshots. These shots are appropriately named because they typically display three-quarters of the body, from the head to the thighs or knees. They are particularly popular with many commercial agents and commercial casting directors because they reveal more about one's appearance. Not only can they see your face, but also your proportions, weight, and overall presence.

It's a good idea to have a three-quarter shot of yourself in addition to the standard headshot because it will give you and your agent an option when submitting for a part. (However, there are some casting people who hate three-quarter shots, and others who like them. Many casting directors say that a good picture, regardless of whether it's a headshot or three-quarter shot, is what is most important.)

Reproducing Pictures

Once you've settled on one or two favorite pictures, you will need to get them reproduced in mass quantities, for auditions and mailings. In L.A., there are two common methods of duplication: photographic prints and lithographs, also known as "lithos."

Photographic prints are reproduced on photographic paper and look the best. However, they are considerably more expensive. The process involves taking a precision photograph of your 8x10 original, which becomes an 8x10 negative. From that negative, duplicates are created in mass quantities on either matte or glossy photographic paper. They come very close to replicating the original. Prices vary depending on quantity, but the average cost for an order of one hundred reproductions runs approximately $50 to $75. Matte paper, which some feel is a bit classier, is slightly more expensive. In addition, there is usually a one-time charge of $10 to $15 for the negative, plus a $5 to $10 typesetting fee if you want your name to appear on the 8x10. Most people do. (At most places, however, you can avoid this fee by typesetting your name on a computer yourself and bringing it in with your order.)

Where to Have Them Reproduced

There are many different duplication houses in L.A., and prices usually don't vary too much because there is tremendous competition. Below is a list of some of the photo-duplicators that many actors frequently use:

Ray's Photo Lab
(Ray The Retoucher)
1328 North Highland
Los Angeles, CA 90028
(323) 463-0555

Anderson Graphics
3550 Tyburn Street
Los Angeles, CA 90065
(323) 460-4155

Isgo Lepejian
257 S. Lake Street
Burbank, CA 91506
(818) 848-9001
Also at: 1145 North La Brea Avenue,
Hollywood, CA 90038
(323) 876-8085

Industry Interview: Advice from Michael Helms, Photographer, on Taking Good Pictures

Could you tell me about your idea of an ideal photo session?

The ideal photo session involves many elements. Before the shoot, you should meet with your agent and/or manager to decide what images are being sought. A stylist should be consulted for clothing and accessories. A hair and make-up artist should also be consulted. All too often, because of budgetary concerns, clients sacrifice some or all of these. With that in mind, here are a few suggestions:

Ultimately, actors should "be themselves." What you wear greatly affects how you are perceived. Therefore, it is important to wear clothing that reflects the "image" you are trying to project. Put your money where you make your money. If you look rather "momish" it would not be wise to compete with "beach bunny" types. Conversely, if you're young, blonde, and blue-eyed, the chance of being cast as a D.A. is slim. Ask your agent, manager, and/or acting coach—"What is my type?" "How will I be cast?" We are all multifaceted, but remember (especially those just starting out), lead with your strength. Decide what "looks" you want well in advance of your session, then dress accordingly for your photos.

There are a few things you should avoid simply because they rarely work well in photographs. Avoid solid white, deep "V" necks (unless a more sexy image is desired), tank tops, tube tops, sleeveless and short-sleeved tops. Avoid busy patterns, i.e., plaids, paisley, polka dots, large checks, big prints; and leave your Hawaiian shirt at home. Generally, the idea is not to compete with your clothes for attention.

Hair and make-up also affect how you are perceived. Rarely can clients "do their own" and have it look as if it were done professionally. Make-up for a photo session (even very "natural" looking make-up) is not what you wear on the street. What the camera sees is different than what the human eye sees, so professional hair and make-up artists custom blend their products to enhance the faces of their clients.

Michael Helms can be contacted at (818) 353-5855.

Industry Interview: Advice from David Muller, Winner, the Backstage Readers' Choice Award For Los Angeles's Favorite Headshot Photographer, 2010, 2011, and 2012 (Award Nominee For 2014), on Summing Up a Successful Session

In your professional opinion, what are some common mistakes actors make when it comes to looking for a good photographer for their headshots? What should actors always seek from a photographer to make sure their photos come out as professional and polished as possible?

Just because a photographer got some good photos of a friend of yours does not necessarily mean they are the best fit for you. When you look at a photographer's portfolio, pay attention to whether or not they'll be the best for your type. If you're a character type and have lots of fun personality, don't go to the photographer whose strength lies in capturing the beautiful leading types, as you won't share the same vision for your shoot.

When it comes to physical presentation of themselves, what's your advice for actors wanting to look their best in a headshot?

Wardrobe really does make a huge difference! An actor who comes in with boring, disheveled, un-inspired clothing completely does himself a disservice. You are competing in the age of the thumbnail, and your clothing is taking up a good part of your photo, so make it count!

How has the digital age changed the way headshots are produced and distributed within the industry? What advice would you have for actors on how to capitalize on digital exposure when it comes to utilizing a great headshot?

There was a day when an actor needed a good "theatrical" headshot and a good "commercial" headshot. Generally, they were black-and-white and most people looked quite glamorous and better in their headshot than they did in real life. Today, it is a complete 180. Casting directors want to see what you look like as a certain type i.e., young mom, business professional, blue collar worker, etc. The general feeling from the actor's point of view is that it makes headshots even less fun than they already were and a little bit more work for them, having to plan different wardrobe choices, instead of just wearing your favorite shirt. Overall, it can be looked at as a positive, since it forces the actor to think somewhat objectively about their type and how they are likely to be cast. Know your type, nail your type!

What do you like to see your actor clients bring to the table when preparing for their headshot session, so you can help them achieve the image that will show them to best advantage? (E.g., taking your suggestions when it comes to poses, collaborating to choose the right finished shot, etc.)?

I love when people come in prepared with great wardrobe, knowing their types, knowing and being on the same page with their agents/managers as to the goal of the headshot session. Know what you want, and know what you don't want. Then, trust your photographer and don't micromanage the shoot; that always yields the worst result.

Also, be flexible. I can't stand when someone tells me they don't want a certain side of their face photographed. It just shows me that you're interested more in how you look than showing a type, so you can get called in for a job! Check your own likes and dislikes about yourself at the door, and experiment in your shoot, have fun and, honestly, don't pick your own headshot! I truly believe that actors should not pick their own headshot, as it's very hard to get past liking and disliking things about yourself. You want a shot that speaks to people, so listen to people who will tell you truthfully, who are in the know about the business.

David Muller can be reached at davidmullerphotography. com.

PUTTING TOGETHER A
PROFESSIONAL RÉSUMÉ

In addition to a great headshot, you'll also need another very important selling tool: a professional résumé. Just like anyone else in the job world, you, as an actor, will need to compose a fantastic résumé that will clearly and effectively help sell yourself to potential agents, casting directors, directors, and producers.

In the entertainment business, actors submit their headshots and résumés together. The résumé is attached to the backside of the 8x10 picture, usually with staples or rubber cement. (Paper clips, tape, or glue that wrinkles the paper are not recommended.) The résumé will include several very important things about you as an actor. First, it will list your acting experience, such as any film, television, or theater work you've done. (It won't include non-acting employment, such as summer lifeguard jobs, congressional internships, or professional employment in any another field.) Second, it will detail your education and training as an actor, which includes any high school, college, and professional experiences. Finally, it will list any and all special skills you have, which hopefully will be needed sometime in the future.

The presentation and format of your résumé are crucial if you want to be taken seriously. I can't tell you how many new people in Hollywood goof up this important step for just getting your foot in the door. So many young, intelligent actors with college and/or community experience come to this town with improperly formatted résumés. Others with little or no experience almost always have a poor résumé, too. The result is that you look like an amateur. And while in truth you might be an amateur, you won't want people to think you are. Therefore, you'll need to know the right way to display your credentials in a professional manner, whether you're the star from Small Town, USA, or just starting out.

For younger, inexperienced actors, the thought of creating a résumé can be an unpleasant one to say the least, since often there is little or no information to give. If you are in this situation, don't panic! There are several honest ways to expand your résumé, and they will be discussed at the end of the chapter.

Following is a breakdown of how to write a typical Hollywood acting résumé. You'll find explanations of how to present information and why you should do it that way. There is also a sample résumé immediately following to help tie all of this information together.

Your Name

This is the very first item on your résumé. Many feel it should stand out, but not overwhelmingly. It can be several font sizes larger than the text or simply bolded or italicized, but whatever you do, don't make it one or two inches tall just to fill space. The general consensus is that gigantic names look funny to agents and casting directors. If anything, it might draw attention to the fact that someone doesn't have a lot of experience.

If you have a fairly common name and are non-union, you might want to check with SAG and AFTRA to see whether or not someone in the union already has it. The reason is that no two people in a union can share names that are spelled or sound the same. Thus, if your name is John Smith and someone else in SAG is named John Smith, you're going to have to use a different name when you eventually join SAG. Therefore, it might be a good idea to start using a stage name now that you won't have to change down the road. For example, if your middle name is Patrick, you could be John P. Smith, John Patrick Smith, John Patrick, or really anything you want. It really doesn't matter, as long as no one else in the union uses it.

Union Affiliations

Underneath your name, any union affiliations are listed (e.g., SAG, AFTRA, AEA, etc.). If you are eligible to join a union like SAG but haven't joined (most likely because you don't have the money), then write "SAG-eligible." This helps to legitimize you in some people's eyes. If you have no union affiliations, then don't write anything. Keep in mind that most people won't be looking only to see whether or not you're in SAG or AFTRA, except for some agents. A killer smile or mysterious eyes will grab someone's attention much better than any union affiliation.

A Contact Number

You'll need to include a telephone number where someone can contact you or your agent. If you don't have an agent, instead of using a home telephone number, many actors opt for voicemail, which generally runs $10 to $15 a month in the L.A. area. The reason is that in the event your picture ends up in the hands of an undesirable person, you wouldn't want to be harassed at home or on your cellphone. This probably won't happen, but nonetheless it's just one reason why most actors (especially females) choose voicemail. Another reason is that you won't have to worry about having your messages misplaced or accidentally deleted by a roommate, friend, or relative. You'll have total control.

Your Website, If You Have One

A lot of actors nowadays, especially younger ones who are computer-savvy, find it easy to establish their own websites. It's a great way to post many more photos of yourself, in color and black and white. You can also list more about your personality and other interests. Most casting people will occasionally check out your website to quickly learn more about you before calling you into their office.

Your Stats

Get ready to reveal some of your most closely guarded secrets. Imagine applying for a job at a company and having to give them your weight! Outrageous? Yes. But in the acting business it's completely the norm. In fact, casting directors—especially those who cast commercials—need to know as many things about your appearance as they can to see if you're a possibility for a part. So if you are going to try to find a commercial agent or audition for a commercial, it's imperative that your statistics are included on your résumé. For roles in television and film, some established actors choose not to include such information. But for now, as a newcomer, you should include it. (Once you secure a theatrical agent, you should check to see what he or she prefers.)

Your statistics should include height, weight, and hair and eye color. It is advised that you be truthful with this information, though with weight, a few pounds here or there won't make a difference. (No one is going to weigh you!) You will not necessarily help yourself by stating that you are much taller or slimmer than you really are, because casting people will discover the truth when you show up—and they will be expecting whatever sizes you've stated on your résumé. Parts are cast for people of all heights and sizes, so don't be self-conscious about whether you're the right size.

However, if you feel you want to be slightly taller on paper, then write down your height when you are wearing shoes with thick soles (excluding platform shoes!). After all, you'll be wearing shoes at auditions. With regard to hair, some suggest using descriptive adjectives to complement your hair color. For instance, instead of "brown" some might put "chestnut brown" or "dark brown." For blonde, it's good to specify, "light blonde," "sandy blonde," or maybe even "golden blonde."

A side note: An agent friend kindly told me one time that "blonde" is for women and "blond" is for men. No one had ever taught me that, so be sure to use the correct spelling when submitting. (But keep in mind that most people aren't going to hold any one thing against you, especially something like the spelling of "blonde." It's just that the more intelligent you are on your résumé, the better it will reflect on you.)

Film, Television, and Theater Experience

These are all fairly self-explanatory categories. While there is no rule carved in stone about how these should be listed, most people with a lot of experience tend to separate each category and then list work under each appropriate heading. Others who are fairly new sometimes combine them into "Film & Television" and "Theater," and still others leave out "Film & Television" completely if they have no experience in that area. In L.A., film and television appear before theatre because they are the main industry here.

Be sure to include all experience, unless you have dozens and dozens of jobs and plays that you can list. Most people generally list the most recent work first, especially for television and film. For theatre, most list the most prestigious work first (i.e., Broadway, Off-Broadway, Off-Off-Broadway, community theater, college, high school, and so on).

Also, if you have any industrial or training film experience, then either list it under "Film" or create a separate category for it. (Industrial or training films are used by companies to train employees or to instruct clients on the use of products/services. For example: The short video you see on airplanes about seat belt safety is an industrial training film.)

Commercials

On 99 percent of all résumés in this town, you will see something like "List available upon request" or simply "Upon Request" after this heading. This is because commercial agents don't want casting directors to be influenced by what you may have or have not done in the past. For example, unlike films and television shows, many ad agencies want fresh, new faces—not someone who's been overexposed in ten commercials over the last year. Therefore, it's wise to just say "Upon Request." (No one will ever ask for a detailed list anyway.) Conversely, if you've done nothing, you wouldn't want anyone to know that either, so "Upon Request" is a good filler.

You should know that at certain times you will never be considered for a commercial if you have a conflict, meaning you've done a commercial spot for a competitor. For example, if you just did a Sprint commercial, you won't be considered for a T-Mobile spot.

If you are seeking commercial representation and you have commercial experience, you should by all means mention it when you contact the agent. Detail all of your commercial experience in a brief cover letter. It will help you tremendously.

Training

Here you should list all professional study, college training, private coaching, and any weekend workshops or seminars that you have attended. If you have a degree, say so—even if it's in another field. (This is the only place to list your non-acting credentials.) Actors with only a college degree in acting, or just a few classes under their belt often list them all. Put down anything you can think of.

If you haven't had any training, then you should probably get some. While training isn't absolutely essential (as several of today's great stars have never taken an acting class in their lives), it gives you credibility, especially if you study with a well-respected teacher or a well-known school. It makes a casting director feel safer when calling you in. It also can make you a much better actor. So train as much as you can afford to.

Special Skills

This is the final category on your résumé. You should fill this area with every activity you can do reasonably well. This category is most often referenced by commercial casting directors who need special skills for commercials.

Below is a listing of useful skills that actors have. While you won't need to know how to do all of them, knowing just a few of them might help you to get a part someday. Use this list to guide you in creating your own.

Sports: any martial art, basketball, football, baseball, ice hockey, tennis, swimming, surfing, soccer, bowling, billiards, fencing, horseback riding, gymnastics, tumbling, boxing, roller skating, rollerblading, weight training, golf, frisbee, archery, rodeo, water skiing, etc.

Arts: dancing (ballroom, hip-hop, jazz, square dance, others), musical instruments, singing (opera/classical, cabaret, pop, rock, jazz, R&B), art (drawing, painting, sculpture), comedy (stand-up, physical).

Unique skills: juggling (2-ball, 3-ball, pins, knives, etc.), contortionist, magician, card dealer, firearms expert, auctioneer, yoga, stilts, tightrope, etc.

Dialects: the more specific the better. (e.g., "Kentucky" is better than "Southern," "Brooklyn" is better than just "New York.")

Accents: (e.g., German, Russian, French, British, Spanish, etc.) You should only put these down if you are proficient at them.

What to Do When You've Got Limited Experience

There are two schools of thought when it comes to writing your résumé. The first is that you should be as honest as possible:

If you haven't had any experience, then be up-front about it and use your enthusiasm to get work. The second is that you should creatively write your résumé, stretching a truth here or there, to make you look like you're not a total novice.

Most industry people advocate honesty for a couple of reasons. One is that it's simply the right thing to do. It shows integrity. Another is that if you're ever caught lying, you could ruin your relationship with a casting director. While most casting directors have never checked the validity of credits on an actor's résumé (because what really counts is how well you do your audition), you might audition for someone who happens to have cast the production you inappropriately listed on your résumé. Therefore, it's not recommended that you lie outright on your résumé if you are lacking credits, especially in the areas of television or film.

The second school of thought encourages beefing-up your résumé in creative ways. For instance, you could stretch the truth a little by including one or two "extra" jobs you've done. Such work is not really supposed to be on your résumé, but many new people include their best jobs (not more than two, or it becomes obvious) to demonstrate they've at least had some experience working on a set. People usually list the part as "featured" or "bit" rather than "extra." If you decide to do this, be prepared to explain if an agent or casting director should ever ask about it.

Another option is to use "Representative Roles" as a heading, instead of "Film & Television." Under this category, list two or three movie or theatre roles that you have studied and would feel comfortable playing. Some believe this is a good way to give agents and casting directors a better indication of your "type." Obviously, choose parts that fit your age range and type. In Hollywood, as a newcomer, you're encouraged to play the parts that fit you. Rarely does anyone want you to play ten or twenty years older or play extraordinary, larger-than-life characters. They leave those roles to the stars. In time, you'll get your chance at them.

A third option that some actors have utilized is to list under your "Theater" section several credits (which include the name of the play, the character, and a theatre) of plays and roles that you know extremely well. If you do this, hopefully you've studied the plays before, in the event you're ever asked about them. (And keep in mind, some people just want to make conversation when they ask about them; they're not necessarily trying to interrogate you.) I've heard some respected agents, well-known celebrities, and even a few casting directors recommend beefing up your résumé this way! In fact, I once heard a casting director tell a group of actors, "Do whatever you can to get in the door." However, know this: Almost all casting directors strongly discourage padding your résumé this way because it's very disappointing and irritating when they think they are calling in an experienced actor and a novice shows up. Most industry people can assess your experience just by the way you walk, talk, and present yourself.

The Finished Product

Once you've written your résumé, you should design it on a computer. If you don't have a computer, consult a friend or a résumé-typesetting service on *backstage.com*. (There are some really great companies, often run by other actors who specialize in creating sharp, eye-catching résumés.) A final option is to go to a copy store, rent one of their computers, and do it yourself. Be sure to set the margins correctly for an 8x10, rather than for an 8½x11 piece.

Once you have a master, you should reproduce at least one hundred copies. It's cheapest to do it at a place like Staples or Office Depot, where one hundred copies are only a few cents a copy.

Some actors opt for fancy, colored paper, but in reality it makes little or no difference. Casting directors aren't going to disqualify you because your résumé is on plain white paper! That is, in fact, what most actors use.

Next, have them cut your résumé to 8x10 size at a copy center. This is very inexpensive and looks much better than if you try it yourself with a hardedge ruler and a cutting knife. But if you really know what you're doing, then save the $2!

If you use rubber cement to attach résumés to the backs of pictures, only put a dab in each corner. This will prevent major wrinkles. If you use staples, one on the top and one on the bottom is sufficient; however, some agents prefer one in each corner so that there is no chance of the résumé falling off.

Once you've got your pictures and résumés together, you'll want to start putting them to use. Keep a few on hand at all times, and start sending them out to agents and casting directors. And have one for an acting teacher, who'll talk about your goals with you and how you might achieve them. Chapter 9 talks about the importance of studying your craft while you pursue work.

And One More Thing...

Despite the fact that we're living in a digital age, it's still widely accepted (and expected) in the industry that you'll submit your headshot and résumé via good old-fashioned US mail. (Once you're signed by an agent, of course, your photo and credentials will probably go up on your agency's website, and info about you and your work may be emailed when it comes to specific audition and employment situations, but that's later on). Here's the standard procedure for how to do it:

- Submit your 8x10 in an 11x14 inch envelope.
- Write a short, punchy cover letter that covers basic 411 about yourself—who reps you if you already have an agent, the role you are submitting for, if applicable, a short bio paragraph if you are using this mailing to try to get an agent, and any references you and the recipient of your headshot and résumé may have in common.

- Now, wait one month. If you don't hear anything, it's OK after that point to send a polite mailed follow-up (a note on a postcard is perfect). Be friendly, but don't nag or plead—and whatever you do, don't call or email, which can really annoy busy power players in the business. Don't be discouraged if it takes a while to get a nibble—keep trying, because if you've got what it takes, someone *will* notice you.

STUDYING YOUR CRAFT

Even though there are stars today who have never had one formal acting class, most industry notables will tell you that it's a smart idea to get some training under your belt here in Hollywood. Training of any kind can only help you! It won't get you the part, but it probably will give you more confidence in yourself and your acting ability, which ultimately will help in getting hired.

Many new actors in town show up with no training at all. Only an inspiration draws them, and that's okay. Others come with a long trail of studies from high school, college, and beyond. It's obvious that the latter individual has somewhat of a head start, but according to many acting coaches, even high school and college training tends to be somewhat basic. (Of course, this depends on where you might have studied.) While some fresh, new, college-trained actors are quite brilliant, many others lack a well-developed craft. Additionally, most aren't prepared for television and film or for the audition process or cold readings (auditioning with material just given to you). Therefore, you should strongly consider taking some classes in L.A., regardless of your high school or college background.

In L.A., you'll find many teachers offering a wide variety of study programs that range from short term to indefinite. The courses explore and develop the acting craft in-depth, and can teach you more about "the Biz" than any high school or college class ever did. Many programs are also specifically tailored for actors seeking work in television and film, not just theater, as in most high schools and colleges. Another plus to studying in L.A. is that agents and casting directors often look highly upon the actor who seeks to improve his craft by studying with a respected teacher.

Acting Classes and Workshops

Virtually every acting coach teaches his or her own particular variation of a method, some more in-depth than others. That means that there are hundreds of different styles to choose from! Your options will include "method" classes (which are usually variations of the Stanislavski System or the Lee Strasberg Method), scene-study/monologue classes, auditioning/cold-reading classes, improvisational/comedy classes, film-acting classes, commercial workshops, and dance or voice classes. All of these are good ideas, if you feel they can help you in some way. The problem is that new people often don't know where they need help, in terms of their acting skills. Therefore, it's best to ask around and get referrals from friends, agents, casting directors, or periodicals when choosing an acting teacher.

Whatever classes you decide to take, you will find that most meet one to three times a week, with the cost typically ranging anywhere from $200 a month upward; a quality program like Stella Adler will typically run you $950 for an eight-week course. There are also some schools, like mini-colleges, that have one- or two-year acting programs. Obviously, fees for extended programs are much higher. While they can't hurt you, attending a one- or two-year school is really not necessary or by any means a sure way of getting your foot in the door. What matters most is that you can act, and secondarily, that you've studied with a reputable teacher.

Below is a more detailed description of the different types of classes you'll find in L.A.

Method Classes. You've heard of "method" actors. They study and utilize a method to help them in their acting. Thus, at method classes actors learn a particular method or system that is designed to give them a technical mastery of the craft. Most programs initially start with classes in fundamental exercises and culminate with the execution of polished scenes, weeks or months later. You will find many different instructors teaching a variety of methods, although generally most teach some version of the Stanislavski System or the Lee Strasberg Method. There are also tons and tons of other "method" classes that have a variation, expansion, or combination of methods. Plus, there are those who teach versions of the Meisner technique (not a method, but a technique), developed by Sanford Meisner. Whatever you choose, make sure that the approach offered is helping you!

Some famous method actors include Marlon Brando, Paul Newman, and Al Pacino. Famous Meisner students include Gene Hackman and Robert Duvall.

Scene-Study/Monologue Classes. These programs focus on developing acting skills primarily through rehearsal and refinement of scripted scenes. As with any class, it is important to have an established and respected teacher who will be able to give you helpful and poignant insights. There are hundreds of scene-study classes with all kinds of teachers, so find one with whom you feel comfortable. Many will let you audit a class for free to see if their style and approach to teaching suits you. This type of class can be very beneficial because you are constantly engaged in developing characters and working with scene partners, whether in class or during the week while you are preparing for class. In other words, it really keeps the "acting" juices flowing in you. Another important benefit of scene-study classes is that you are inevitably exposed to many, many important plays and playwrights you should know.

Auditioning/Cold-Reading Classes. Every actor new in town should take one of these classes, regardless of background. In Hollywood, your brief audition gets you the job, not the fact that you might be a brilliant actor from high school or college. Even if you are an established actor but feeling rusty, you should take a cold-reading class. I can't tell you how important it is!

Concentrating on mastery of the audition process, most classes consist of weekly, videotaped auditions with an instructor. Sometimes a guest casting director, along with the instructor, offers you wisdom on how to break down your script and refine technical aspects of your audition. Just be sure that the teacher is recommended and respected.

Improvisational/Comedy Classes. For those seeking to develop or polish their comedic abilities, improv/comedy classes are the way to go. Not just for stand-up comics, these classes have helped many actors land roles in commercials and sitcoms. They require some courage, but many find them to be extremely entertaining and uplifting. Some commercial casting directors even specifically state in their breakdowns that all actors being submitted must have comedy/improv training, usually from a school like The Groundlings or Second City. So taking some of these classes will not only help you develop as an actor, but it might help in getting you called in by a casting director when he or she sees that training listed on your résumé.

Film-Acting Classes. These classes usually operate like scene-study classes, except that the scenes are taped, hopefully professionally, as if they were appearing on television or film. This helps people fine-tune technical aspects. While some of these classes can be good, they sometimes offer newcomers little instruction on the process of acting, which is usually what they need the most. However, good film acting classes can, and will, sometimes provide you with nice material for a reel if you don't already have one.

Commercial Workshops. Sometimes these are taught by commercial casting directors as weekend events. Other times, independent teachers might hold six- to eight-week classes devoted entirely to the process of "commercial" acting and auditioning. These are great for refining your commercial technique on camera. But beware of any workshop that leads you to believe you have a strong chance of landing commercial representation just by taking the class. (Some classes invite agents to come to class one night.) Some students have gained representation that way, but I've heard from too many others that didn't. Therefore, if you take one of these classes, make your goal to develop a better auditioning technique, and let "landing an agent" be icing on the cake. Ask around for classes recommended by agents.

Dance and Voice Classes. Any class that expands your performing ability is a great thing. This is why many actors also learn to dance and sing. While not essential for success, classes devoted to other performing arts help you to become a double or triple threat when in the arena competing with other actors. Many actors have landed roles because they had that additional talent that allowed them to stand out from the crowd, and some simply find these classes to be great stress relievers.

Choosing a Teacher

The best source for finding a teacher is through referrals. Nothing beats a good recommendation from a friend. Lacking that, you will find a myriad of teachers advertised on *backstage.com*. Listings of acting teachers and their backgrounds can also be found in several publications, including *Acting Coaches* and the *Working Actors Guide* at Samuel French Theatre & Film Bookshops. Google "acting coaches in Los Angeles," and visit the websites of at least five teachers to read in-depth about their experience and teaching styles before settling on a specific person.

When searching for the right teacher, try to meet with several before deciding on one. Most important is to have a teacher who is not only well-respected but capable of helping you. He or she must also be compatible with your personality and be willing to treat you the way you want to be treated. After all, you are paying them! Just like in every other profession, you'll find acting teachers with a wide range of personalities. Some are harsh, others are more gentle. Just find a teacher who works for you. Finally, take a look at some of the students in the class. Find out if they are serious actors and if they are working. If they are, it will not only ensure that you get much more out of the class, but also indicate that the instructor is a good one.

You'll find that some acting coaches feel that college training is essentially garbage and that you should try to forget everything you learned and start over. Other teachers might feel your prior training has served you well and that you are ready to fine-tune your craft and work on scenes in a scene-study class. It can sometimes be a subjective call, depending on who you talk to. Therefore, talk to several teachers to see what course of action might be best for you.

A Checklist of Questions to Ask Before Enrolling in a Class

To help you find the most appropriate teacher, it's a good idea to get answers to the following questions before enrolling:

- How long has the instructor been teaching?
- What is taught/What is the format? Is there a method?
- What is the maximum number of students per class?
- How long is the course of study? Is it ongoing?
- What are the requirements for attendance?
- How often does it meet each week and for how long?
- What is the cost of the class?
- Are there any additional materials to be purchased?
- Are there any prerequisites for joining the class?
- Are there different levels? How will you be placed?
- Will assistants be teaching the class or the instructor?
- May you audit the class first before joining?

Don't Be Fooled by False Promises

In this town, there are a few people who prey on young, naive actors by promising them the world. Be aware that legitimate acting teachers will never guarantee you work. If they do, then you should probably turn around and go the other way!

Some organizations sponsor acting workshops taught by industry insiders—casting directors, agents, directors, producers, and the like—and while no guarantees are made, there is an implication that you'll get connected with the right people. The truth is that you might, but very often these are busy people (who see actors all day long anyway) who are simply trying to supplement their income, not trying to find new talent. Sometimes, but not always, they are horrible teachers, too. Also, occasionally a casting director's name will be mentioned as a teacher, but instead an associate or assistant will show up to teach the class. Therefore, ask questions beforehand.

There are mixed feelings among actors and casting directors about these types of workshops. Some feel that paying to audition, which is essentially what many believe it boils down to, is unethical. Others feel that with so much competition, you have to do whatever you can to gain an edge over other actors, even if it means buying access.

If you decide to do one of these, then be sure to inquire about exactly who will be teaching and what kind of attention you'll be getting. Such investigation might keep you from feeling that your money has been wasted.

Keeping Up-to-Date with the Biz

In addition to staying in shape with acting classes and workshops, you'll also want to be "in-tune" with what's happening in the industry. Several trade papers that you should read on a regular basis to be an informed member of the entertainment community include *The Daily Variety*, *The Hollywood Reporter*, and especially for new actors, *Backstage* magazine. *The Daily Variety* and *The Hollywood Reporter* are published daily and cover all types of entertainment-related news, including deals, mergers, grosses, stocks, executive shuffles, productions, and gossip. *Backstage* contains casting notices, interviews, and stories, along with ads for instructors, workshops, photographers, and others. All of these periodicals can be purchased at any nearby convenience store, news-stand, or bookstore. You can also find them on the Internet at *www.dailyvariety.com*, *www.hollywoodreporter.com*, and *www.backstage.com*.

Though there is no need to become a database of infor-mation, it's really important to know what's happening in Hollywood. It helps your credibility when you're familiar with the various studios and their heads, film schools, arts organiza-tions, current and future films, and stars who are the talk of the town. It shows you are an industry player, and not just the new kid in town.

In addition to reading papers, you should stay informed and knowledgeable by watching television and going to see movies and plays. As an actor, part of your job is to know the work of other actors, directors, and writers. It's good to know every show on TV, in the event that you get an audition for one of them. You'll feel much more confident going in to read. You'll know whether the comedy is supposed to be subtle or over-the-top, or whether the character is supposed to be real or more like a caricature.

So sponge up as much as you can about the industry, but maintain a sense of balance. Don't be so over-consumed that you live, eat, and breathe Hollywood! Just maintain an eager and enthusiastic attitude. You'll feel more and more like you "fit" into this town as you come to know more about it, and you'll find that the more you know about the business, the more people will take you seriously.

Industry Interview: Advice from Eric Morris, Acting Coach, on Acting and Acting Classes

What is your impression of people who come to this town with college acting training? I know it varies a lot, but what is your overall impression?

Well, after teaching tens of thousands of people, I have a real cross-section. Here's my feeling, and it's a little bit elitist and a little bit hard: Most of the people who teach in universities and colleges are academics who never really went out there and worked in the field as professionals. They are academics, they learned their stuff in college and then went on to get their M.A.s and Ph.D.s and M.F.A.s, and they stayed in academia. They haven't a clue about what goes on.

Also, I think being a fine or great teacher is a God-given gift, predicated on your knowledge and talent. The talent without the knowledge is as dangerous as the knowledge without the talent. But I find categorically that college-trained actors are ill-equipped to deal with creating reality in front of the camera or on the stage. There are only a half a dozen teachers I think in the entire country that I have respect for in terms of what they're teaching. I think there are probably hundreds of teachers who are ethical, committed, involved, and want to do the right thing, and are really committed to coaching and teaching and sculpting people, but they don't have a process. They haven't anything to teach.

So what I would say is, if you go to college and you want the degree, that's all fine and good, but I've never had to use my degree (and I was an associate professor at USC, hired for my attainments in the industry). I was there for eight years, part-time. But if you want to go to college to get a degree or you want to get a background or you want to be well-read, then read a lot of plays, and get a good theater background. More power to you. But if you're really serious about being an actor, and particularly coming to California, you should find a really seasoned professional coach/teacher, not a college teacher.

After college, you should really spend two to three to four years training regularly, consistently with a professional, well-established teacher with a good reputation and a process. It's the only edge you have when you come to Los Angeles. The only edge you have is to be able to push your buttons with professionalism and a certain kind of mastery, and come up with a result. Because that's all they care about: what comes out on that screen. And if you don't know how to access your emotions, and you don't know how to create an inner, organic, authentic life on the stage or screen, you're in a pool of thousands and thousands of actors and then it becomes like a roulette wheel. Does the ball land on your number this time? Do you get a job because of that? To really call attention to yourself, and create and build a reputation in this business, you have to have an edge, and that edge is being a craftsman. No matter what talent endowment you have, you've got to be able to access it.

I really want to reach people and communicate, and help people to make our business, our theaters, our films better and more authentic and more meaningful. Because the richer our industry and our theater are, the richer we all are. And everybody has to collaborate in that. You cannot take things out of the world without putting something back. You have to do that, and I'm really committed to that.

What advice do you have—mental, spiritual, physical—for actors?

Well, mentally, first of all, if you're going to go into this business, don't do it unless you need to do it. It's a calling, something you want to do. It's something you're inspired to do because you love it and you're going to make a commitment to it, a life commitment to it, not "I'm going to give this a try for one or two or three years." Listen, before Jack Nicholson did *Easy Rider*, he had been in the business eighteen years and had done thirty-one films, and nobody really knew who he was. Do you know what I'm saying? In the larger scale, we know who he was. But until he did *Easy Rider*, on the worldly level, nobody really knew who he was. So what I'm saying is that you can't come here for a year or two and "give it a try" because it isn't that kind of business. You might be here three, four, five years before they even know you exist! That's the first piece of advice.

The second is to look out for the charlatans. Parasites. People who want to take your pictures and manage you and coach you and shoot reels for you, and promise you work. They survive parasitically on the young, impressionable, needy, unschooled, and naive actors. Look out for the charlatans! Don't go with a coach unless you check them out with Screen Actors Guild or you get references, referrals, you've heard of their reputation, or you've read their material. Don't go with an agent just to be with an agent. Find out who he represents, what he believes in. And don't go with an agent because he takes you because he likes your blue eyes. You want to be with an agent if he sees your work and he's turned on by what you do, and he has a good reputation and is recognized, accredited, and licensed to practice. Don't go with a manager. I don't think people should be with managers until they are at a certain place anyway. But don't go with a manager unless you have his credentials and know who he is. So many people out here want to reach into your pocket.

You should be well prepared. If you don't come into town well prepared as an actor or craftsperson, you should get with a really good coach who has a good reputation, and there are some really good people out here—it doesn't have to be me.

The other thing is, I've seen more people spin out in this town and fail because they did not recognize their financial responsibility. They got too deep in the hole and couldn't dig out. So finally, they had to get a job and give up. You should come here with some money if you can, at least enough to hold you six or seven months. Don't depend on it, but look for employment in that period of time. Don't over-extend yourself. Don't rent an apartment or condo that is too expensive, because this is a feast or famine business. You might get lucky and get two or three jobs and then not work for six months or a year. I know some incredibly good actors who have gone two or three years without a job. It had nothing to do with their talent. It had to do with being in the right place at the right time and being up for the right role. So fulfill your financial responsibility so that you don't get sucked into the quicksand.

Spiritually, mentally, and psychologically: Keep optimistic and up. Any kind of spiritual involvement is good: yoga or other positive involvements. After you get some training, get yourself into a theater company, audition for plays, and be seen. If you're looking for an agent, get into a play and invite a few to the show, so that they can see your work. Start working on creating a reel, which is a videotape that shows people your work. The first thing an agent will ask you is, "Do you have anything I can show anybody?" So start working on the reel as soon as you can.

It's a very competitive business, and I've seen too many people die of a phenomenon that I call "theatrical immortality." And the phenomenon is that everybody has to work really hard and really struggle. "But not me, baby. It's going to happen for me!" That's a real dangerous mindset. You have to work. You have to make a commitment. You have to be prepared. You have to keep positive about it and you have to fight discouragement and depression by keeping productive, active, and creative. And if you do all of that, somewhere down the line, opportunity will knock. Because it knocks more than once. Opportunity knocks so often that its knuckles get bloody. You've just got to be there for it. And don't take it personally. Rejection is part of what you are facing. Don't take it personally! It is personal and it is not personal. Of course it's personal: It deals with you. You may not get a part because you are too tall, too short, too blond, or because you've got brown eyes instead of blue eyes. Or it might be because you don't have the right quality for what their concept is. You may be perfect for the part but they have a different concept. So you can't take it personally.

In your opinion, when one hundred actors audition for a role, out of that one hundred, how many have got the right stuff? And how do California actors compare to New York actors?

It could come down to something so minuscule as a vocal quality. You never know, but out of the hundred, I'd say it comes down to maybe 3 percent.

When I got here in 1954, there was the myth of the New York actor: that a New York actor was always better than a Hollywood actor. They were serious, well-trained actors. Well,

I taught in New York for fifteen years, and they aren't any better there than they are here. It's a myth and a fantasy. It's not true. As a matter of fact, there are probably more good actors here just by number. But what created that myth is the struggle, the commitment, the willingness to suffer for your art, the old Stanislavski addicts. But I have found some of the best actors in the world right here in Hollywood.

The best advice you can give anybody is to tell them to befriend somebody who's been in the business actively for five or more years. They can save them grief. They can save them a lot of grief!

Eric Morris can be contacted at Eric Morris Workshops, 5657 Wilshire Boulevard, Los Angeles, CA 90036; (323) 931-9245.

Industry Interview: Advice from Julian Neil, Acting Coach, on Acting and Acting Classes

Julian Neil has been an international award-winning playwright and a director of theater, television, film, and music videos. He is also the creator and producer of network television series.

Could you tell me a little about the California mentality that you've noticed, in terms of actors and acting?

Many California people have an understanding of the craft, but they just want to be stars. They just want to make it—and that's possible because people can see you. For example, I have a student who the other day was working in a pizza place and the head of Disney saw him there and liked him. He thought he was incredible looking and so on and so forth, and is now setting him up with things. So, that happens and people expect that a little bit out here. I am leery of that because it doesn't give you the foundation of the craft and I think it's all about always being able to deliver.

So are you a strong advocate of theater?

I think theater is like classical music. If you can play classical music, you can play jazz, rock-and-roll, boogie-woogie, swing, it doesn't matter. It's funny—in other arts, dancers don't even get on stage unless they've trained for eight years. Musicians play their instruments every day for hours and hours and hours. But actors—a lot of them, not all, but a lot of them—feel like they can just not practice, not constantly work on and be opening up the instrument and stretching it, learning and developing. I think that's a big problem because acting is a craft, and as in any other craft, it's what is necessary. So I'm a big advocate of training and theater, really knowing your craft and always working on it.

In terms of theater versus film, if I move my hand largely, it's fine on stage, but if I do that on film, I'm out of frame. So there's a very different technique involved. With stage you're on two hours straight. With film, you sit around for two hours, and then you go for thirty seconds. So it requires a different technique and approach in a sense.

In addition to the training, what are the other important issues that actors should keep in mind as they work on their careers and acting?

I think that being focused—incredibly focused—is a must. Most everything you do should be geared toward acting, if you really want to get a hold on it. However, I believe in balance. I tell my acting students all the time that they need to know classical plays (not only by Shakespeare and Strand and people like that, but Arthur Miller and Tennessee Williams, some of our American playwrights as well), but they should also be versed in music and literature and painting, etc. I think that is all very important: that you understand all kinds of crafts. Many times you can look at a painting or a photograph and you understand characters and you become a character just by that exposure. It gives you an experience that you then can translate through your instrument. And that's part of what I mean by being focused. What you do artistically and creatively ultimately feeds the instrument.

Emotionally, you have to understand that you can only do your part, and that so often there are so many other variables.

The best actor does not always get the part. There are just too many other variables. So, learn to emotionally stay balanced with yourself and understand that all you can do is do your part. It's about just doing the best you can each time—being able to stay focused, patient, and growing.

Spiritually, don't get caught up in the illusion of the business. I think integrity is the most important thing. For me, integrity is not being able to be bought or sold, which means whether they offer you the Mercedes or they tell you to go be a waiter, that won't change the integrity of where you are creatively and your desire to have that creative expression. Be a contribution, and to me spiritually, this is the most important thing. See yourself as contributing something valuable to the industry, and therefore, to people that view the entertainment industry.

If you fall under the illusion of acceptance and rejection, it's a detrimental trip. You get tossed around. It's hell on earth. Every time they say you're "great," you shoot to the moon, and every time they don't give you the part, you fall to the depths. Your life will be hell. So I personally recommend a lot of yoga and meditation for actors, because it's very balancing and healing. It puts you in touch with yourself, and combines the body's spirit and mind, which is the instrument. We are our instrument. We don't put them away in a case, we carry them around with us. Just like I wouldn't want to take my sax and drag it on the cement and bang it around, we as actors have to treat our instruments with the same respect. So eat good food and exercise. This is why California is great—the sunshine! These are things that help the body. So find those spiritual practices. It can be walking on the beach. It doesn't matter, just so you stay balanced and that you stay connected beyond the illusion, in a state of serenity and peace.

Also, we're in the business of illusion. Hollywood is like Detroit. They make cars in Detroit, and we make movies and illusion here in Hollywood. I think you have to be careful not to get sucked up into all of that.

As an actor and a teacher, how do you recommend that people go about finding an acting teacher?

One way is to get a periodical called *Acting Coaches* at Samuel French.

I have a spiritual view on it: You find your teacher when you're ready, and you get the right teacher. But I think you should still look around. It doesn't mean that the first teacher someone recommends to you is "your teacher." I tell all my clients that I'm not the teacher for everybody and I know that, and I expect them to know that. But I might be the right teacher for them—it depends. We need to see how it is.

So Samuel French is a good place to start if you know absolutely no one. *Backstage*, and the trade papers are also places where you can get names or read testimonials from actors that you like. Agents often have a certain number of acting teachers too. Most agents will give you three or four different acting teachers that they recommend for their clients. That's another good way. Also, try asking at auditions or going around to the theaters and talking to people—Who do you study with? What method is he/she teaching? How do you like it? Can I come and see it? Can you give me their number? Can I call and get an interview?"

I think you have to be systematic about it and try to get as much information as possible. And when you feel an affinity toward a teacher who is saying and doing the kind of things that you want to experience, and you feel they can really train you, then that's who you should start with.

As a director, what do you look for in actors? What turns you on and off? What inspires you to want to work with an actor?

There's an energy that comes from confidence. You can feel actors when they audition. You know when they're worried about what we the auditioners think of them and their work. It's a neediness, and an insecurity that we feel. And I will say that's a turn-off. Right away you've lost us.

So I'm always looking for somebody who is really able to bring out the truth of who they are. The more you can use yourself and your own truth, and you can do that without your own judgment, this is what comes through. Don't worry about what we are thinking. We watch actors who won't go into certain areas because they judge themselves, or they think they're going to look silly or that feelings make them weak. So they don't show their feelings or else they don't know how to.

A truth and a precision of craft—skill—is very important. It's a combination of both. Skill can be taught to anyone, and repetition is the mother of skill. So if you practice every day, you will gain skill. And I want to see a skilled actor. But I also want to see someone who really knows how to bring life to something—that's the truth part—sculpted through the text given them. That's the skill part.

What would you tell someone who's just moved out to Hollywood? What advice or words of wisdom would you offer about the way this town works?

You have to be prepared to support yourself financially. Finding a good foundation right away is almost more important than anything else. Finding a good place to live and a good job is practical advice. Get in a class so that you can be part of what's happening. Meet people who have been established and find a teacher who is established. Network, because in this town, it is very, very important. I would pick up the trades and books on agents, and again network. If you have a brother, or sister, or friend, or a distant cousin, or somebody you know, make the phone call. Don't be shy. If you don't ask, it won't come to you. No one's going to find you in your apartment. They are not going to say "Oh, you finally came here!? Great! He's here!" So ask. The worst they can say is "No." And you're no worse off than when you started. So I think a lot of times, we want to stay humble. Humility is good. But we also have to be aggressive, and by that I mean, we simply ask for help. It's okay to ask for help. And to listen a lot and seek advice. Stick with the winners. Look at the people who are doing the kinds of things that you want to do, playing the kinds of roles or working in the kinds of arenas that you want to work in. Look for those things.

And don't be frightened of the town. It can be overwhelming. These are practical things. In general, I say to anyone, if you can do anything else and be happy, do it. This is the business with the greatest highs in the world, but also very hard and tough, depending. Some people have an easier road. I look at it spiritually as karma, destiny, and those kinds of things. And if it's not going to be fun, don't do it. There's a certain sense of fun people have to have.

I also think that, in this town especially, going places, meeting people, learning to do the schmooze are all important. Being places. Showing up. You have to start to just be places. And don't turn down an opportunity because of too many opinions, especially when you're new. Know less, I say, and then you can experience more. Don't come with an attitude of "I know how to act. I know how to do this. I just need this and I just need that!" The people who come and say "I don't know anything. I just want to work and I'm willing to do . . ." are the people who have a greater experience. They stay open enough to get the experiences, to be places, to do play readings, whatever. I'll give you an example: I'm directing a play that just opened and the actress in it has a wonderful agent now. She's an incredible actress, and a while back she did a reading, nothing more than a reading of a movie script—just a "Can we get together in a room and read it for some industry people?" Well, it just so happened that there were a couple of agents who saw the reading and they signed her as a client based on that reading. That's how good she was. So I say, look at all the opportunities that present themselves.

Industry Interviews: How Training Shaped My Career
Kyle Walters

What's your philosophy on acting classes?

I think training is great. I studied with John Rosenfeld, plus at Upright Citizens Brigade. I think the thing to do is to sit in on several classes to make sure you find the one that covers what you want to learn, and that you like. Another thing I found that was very helpful about my training was that it helped me create a real nice community of actor friends I'd meet. For me, it was building a web of trust with those actors. Training's not free or cheap, but it's important for an actor in a number of ways.

Ben Whitehair

What are you personal thoughts on training? How do you suggest using it to your best advantage?

Training is imperative, but for every actor, the way it looks will be different. There is no specific right way to train. Of course, there is a baseline standard everyone needs to meet, but what you study depends on what you're looking for. Maybe you've done a lot of theater, so you need a class to help you when it comes to adjusting for camera. You might want to take commercial classes, or improv classes. I suggest auditing at least ten classes before committing, because you're going to be paying a lot of money to study.

I like the analogy of actor as athlete when it comes to studying—classes are like a daily workout. If you're a football player but you don't work out every day, it would be crazy to think you'd make it to the NFL! So study, and figure out what you want to focus on, careerwise. I think it's important to understand that the entertainment industry in Los Angeles is actually forty-three different industries. There's the commercial world, there's the world of hour dramas, the world of live theater—everything is so different, it can be overwhelming. So try everything, but narrow yourself down in order to be super-effective. Maybe two, or maybe three areas of the industry—know what you want to focus on after that exploration.

FINDING AN AGENT

It is essential to be represented by an agent if you want to work as a professional actor in Hollywood. While you might be able to seek out work in student films and small independent projects on your own, you'll definitely need someone else pushing for you if you want to play in the big leagues of television and film.

What Agents Do and Why You Need One

In the simplest terms, an agent submits actors for roles, coordinates their auditions, and then negotiates their contracts when they are cast for parts. One reason that you, as an actor, need an agent is because only agents (and managers) have access to the full Breakdowns, a service that many casting directors use to list roles they are casting. Also, having an agent legitimizes you by showing that someone believes in your acting ability. Additionally, an agent can open some doors by using his or her connections, which hopefully will land you more auditions and ultimately more work.

Getting an Agent to Represent You

Fortunately, it costs nothing to get a legitimate agent to represent you. All you need is for an agency to think that you have strong potential to make money as an actor. Any legitimate agency makes money only when the actor works, with the compensation being 10 percent of the client's earnings. This is regulated by the Screen Actors Guild and is standard throughout the industry. There are never any additional charges or fees that an actor can incur. This is great news to newcomers!

However, some say that every rose has a thorn, and that thorn is that it can be somewhat difficult to actually find an agent to represent you, especially if you are a newcomer here in Hollywood. The reason is that there are thousands and thousands of actors seeking representation. SAG members have a far better chance than non-union folks, but even most of them have to work hard to attract an agent.

So how do you do it? How can you get an agent interested in you? Following is a discussion of some of the most common ways actors—even those with little experience—have grabbed the attention of agents and landed representation.

Showcasing Your Talent. There are many theaters in Los Angeles where you should try to get the opportunity to showcase your talent. Every week *Backstage* has numerous listings (both Equity and non-union) for upcoming theatrical productions. So read the notices! Often auditions are open to the public, and all you have to do is show up. You'll be guaranteed the chance to try out for whatever part you want. When you are cast in a play, it's a perfect opportunity to invite agents and casting directors to come see your work. But make sure the play is a quality production that shows you in a good light. And make sure you have a sizable role that warrants their coming to see you. They won't be very impressed with you as "Crowd-member Sixteen," who's got one line in the Second Act.

If you feel you're pleased with the production, then send out postcards or flyers inviting industry people with an offer of complimentary tickets. Take the time to send something nice. A professional invitation runs circles around a sloppy handwritten note on spiral notebook paper. Some actors even follow up their mailings with phone calls to the people they especially would like to attend.

If an agent likes your performance, he or she may want you as a client! Casting directors, who frequent theater regularly, might even call you in to read for roles they are currently casting! Lots of actors have been noticed this way. In fact, of all the methods of obtaining agents, this is probably the best way. The reason is that you are giving them an opportunity to see your polished talent. Additionally, you will be demonstrating that you are capable of getting work, as evidenced by landing your role in the production.

Mailing Out Pictures and Résumés. This can be costly and time consuming, but it can be successful, too. Though agents receive tons of mail on a daily basis from new faces, many actors have obtained representation this way.

Start by sending out pictures to about twenty or thirty agents at a time. Hopefully, you'll get a call from one or two. With your picture, attach a brief letter explaining a little about yourself and that you are seeking representation. Short, direct, and polite notes are best because they seem most professional. Let some of your personality come out too, but don't go overboard! Silly and absurd notes often are inappropriate and ineffective—unless, of course, you are a very eccentric character type who might be expected to send something a bit nutty.

If you have very little experience, you might consider going after a commercial agent first. This is because commercial casting is based more on looks than acting ability or experience, so agents will be less concerned about your background. Take a good look at all the commercials on television; more than half of the principal actors aren't even speaking, so a long theatrical background isn't always necessary. All that's needed is an ability to be professional, coupled with something distinctive about yourself, whether it's stunning beauty, warm and fuzzy energy, unique skills, bizarre looks, or pizzazz.

Referrals. It helps tremendously if you have a friend or relative who is already signed with an agency. He or she can assist in getting your foot in the door to meet an agent. By no means will that connection guarantee you representation, but it's definitely an opportunity that many new actors have to work hard to get.

Remember, much of this business is knowing the right people and the right people knowing you. So if you have connections you might give serious consideration to using them. A friend saying, "Hey, this guy is really great. I definitely think you should meet him," goes a long way.

Sharpening Your Approach

The trick to getting an agent is clearly setting yourself apart from the pack. This probably sounds pretty difficult to do—after all, aren't there a zillion 5'7" brown-haired brown-eyed ingenues just like you roaming the streets of L.A.? Maybe in type, but not in essence—only you are you, and you need to emphasis your best qualities, both personally and professionally, to make a great impression on an agent who can take you places. Here are five points to focus on:

Perfect Your Demo Reel. If you've done enough work on film to cut together your "greatest hits" package of scenework, terrific—now use it to best advantage, so when you show it to a prospective agent he or she will instantly get how to sell you. Your reel should be no longer than a minute; agents often have far shorter attention spans than that, so put your best work upfront. Your face should be the first (and final) image seen on the reel.

Cut the scenes you include to be short and sweet. It may sound a little cold and calculated, too, but it's just common sense: don't include scenes with even "give and take" between you and another actor. Make sure *you* are driving each scene/clip you use! (The friend you're performing with in your scene can spotlight himself in *his own* reel.) There's a technique called scene splitting that's becoming more standard in the industry—essentially, labeling individual clips (like "Mother Searching For Lost Child") so that again, the intention of the work you're spotlighting yourself in is crystal clear at first glance. This can be a good idea if you have a range of strong characters under your belt. Make sure you look as marketable as possible as

Narrow Your Possibilities. Many actors send out scores of headshot/résumé packages, cross their fingers, and wait for the phone to ring. This *can* work, but know that your odds are about one interested agent per one hundred send-outs. Consider targeting between ten to twenty agents instead; research who they represent, and what films/TV shows/plays they've sold performers to, to find an agent who might be interested in what you bring to the table. Check out individual agency websites; Google and IMDb (Internet Movie Database) are of course other great web resources. Pursue a mix of agents for your best odds—small boutique agents, a medium-sized agency rep, even a rep with a large, well-known agency if you feel you're really ready. (It's OK to dream big—just don't be disappointed if it takes a while to have your dream, and your talents, acknowledged.)

Use electronic communication wisely. Don't email an agent cold. They hate that—it's the same as showing up at their office, grinning widely, with your headshot. Don't try to hook up over Facebook or Twitter unless you use a subtle, cautious opening. For instance, you could add your two cents to a point the agent posted about a film you happened to work on (even if you had a tiny role), if the agent liked said film. That could open up a fruitful conversation. Flattering an agent slavishly, or being a pest, won't serve you at all.

When an Agent Calls You In: The Interview

If an agency is interested in you, one of its agents or owners (usually their assistant) will call you and usually set up an interview. If the meeting is for theatrical representation, you might be asked to prepare a scene or monologue (unless you already have a video reel of your work, which they'll probably opt to see instead). This is usually something most actors dread because the monologue takes place in a cramped office and you have to perform solo for several minutes to an audience of one person who happens to be judging you. To ease this situation, some agents will read sides with you, instead of asking you to do a monologue. This is actually more like a real casting session. Also, some agents will want to see you in a showcase, instead of having you read in their office.

If a commercial agent has called you, then you will most likely have to read commercial sides that will be given to you sometime during your meeting. Whatever an agent asks, it's best to try to accommodate his or her wishes, as long they are strictly professional. As a new person, you really won't have any clout to do things your way.

During your meeting, you will probably talk a lot about yourself: your experience, your acting background, your goals, your hometown, and your acting teachers. In addition, standard conversation starters like sports, the weather, Los Angeles, and current events may come up too. Most agents are really just trying to get a sense of how well you communicate and present yourself. Some agents really could care less about your experience; they just want to see if you have some indefinable sparkle in your eye, which they usually notice in the first twenty seconds.

After your meeting, you will probably have some idea about whether or not they are interested in representing you. If they are, they'll definitely tell you. If they aren't interested, or just not sure, they'll usually give you an excuse and say they'll get back to you.

If they inform you that they would like to represent you, but you still have other agency interviews scheduled, then tactfully put them off. Express your immense interest (even if it's only moderate) and let them know your situation. Most agents will understand and would never pressure you. In fact, most will encourage you to interview with other agents too.

If an agent chooses not to represent you, for whatever reason, be very polite and thank him or her for spending some time with you. Reasons an agent may not want to represent you are varied: It could be that she already represents too many people that are your "type." (But then you have to consider, why did she call you in?) It could also be that you didn't click, that you reminded her of a bully in high school, or perhaps you're not as polished as she wants you to be. Regardless, it is not the end of the world. There is an agent out there somewhere who will believe in you.

Signing with an Agent

In Los Angeles, actors are supposed to have only one agency representing them theatrically (television/film/theater) and one representing them for commercials, though the same agency can represent an actor for both. Thus, you would never have two theatrical or two commercial agents at one time. It just depends on what you want to do or what a particular agency wants to do with you. A high-clout agency might want to represent you only commercially, because its agents feel your theatrical credits aren't extensive enough. Sometimes agencies are only franchised to represent actors in one area, so they can't cover you in both. As a newcomer, you'll take what you can get.

When you are fortunate to find an agency that wants to take you on board, they will either "sign" you immediately or operate on a verbal agreement, usually until you book your first job. Then the agency will probably sign you. When you are signed, both you and the agency will sign a SAG Talent Agency Contract (either TV/Theatrical and/or Commercials), which will be valid for one year. However, after the first 151 days, if you have not worked for at least ten days in the preceding ninety-one days, you may be released from a TV/Theatrical contract. With commercial contracts, if you have not earned $3,500 including residuals in the preceding ninety-one days, you may be released. (If your contract is a renewal contract, then the 151-day initial period does not apply.) Many agents don't like these clauses because they might work like a beaver for you for six months, with no compensation, and then you can leave them.

Though most actors prefer being signed because it solidifies a relationship and shows some kind of commitment from an agency, if you have obtained a verbal agreement instead, it's not necessarily a bad thing. Many agencies do this with relatively new talent and it's a way of setting up a trial period. Hopefully, your agent will send you out on a number of auditions, and hopefully you'll book something, which will establish a deeper commitment to you by the agency. However, if the agent receives mostly negative feedback about you from casting people, then he or she will probably conveniently forget about you, and you'll have to go looking for a new one. Likewise, if your agent obtains only one or two auditions for you over a period of several months, you'll know it's definitely time to go searching for a new one. And since you only have a verbal agreement, you can leave whenever you feel it's necessary, without having to meet contractual obligations. All it takes is a phone call.

Once You Have an Agent

Once you have an agent who is interested in representing you commercially and/or theatrically, don't break out the champagne just yet. It won't mean a thing until you start going on auditions and you start to book work. There are many actors who have landed representation with a power agency and then waited six months only to go on zero auditions! The reason this happens is either because the power agent is not submitting you or because the agent is unknown, a poor worker, has a bad reputation, or you have really bad pictures.

The time to start getting happy is when you are auditioning on a regular basis. This means at least once or more a week, or every couple of weeks during slow periods. Then you will know your agent is working hard and has a strong interest in promoting you.

To keep up your relationship and stay fresh in your agent's mind, it is nice to stay in touch at least once a week. It's especially important to do this if you are not being sent out often. As a premise for contacting an agent, many actors will call to check if any more pictures and résumés are needed. Other good topics of conversation include any roles you've heard about, or any classes or projects you're involved in. You will find that just a brief conversation is sometimes all that is needed to rekindle the fire.

It is vital to have a nice working relationship with your agent. If you can't stand the person, or if you feel very awkward or unwelcome every time you call, then it's obvious the agent is not the best person for you. An inability to communicate will probably lead to more trouble down the road. But don't feel as though you should be able to discuss with your agent, at length, details of your crisis of the week. Agents are agents, not therapists, and most agent/client relationships are fairly professional. As you get to know them, they may seem more like friends and your relationship may become more open, but basically they are busy business people who are trying to make a living. Just keep that in mind.

A Final Note: Remember to Keep Hustling

Even after developing a solid relationship with an agent, many successful actors don't just sit around waiting for a phone call. They are constantly searching for work themselves. They scour the trade papers, send out pictures themselves, network, and do just about everything to get some exposure. They are true "hustlers" who will stop at little for an audition.

It will be important for you to develop and maintain such a mentality. Remember that professional acting is a business. Like any businessperson, you need to cultivate leads and contacts. This means going on as many auditions as possible and meeting as many casting directors, directors, and producers as you can. It's a numbers game: The more you show off your talent to people, the more opportunities people have to buy it.

Industry Interview: Advice from Mark Measures, President, Kazarian/Measures/Ruskin & Associates, Speaking on Actors and Commercial Success

Could you tell me a little bit about yourself and what your day consists of?

Well, I'm a commercial agent, and I work with actors, actresses, celebrities, and sports figures doing television commercials. There seems to be a greater volume of work in TV commercials than in the theatrical world, and by that I mean that the agency will work on maybe forty, fifty, or sixty jobs in a day. The turnaround is very quick.

Before I was an agent, I was actually a production manager and stage manager for touring magic shows. I then started at an agency called Richfields-Freed, which merged with TGI, where I was in the on-camera and voice department for five years. Then I went to Special Artists where I worked for six years, and then I came to Abrams Artists just about six months ago and took over the department shortly thereafter.

My day basically consists of a lot of things. It consists of doing the Breakdowns (the commercial Breakdowns), selling actors, getting actors in on their auditions, meeting prospective clients—we meet anywhere from three to four people a day, sometimes as many as six—between the four agents here. I might also be negotiating contracts that are up for renewal, negotiating over-scale contracts, those kinds of things.

I think the Screen Actors Guild figures that 53 percent of the income made by actors in commercials comes from the Los Angeles branch. About 30 percent comes from New York, and the remainder comes from the other branches, like Atlanta, Chicago, and Seattle. So we do a tremendous amount of work out here.

Are most of your clients over-scale?

No, I would say that most of them are scale. There is a group of over-scale, or celebrity, clients, but the majority of the commercial work is scale.

What do you recommend to actors looking for representation?

Most actors come to town and they send out a mailing to look for representation, and I usually tell people that if you get a response or get an agent from a mailing, it's probably an agent you don't want. And that's always the discouraging part of what I usually tell actors, because doing a mailing is the way you are told to find an agent. I generally tell actors to use that same time and money and send to the casting directors. Get in to meet one, two, or three casting directors, just on a general basis, and they can then refer you to an agent. It's hard to get a really strong agent just by sending your picture in the mail. If I pull out one headshot a month from all the mail, it's a good month. The reason is that I have so many referrals from clients, theatrical agents, managers, and casting directors, I don't have time to pull out of the mail. You don't know what you are getting. And those agents that have a tendency to pull out of the mail, sometimes they are the ones that aren't that busy and don't have all those people referring to them. So they probably aren't going to be as strong as you want. But if you go in and meet a casting director and he talks to you and says, "You know what, such-and-such agency needs you. You know, Abrams Artists could really use a comedic woman like you. Let me give them a call." Then if you come in on a casting director referral, it makes it a little stronger to get in my door. It's about using who you know. If you have a friend who is an actor and he is really happy with his agent, see if he'll walk your picture in. It's an easier way to see me if a client brings me a picture of you. Don't do it just because someone says, "Well, I can bring your picture in to my agent." If he is not getting out to auditions and he is not happy with his agent, what's the point? Just to meet an agent?

Once you've chosen a new client, what turns you on and what can start to annoy you?

Well, there are clients who are high maintenance and there are clients who are not high maintenance. I have a client who called me so often after she first came in the office to see me that everyone was saying, "Is that your girlfriend?" She was the kind of person who just needed a lot of attention. Would that annoy some agents? Sure. Some agents aren't going to want to spend all that time on the phone, babying a client. But there is nothing in particular that really annoys me. Clients who get a "star mentality" are always annoying. But you know, you are in this for a reason and, hopefully, it's because you like actors . . . and I like actors. So you learn their foibles and you learn how to deal with each client on an individual basis.

If you had friends or relatives moving out here, what would tell them?

Make sure you come in with all your guns firing. This is the place where everybody is getting off the bus to come out and be a star. In New York, actors go to train and they start in the business that way. Out here, everybody getting off the bus is here to be a star. So have the best picture you can have, get into classes immediately—acting classes, commercial workshops, improv classes, whatever it is. And take classes with high-quality teachers. Find out who the high-quality teachers are. Get into those classes so that you are well-trained and prepared with a great picture. If you do that, then you'll be ahead of the game, especially commercially. When a Breakdown comes out to agents and a casting director is looking for "young girls, twenty to thirty, who are pretty," how many thousands of girls do you think are going to be submitted for that? Thousands! You've got to stand out from those thousands. So if you are not trained, or if you don't have a great picture, then you won't stand out. If your picture is something your friend took in the backyard and you took a commercial class at your local modeling agency, that's not going to be enough to get the job, or even get you in the door. You need to come out here and have the best training, and the best pictures, and the best agent you can have at the time so that all of your ducks are in a row.

That's great. Any other final words of wisdom?

I also tell people don't take it personally, especially in the commercial part of the business. It's not personal. They're sometimes seeing three hundred actors for one role. You'll be on a videotape that gets sent to an ad agency in St. Louis, and they'll be watching it while they are eating lunch and looking at story boards, and somebody will glance at the TV and say, "Oh my God, she looks like my ex-wife!" and they'll fast-forward past your face. So you can't take this business personally. Just go in and do the best you can do, and walk out the door and forget about it. Always do the best work you can do and be happy with the work that you are doing. If somebody "gets you," they'll get it. And if they don't, it's just one more person with an opinion. You can sit in my office and sit with the four agents here and walk out and none of us will "get you," and you might go and become the biggest star that ever walked the face of the earth. There are 120+ agencies in town: if one doesn't "get it," someone will at another agency. And find those people who understand you.

And know that some casting directors won't "get" you either. You'll go in and they'll look at you like you've got three heads. But you'll be attracted to those casting directors that "get" you. And we all have felt that way about actors from time to time. You might look at an actor on screen and think, "I don't get so-and-so. Why is that person a star? Why is that person starring in a movie?" That's your opinion. Just remember, there are obviously thousands of other people who do get it. So that's what I tell people. Don't take it personally.

Industry Interview: Advice from Chris Nassif, Former Owner of CNA & Associates, a Talent Agency (Now "The Diverse Talent Group") on Succeeding in Hollywood

Could you tell me when you became an agent and what you like most about it?

Well, I started this agency in 1982 right after I graduated from USC, and the agency has grown ever since. What I like most about being an agent is that I get to be involved in many things. I put projects together, I help clients' careers grow, and I get to see them go from rags to riches. Being responsible for all of that and having an impact on a person's life is very rewarding and enjoyable for me.

Could you tell me about a recent success story?

Ricky Martin is one of our successes. I took Ricky Martin as a client when he could barely speak English. I saw the hysteria that he had created in the Latin world, and at the time I was trying to get Hollywood to notice the power of the Latino market. Latinos buy tickets, they watch TV; they are a huge consumer group. And eventually we were successful in crossing over Ricky Martin into the U.S. market. We were able to get him on *General Hospital* and then on Broadway. So I was able to make my point.

But there was always a hesitation, and still is, in Hollywood where people will say, "Oh, we don't want so-and-so for this," or "We don't want so-and-so for that." And what it goes to show you is that people are always afraid to take a chance. But eventually someone does take a chance, and most of the time for me, I prove to them that I'm right. I proved that I was right with Ricky Martin.

What general advice do you have for new actors in Hollywood on finding representation?

Well, there are several steps you have to take. The first is that you have to have and maintain a positive attitude. It's essential.

Then, once you get to Los Angeles, if you have few or no credits and you are looking for an agent, the best way to get representation is to get into a workshop, a showcase, or an equity-waiver play. That way people—agents, casting directors, producers—can see your talent.

If you are coming from a place of strength, and you really are a good actor and you're confident that you are going to make it in this industry, then you shouldn't have a problem getting into a play somewhere in town.

What types of qualities do you look for when you meet with an actor for the first time?

When I'm meeting with an actor, my impression of them is based on how real the person feels. It's just a general feeling that I get. Do they feel like a real kind of person, where they are very sincere and serious about what they are doing? Are they in this business for the right reasons? Acting has to be the profession that they want to get into not because they want to sign autographs or get a great table at a restaurant. They shouldn't want to be an actor just to be recognized. Sure, that's the gravy, that's the fun part of being a successful actor. But the real reason for acting is because one has a die-hard desire to do it and because one totally loves it and one could be just as happy doing it in theater. You see, that's the kind of real actor that I am looking for.

What qualities tend to turn you off?

I suppose a turn-off is an actor who's not willing to take the proper steps. First of all, an actor brand new in town with little experience is not usually going to get with an agency like this. It's just very difficult to do that. You have to start somewhere—get some training, build some credits, take the proper steps. However, if someone is very young, we can be very open to that. You know, when actors are young and they are willing to train and if they have a certain type of charisma, we sometimes are willing to take that chance and invest in them.

What do you tell actors about how to stay balanced?

I beg actors not to get caught up in all the hype. You know, success is a by-product of their hard work. I try to tell them not to care about being a star, but instead to strive to do good work and become as good an actor as they can be. If they focus on that, then once the success comes, hopefully their head won't swell. If they've been focusing on their craft, then when they make it big they hopefully won't become unrealistic or hard to deal with. The truth is that very few people keep their feet on the ground when success comes. Very few people.

How would you sum up your advice to newcomers?

Well, if people are dead-set on coming to Hollywood, the advice that I would give them is that they have to be very serious about the craft of acting. If they are really, really good and they work hard at it, and they've got a lot of talent, then everything will eventually unfold as long as they take the right steps. And those steps include getting the right agent, getting into the right theater, getting into the right class, and doing great work in front of casting directors, directors, and producers.

Industry Interview: Advice from Buzz Halliday, Owner of Buzz Halliday & Associates, A Talent Agency, on the Business of Acting

What advice would you give to new actors who are seeking representation? How should they go about it? What should they do if they only have a few credits? What things can they do to help improve their chances of finding representation?

Number One: The actor should really want to be in this business. I mean that "not to act" would be life threatening. You have to have that desire and have that determination of "this is what I am, this is what I have to do." That's got to be there. If you don't have that, I don't care what else you've got to offer. That is what will get you through some of the leaner and more frustrating times.

Number Two: You've got to believe in yourself. You've got to feel that you are truly talented and that you're not approaching this as a fantasy. The entertainment industry does not have one set path. Acting school is not like going to law school, where after graduation you pass the bar exam and work for a law firm. An actor can go to acting school but that does not guarantee your future as a successful actor. So you have to really look at the big picture—which it is—and really feel that "this is truly what I want to do and that I am really talented."

Number Three: An actor has to understand where they fit into a casting situation. If a young character man comes into my office and I ask him, "Where do you see yourself?" and he says, "I want to do romantic leading roles," right away I know that this is not somebody I want to invest any time in. He is not seeing himself.

If you are new in town, showcases are a terrific way of being seen. Do not choose a scene or piece that you fantasize about doing. This is your opportunity to show other people what you think you are right for now. If you are a "young upscale person," you do that kind of a scene. Please don't play an older person or do material that you can't relate to. You'll confuse people and casting people won't get a sense of your talents because they'll be watching your choices and not your acting ability and you've wasted a great opportunity.

What makes an actor better or more distinctive? The choices that you make. You have to help by showing yourself through your pictures, presenting yourself properly, and by choosing good material. Your life as an actor is filled with choices. Filled with agents, pictures, material, wardrobe, classes. . . . The list continues forever.

What do you look for in a client and what turns you off from a client?

I'm turned on by an ambitious person. I can sense it immediately. I'm turned off by somebody who I feel lies, who's got a game going, who comes in with an attitude about instant stardom. It's not necessary. That's living in a fantasy world. They saw it in a movie, or they heard about it.

I'm sure that goes on, but if you're starting out and you don't know who people are, it's in your best interest to listen and ask questions. You should be in control of yourself and try to be in control of the situation so that you don't do something that you might look back on and regret.

What would you recommend to actors to stay active, to keep their creative juices flowing?

If you sit home waiting for your agent to call, it's going to be a very long wait. You have to read all the trades every day and circle the names of people you know and who might also know your work. I'd watch every new television show at least once. Make a list of shows that you'd like to be on and films you see and be able to say, "These are the kinds of parts I want."

You have to be constantly working at your craft. Do a showcase or two at a reputable theater. Join a theater group. You should take a good cold-reading class, because auditions come up last minute and you've got to be able to feel comfortable winging it. Don't be afraid to find out what your peers are doing. Also, I don't know how many people do this, but I think probably one of the most constructive things you can do is to form a group. I don't mean a self-help group but a support group. The group could get together at least once a month. Talk about what you've been auditioning for, how you're doing with your agent, and anything else that's been happening. I'm aware that some directors do this. They hang out and have lunch together at least once a month and they've helped one another with leads. That could help with actors too. But I don't advise meeting with people you may be in competition with. In other words, they may not be telling you the truth and why risk damaging a friendship?

What things should actors keep in mind mentally, emotionally, physically, and spiritually as they pursue their work?

The best thing, I think, is to know how to handle stress. I think all people have to find their own way of handling it, whether taking a yoga class, hiking, or learning another language—do whatever works for you. You have to deal with the physical part of yourself because there's so much mental stress in the acting profession.

I think it's terribly important to have something away from the business. It's what's kept me sane my whole life. You should always develop other interests because this business can become your life. It can just take over. When you are in a long-running situation like a television series, those people become your family and you have to become very careful, because the show will end and you could feel lost.

Actors can have a problem being well-rounded people. I actually had this problem early on when I first started out. I loved the business so much that the only things I read were about the business. I only hung out with industry professionals and I was becoming a very boring actor. I couldn't bring anything to my work except what I knew about the business. Every experience you have or create will add to the richness of the work. When you see some of the older actors who are around, why are they so interesting? Well, they have lived so much longer and lived so many more experiences, that they have that advantage over the young actor. If you get interested in other things, that's going to add to the wealth of your work.

Anything else you can recommend?

Oh yes, pictures are your passport! They not only have to look like you, they have to project the kinds of roles you feel you are right for. It's important for the actor to have control of his or her photo session. That has to do with choosing the right photographer. If you feel comfortable with a photographer, you should tell him or her, "This is what I need and this is what I want."

Industry Interview: Advice from Jay Bernstein, Star-Maker, on Succeeding in Show Business

To understand the influence that the American entertainment industry has had on the world is to understand Jay Bernstein. *The Hollywood Reporter* said of him, "Jay Bernstein must have a direct line to God. When Jay starts talking, Hollywood listens."

As a television producer, Bernstein had more shows on prime time, in one particular season, than anyone else, and he has produced fourteen movies for television. Labeled the "premiere star-maker," Jay not only has represented America's biggest television and movie stars; he's produced them. The list of stars he's represented and/or produced include Farrah Fawcett, Suzanne Somers, Drew Barrymore, Sharon Stone,

Brooke Shields, Pamela Anderson, Michael Jackson, Stacy Keach, Lee Majors, Michael Landon, Kristy McNichol, Delta Burke, Mary Hart, Linda Evans, Ray Liotta, Jim Carrey, and many others.

Jay's goal has always been one of accomplishment—to combine quality entertainment with the creation of role models who would represent commitment, responsibility, and success. He has dedicated his life to that task and the results of his work will outlive us all.

What advice do you have for new actors in town?

One thing to remember for people who come to Hollywood is that rejection is pretty much the name of the game. You have to have a very thick skin to go through it. But the good news is that everybody was nobody until they were somebody.

Most of the actors that I've seen that seem to do well are those people who did not do well socially in high school or in college. They were either too short, they were too nerdy, or they were too "something." For example, if you are 5'7" and you've got a good-looking face, you certainly were too short for the basketball team in high school and you probably weren't going to be on the football team 'cause they'd kill you in the first five minutes. But Hollywood can be a good place for you if you are 5'7" because you can be sixty feet tall on the big screen.

It seems that as I look at the backgrounds of most of the successful people in this business, they were people who wanted to show others back home that they were worth more than the credit they'd been given at the time. Sometimes it might be a minority person living in a city where that particular minority wasn't looked upon as "number one." For example, in Mississippi, if you are an Italian, it's not the best thing to be. We still haven't had an Italian president and we haven't had a Jewish president, etc.

So a lot of the people are minorities of one kind or another who wanted to be accepted and they say, "Okay, you're treating me like I'm different here in high school or in college. So if I'm going to be different I might as well be better." So they come here with a burning desire to make it. That's the kind of person who usually does make it.

What's the kind of person who usually does *not* make it? It's the beautiful girl or very handsome guy who comes to Hollywood. The beautiful girl is told in Omaha, Nebraska, "You're so beautiful . . . Why aren't you in Hollywood?" She might hear this often enough, so to be a teller at a bank and keep hearing that is pretty depressing. So she looks at her options, and says, "Well, I could marry the president of the bank or maybe everybody's right. Maybe I should go to Hollywood and be a star." The problem is that these types of people get to Hollywood but they don't have anything but the looks. And they are not used to studying hard because everything came so easy to them in their lives. They aren't used to putting in twenty-five hours a day to make certain that they are going to be the best. So most of them end up very sadly.

Once most of these types of people get here, they learn that it's not so much what you can do, but who you know. And, in truth, it's two-thirds "who you know" and only one-third "what you know." But the problem is that the one-third of what you know has to come first. So if you're a very pretty girl and you meet everybody important in town, and they all test your abilities and you are no good, then that's the end of you. You're back home.

So the best thing is to stay out of that until you feel you could compete with anybody for any role, and that the only way you're going to lose a role is because they wanted someone with another hair color or someone shorter or taller or a different race.

It's all about being the best you can be. So how do you do that? Well, the first thing to do is find an acting class. How do you find an acting class? Well, you go to Samuel French Bookshop in the Valley on Ventura Boulevard or in Hollywood on Sunset Boulevard and you get hold of a list of the acting coaches in town. You read who some of the best people are and who they've coached who have become successful. Samuel French also has books on personal managers. They have books on agents too, and some of those books tell you who the agents have handled. You don't want to necessarily go with an agent or manager who says, "I've never done this before but I know I can do it for you," because you need somebody who's been through the Hollywood jungle. You need someone who can get you through to the other side safely. It seems like you can just go straight ahead and get from one side of the Hollywood jungle to the other, but what you don't know is that in the middle there's the quicksand. So you need somebody to guide you around that quicksand. And if they take you to the left, the problem is that's where the crocodiles are. So the logic is that if you don't want to get eaten by the crocodiles or die in the quicksand, you might as well go to the right. But that's the cannibal village. Well, how do you get across? You get someone who's been there before, who can take you just to this side of the quicksand, around the crocodiles, just over and in front of the village of the cannibals, and around to the other side. So that's a pretty difficult thing to do for someone who has never done that before.

But it's way too soon to worry about that when you first get here. You don't want to have a representative when you first get here, when you don't know what you're doing, or when you don't know yet that you are the best. Anybody who would sign you at that point would not be anybody that you would want to have years later, and you might not be able to get rid of them. It's like the Groucho Marx line that Woody Allen used, "Any club that would have me, I wouldn't want to join." So you want to wait until you are good enough to get the right people.

Another important thing is to start young. The younger the better. Do I think it's important to go to college first? Probably not. I used to think so, but now I find that college doesn't really make up for the four years you are losing, unless it's going to give you the maturity to make the ground more firm under your feet when you get the rejection that you're going to get. But if you feel that the maturity is there and that you're just going to college to learn, you're better off coming here and learning by doing it. We don't learn from what we do right, we learn from what we do wrong, and it's better to start early doing things wrong before we get too old to make those kinds of mistakes.

One of the things everyone should know is that drugs will stop an actor's career more quickly than anything. Stay away from drugs, alcohol, and any kinds of addiction, whether it's sex, whatever. Because that will take you on a whole other road and will waste all that time when you might as well have gone to college. And then by the time you become success-ful, those addictions will have taken over. It's really a shame that this happens. But there can be so much pressure. So much peer pressure. And people get lost very easily here. Everybody's offering you something that usually doesn't even exist. If you are a pretty girl, you could go out for a week and probably get 3,000 cards that say "Producer" given to you.

It's also important for anyone who is going to make it to have a mentor. I've mentored a lot of people by showing them how to get through the Hollywood jungle and by doing the fighting for them.

If you had friends or relatives moving out here, what would you tell them?

The first thing I would tell them is, don't come! But, if they do come, then I'd reiterate to them that there's no time for major or minor vices because you'll be too busy studying. I mean, when you get to Hollywood, that is the time to study and get good. I have people I give advice to who are in classes every day and every night.

Training is so important, because how are you going to get a part if someone else is better than you are? You have to be the best, unless you want to be in some kind of show that is totally surface. I think if you want to be an actor with any kind of significance, you must study and be the best and know that you are the best.

Also, I think people should be aware of who they are and how they come across. I had this client who used to dress like a rock star. The people in casting sometimes are not that creative. They aren't going to say, "Well, she's got bleached hair and a man's suit and tie, but yes, she can play a nun or an advertising executive or a sorority girl." It doesn't work like that. I've cast over 300 shows, and I think in most cases you have to be a blank blackboard who can act. So when you come in, don't give them anything that will throw them. Let them see your talent and let them build on the building blocks of what they want you to be. If you're lucky enough to be wealthy, don't wear your diamond earrings or your Rolex watch or your Cartier watch or your diamond bracelet. A lot of the casting directors used to be secretaries, and even as casting directors, a year's salary wouldn't be anywhere near the cost of the jewelry that most of these girls are wearing when they come in. So if the part was between that actress and someone else, they would probably give it to the someone else. They'd say, "Well, that someone else needs it more."

And remember that you are as strong as the weakest link of the team. Every team has the actor, the talent agent, the personal manager, the public relations person, and the lawyer—because there is an awful lot of small print in Hollywood. The agent gets 10 percent to get you the job, the manager gets about 15 percent to tell you if he thinks it's a good job, the press agent promotes the fact that you've got the job, but you've got to do a good job. And sometimes the weakest link in the chain is the actor. So that's something to consider.

Industry Interview: Advice from Garry Purdy, Co-Owner of Monumental Talent Agency, on Making a Great Impression on an Agent

When considering whether to represent a new actor, what three qualities do you most like to see this actor bring to the table?

Most importantly we look for that special spark. Something that stands out in a crowd. Very few people have that magnetic energy when they walk into a room. The ability to make a script come to life. We need to believe they believe in what they are saying. We don't want to see them acting. We want to see them believing. This business can take even a strong person down, so we look for an immense amount of discipline. Additionally we look closely at who the actor is as a person. Success tends to magnify whatever personality traits are already there, so we're looking for people of character and we're looking for people we will enjoy spending time with when the success comes.

What questions do you like to hear an actor ask you before you commit to representing this performer?

What can I do to help you?! Actors should be prepared with their materials and give us everything they can to help us market them the best. You can tell when an actor knows what they're selling; their headshots and demo clips clearly indicate the four to six types they feel are their "wheelhouse" and they're proactive about modulating and updating their marketing materials in an area/type when the industry is not responding.

When it comes to an actor's first significant or breakthrough role/deal, how would you advise actors to proceed on the following two fronts? (1) How should this actor keep his/ her expectations realistic and practical from a business perspective? and (2) How should this actor build on a first success most shrewdly, for maximum benefit to his/her career long-term?

In this business you can rarely predict with certainty the outcome of a project. Those projects heralded to hit big, don't, while other projects that haven't garnered particular attention blow up. There's also the challenging period between when a client completes their first significant project and its release date. During this interim period, when the client is usually the most anxious to leverage the immediate results, no one has seen the project, there are no reviews, there are no DBO numbers to present or leverage from, so often it rests squarely on the shoulders of the "breaking agency" and their ability to parlay this initial opportunity into the next. We generally look for the follow on/interim project to be a significant (ideally the title) role in a medium budget project where those producers are willing to gamble on being able to leverage the success of the client's previous studio film to distribute their own project. If the script and the role are right, this can set the client up for even more accolades from a brilliant story/cast-driven independent film right on the heels of their studio film success (followed then by another significant studio film if all goes as planned). During this interim period we're also working with the client to secure the rest of their team (their publicist, their attorney, their business manager, etc.) as well as working with their manager on the long term plan.

What do you find most rewarding about helping actors achieve their career goals?

The process. Taking on an actor because we believe they have that special something, getting that actor the opportunities, and then watching that actor land the job. It's a rush like no other to see that actor in the final performance, because we know the hard work and determination it took. It's also rewarding to watch the clients give back. To watch them help their families, their friends and their fellow actors. Some of our most successful clients have come into the office to read with prospective new talent, and we've watched our highly successful clients "give their all" to try and get a performance out of the potential new talent that will cross the finish line. It's that kind of generosity, in resources and spirit, that we're truly proud to be a part of.

Industry Interviews: Actors on Agents
Ben Whitehair, Actor

What's your philosophy on agents?

I think a lot of times, actors give all their power to their agent. For me, I always think, I'm the one in charge. I'm the one who's going to be responsible for making my career happen!

I spent years without an agent, and during those years I got some of the biggest jobs I've booked—through relationships I had developed with people, not through an agent doing that for me.

To every actor who wants an agent, you want a *good* one. An ineffective agent will harm you; your agent needs to move you forward. So if you're thinking about getting an agent, know first that there's a difference between commercial and theatrical agents. Again, we're talking about the industry being *different* industries. If you want a commercial agent, you need to be super clear on what your type is—being a good commercial actor is less about talent and more about what a split-second glimpse of you gives the person casting for a job. Do you instantly give off the vibe of what they're looking for?

A lot of actors get a commercial agent before a theatrical agent, and there are some ways I recommend to do it. You can consult written guides, talk to every actor you know about who is good, and if you're on set or at an audition, you can check out sign-in sheets to see who is represented by whom. You start to see the same agents' names over and over, and you figure out which agents are good that way.

For theatrical agents, I'd say if you're super young and beautiful and under twenty-one, that's one way to get an agent. More often, someone believes in you, and will give you a referral—like a good casting director. You have to remember that when it comes to agents, the supply of actors to be signed is so much greater than the demand, too. Friends of mine who are agents tell me that actors can be really arrogant—you have to have realistic expectations, and you need to ask your agent what *you* need to do to help that agent get you work. Oh, and don't look for an agent without a killer one-minute demo! It should look like something straight off TV, or straight from a movie!

I've had friends who were represented by CAA, WME, ICM—and never worked. A lot of actors go with a non-name agency, and they get lots of work because their agent is hungry and works his ass off on the phone all day. You need to have the mindset of, "This agent is coming along on my journey, as a business partner." And that means if you need to have a tough business conversation, you have it. My dad's a lawyer, so I will always talk about my contracts—I would never be afraid to say, "I'm taking this contract to an attorney." It's an agent or manager's job to negotiate, and if they can't have that kind of conversation with you, that's a red flag.

Deanna Meske, Actor

How was your first experience signing or working with an agent? What advice would you give aspiring actors about evaluating an agent to make sure he/she will be good for you and your career?

My first experience was not so good. I waited and waited and for almost a year I did not get one film or TV audition, just low budget commercials. I didn't know that other actors were getting called in for roles I fit until I started talking to other actors, and then I dropped that agent. [When dealing with an agent], first of all, you need to be proactive, have some experience, know how to audition and go with your gut feeling. If you are wrong, be willing to drop the agent. It's a relationship and a business—if you don't see results, find out if it's your headshots or résumé If it's not, look for a new agent.

Kyle Walters, Actor

In my mind, agents and managers are your employees. They work for you. It's not about, "Will this agent take me?" It should be about, "Is this agent a good fit for *me*?" Also, is this agent a good person? I wouldn't want a womanizer, or a guy who talks badly about people all the time, representing me in this business. Building your team and brand means working with quality people, and in the end, that's the best way to get work.

BUILDING YOUR CREDITS AND GAINING EXPOSURE

What's the best way to get people to take you seriously as an actor? It's very simple: work. A pretty face and great headshot will help you to get noticed, but when you can tell people you're currently doing a play, or you just finished a part on a television show or a movie, it really catches people's attention. You don't have to convince anyone that you're great; you can just tell them to go see your work.

Even performing in smaller-scale productions like student films, independent films, and cable television can be worthwhile endeavors that will help to kick-start your career and make you more of an attractive commodity in the eyes of talent buyers and sellers. And as a professional actor, that is an important goal. Therefore, this chapter will detail these and other important ways to build your credits and gain some exposure.

Student Films

For a newcomer to the business, this is a fantastic way to introduce yourself to the process of filmmaking. It's also the best way to acquire film of yourself for a reel, which can be shown to agents and casting directors.

Luckily, student films are prevalent in this town and very easy to find out about. All you have to do is check out *backstage.com* and you're halfway there. Every week, casting notices are posted by film students seeking actors for a multitude of assignments, which include short films, videos, and mock commercials. Most often these projects run anywhere from two to fifteen minutes in length, but occasionally you'll find a graduate student shooting a feature length film. And fortunately for you—the actor living in L.A.—most of these budding filmmakers shoot these films in L.A. because they attend one of the local colleges or universities, including the University of Southern California (USC), the University of California Los Angeles (UCLA), the American Film Institute (AFI), Los Angeles City College (LACC), Loyola Marymount University (LMU), and the California Institute of the Arts (Cal Arts).

You'll benefit in several ways by seeking out parts in any student film. First, you'll gain more experience with auditioning, which is an essential procedure with which every new actor needs to feel comfortable. You'll learn to deal with all kinds of people, all kinds of audition situations (improvisation, monologues, scenes), and all types of material. Second, if you are selected to act in a film, you'll get experience working with a crew, though probably a small one, and you'll learn the process by which film is shot—a very important thing to know before you're hired professionally. And finally, as already mentioned, you'll get a copy of your work, which can later be added to a personal reel to show people.

As you might expect, there is no pay for working on student films, basically because students don't have any money. However, you probably can expect a sandwich and a soda for lunch, as some form of appreciation. The payoff is really the experience, which is invaluable.

Fortunately, you won't have to worry about giving up too much of your time for these types of projects. Since students have to attend classes during the week, they frequently shoot on weekends. This is a blessing because it won't interfere with your weekday auditions and/or job. Plus, most shoots don't last more than two to four weekends, so your time commitment overall will be minimal.

Non-Union and Independent Projects

In addition to students, many independent filmmakers also advertise in *backstage.com* for films and videos they are producing. In fact, *The Blair Witch Project* got its actors through a casting notice in *Backstage.* So you never know what you might find.

As with student films, often there is very little or no pay, maybe $25–$75 per day at most. (Sometimes advertisements will say "Possible Deferred Pay," but that usually translates into "Chances of ever getting any money from this thing are very, very slim.") But in the beginning of your career, your intention should mainly be to do these for experience and not for money anyway.

Just as you, the actor, are trying to acquire some film of yourself, the director very often is trying to develop a director's reel that he or she can show people. Sometimes the director also has hopes that the project might make it to film festivals or video stores, which would be nice for you, too. In addition to getting some footage of yourself, you might get some great exposure!

Like college films, small independent films typically don't shoot for very long either—maybe a few days or a couple of weeks. Occasionally, I have seen announcements where actors are needed for up to two months with no pay, but that is a rarity. Most actors cannot do those because of time and financial constraints. So just look out for the jobs that you can manage to do, and send out your pictures every week.

Public Access Television

As you already probably know, public-access cable television shows have a reputation for being pretty bad. People more often laugh at public-access shows than actually appreciate them. But don't let that discourage you if you have an ingenious idea. As long as it's original, entertaining, and a quality product, it has every chance of helping your career. Even if no one ever sees it, you'll get experience in front of a camera, which can only help you polish your skills, and you'll get some video of yourself.

The sky's the limit with what you can do. In Los Angeles, there are numerous cable franchise areas that are required to provide public access facilities and equipment at no charge (or very little) to users. In addition, all airplay time is free. The only restriction is that the material you produce must be non-commercial, meaning you can't be selling products or services. To get started, all you need to do is attend a seminar on how the process works, and additional seminars if you want to be able to rent video equipment.

There is a wide range of public-access entertainment airing throughout the day in L.A., including talk and variety shows, mini-movies, spoofs, and just totally bizarre programming. Talk-show hosts discuss anything and everything, including sex, spirituality, race, nationality, health, and hobbies. Actors produce a smorgasbord of half-hour skits, scenes, and video-movies. Occasionally you'll even see something so weird you won't know what's going on. Try channel hopping and you will surely find some of these programs.

For more information on how to produce your own show, you can contact the City of Los Angeles Information Technology Agency at (213) 978-3311 to receive a brochure (or go to *www.lacity.org/ita*). You can also contact individual cable access entities listed below:

L.A. Cable Access Corp (LA 36)
www.la36.org

California State University Los Angeles Educational Access
(Channel 26)
www.calstatela.edu

Putting on a Showcase

Though it can be costly and time consuming, some actors have had excellent success by putting together their own showcases.

It's a way of gaining total control over a project, and ultimately your career. You and your cohorts pick the material, cast yourselves, rent the theater, and do the advertising. In short, you do everything.

The most important rule to abide by when doing your own showcase is to do it professionally. In addition to having quality material and a clean theater, you must also have adequate money set aside for advertising and publicity, which are frequently neglected by producers of small productions. Why go through all the trouble of rehearsing, renting space, building a set, and then not take time to draw people in? It's pointless, but it happens. Many actors have performed shows to an audience of one or two people on a Friday night! So make sure you have classy invitations and ample publicity to attract both industry people and the public. Make sure you invite industry people to come for free! You might even consider hiring someone to create invitations and even a publicist to promote your production.

Realize, too, that if you want agents and casting directors to come, you will have to perform somewhere close to town. Very few people will drive to northern parts of the San Fernando Valley, but you'll probably get a high turnout if you do your show in places like Hollywood, West Hollywood, Studio City, or any of the neighboring vicinities. Of course, theaters are more expensive to rent in these areas, but doing so might be worth it.

Many casting directors have said that they like to see new material too, so writing your own material isn't a bad idea as long as it's good stuff. High-quality material is vital or it will tarnish your performance. To ensure that it's brilliant, you should get second and third opinions of your material before you showcase it. If you decide to perform an already written work, you may have to pay a royalty fee that will be another added expense, albeit small.

Depending on the theater in which you produce your material, you may also have to contact Equity to apply for showcase status, which involves submitting light paperwork. Many of the smaller theaters in L.A. fall under the AEA (Equity) 99 Seat Plan. However, some of the tiny theaters with thirty or forty seats don't fall under any plan, so you won't have to worry about such technicalities.

If you've never put together a showcase before, I would recommend hooking up with another actor who has—maybe a friend or someone from an acting class. It will save you a lot of headaches. They will know how to handle many of the details that come up.

Joining a Theater Company

This is another way to gain exposure, while also making friends, improving your acting, and learning more about the business. Most theater companies in L.A. have anywhere from fifteen to fifty members. Some have more, some less. To join a company, you typically have to audition for a membership board or committee, and most companies hold auditions once or twice a year.

The standard way to seek out membership is to submit a picture and résumé to the company, and then you will be contacted when auditions are held. Usually auditions consist of performing one or two monologues along with a brief interview. If you are accepted, which might be on the spot or after a few days, then there is almost always an initiation fee of approximately $25 to $150. In addition, there are monthly membership fees ranging from $20 up to around $175. Also, you sometimes have to work a few hours a month for the company.

There are wonderful benefits to being in a theater company. A good company will have many productions throughout the year in which its members can appear. Many groups also have helpful workshops on acting and the business of acting. Some even have play readings, to which industry people are invited. You'll also meet other actors with whom you can swap stories and develop friendships. One other benefit is that many companies are always seeking material, so if you are a budding writer too, you might have an outlet for your work.

Addresses and contacts for theaters and theater companies, some of which have been around for years along with new ones that form on a monthly basis, can be found in resource periodicals at Samuel French Theatre & Film Bookshops. Additionally, there are more comprehensive resource guides with addresses of all kinds that can be purchased. Also, some theater companies advertise on *backstage.com* when they are seeking new members, which is one more avenue to pursue.

Volunteering Your Services

In the entertainment industry, there are many opportunities to volunteer your services, where you can gain exposure. Some casting offices and talent agencies hire unpaid interns to work a few hours every week. The "pay" is obviously the learning experience and the connections you make. Production companies are always looking for help too. Even the Screen Actors Guild needs people to help coordinate events and seminars. There are so many places to which you can offer your services!

I really believe that great things can come from volunteer work. For example, a friend of mine volunteered to work as a production assistant for a week at a company that produces late-night thrillers. Out of that came several paid production jobs. In addition, he not only learned a lot about behind-the-scenes work, but he got to know several casting directors, directors, and producers while working. It was a great experience for him.

So I would recommend calling or writing those people with whom you'd like to work. Keep calling people until someone says "Yes!"

Sending Out Postcards

In addition to getting headshots reproduced, many actors also get postcards made of their headshot, which we've mentioned before. Postcards are a nice way to make people aware of your presence in L.A. Every few weeks, send them out as reminders to industry people you have met or would like to meet eventually. Doing so helps lead to employment sometime down the road, if not right away.

One of the smartest reasons for sending postcards is that they are much less expensive than headshots. The average cost for 500 is about $65–$70. Another good reason to send postcards is that the required postage is much less than when sending an 8x10. The savings really add up when you're doing a mass mailing. Finally, the best reason to send a postcard is that casting directors will see your face immediately. Unfortunately, sometimes manila envelopes never get opened. It simply takes too much time for a casting director to open up twenty or thirty new manila envelopes every day from actors, when they're already trying to process all the agent submissions that they're receiving.

It's true that casting directors get tons and tons of mail every week, and that the chances of being called in from a postcard are slim. But it has happened plenty of times! I've heard many casting directors say they've called in actors from postcards when they happened to be looking for that particular type the day an actor's mail arrived. Some call it destiny or just pure luck. But even if you don't get called in immediately, sending postcards helps to slowly build your name recognition, either consciously or subconsciously, which someday might inspire a casting director to remember you when your agent has submitted you for a part.

When doing your mailing, it's a good idea to include a brief message on the back because it helps to reinforce that you're a real person and not just a picture. If you already know the individual to whom you're sending the postcard, then update him or her on what's been happening with your career. Say something like, "I just finished doing a play at Theatre XYZ, and I'm still studying with (Acting Teacher). I'd love the chance to read for you again sometime." If you haven't done anything lately, then just say hello and ask to be kept in mind for any upcoming parts. If you know him or her really well, then be as personal or funny as you like.

Of course, if you've never met the person to whom you're sending a card, don't write a real cozy friend-to-friend message. That's totally inappropriate. Just be polite, professional, and concise. Write something like, "I'd love the chance to audition for you sometime" and then briefly mention any of your recent achievements. Anything you can say about your success will always boost the effectiveness of your message. Just use good judgment, don't be cocky, and remember to write neatly and without spelling errors.

The Players Directory

If you have obtained agency representation or you are a member of SAG-AFTRA or AEA, it's a good idea to include yourself in this publication, which was published by the Academy of Motion Picture Arts and Sciences until 2006, and is now published by a private company. (Those are the requirements to be included.) The directory comes out multiple times a year in print and is also available online. It lists men, women, characters, and children, with tiny pictures of hundreds of professional actors. While being included isn't a guarantee you'll get work, it can only help you. I've heard many reputable casting directors say they've thumbed through it, especially when looking to book actors on a last-minute notice. So contact the directory to find out when the next filing dates will be. The cost to have your picture included is only $18 an issue if you elect to make a recurring online payment, and you are also able to submit recent credits and a résumé for their online publication. For more information, contact Academy Players Directory, 2210 W. Olive Ave., Suite 320, Burbank, CA 91506 .(*www.PlayersDirectory.com*)

Getting Online

As the Internet comes to play more and more of an important role in our lives as a whole, it inevitably is changing the way the acting business operates. If you search the Internet for acting-related sites, you'll probably find dozens and dozens where actors can now find work. Here are a few great options to check out:

Actors Access (breakdown services)
www.actorsaccess.com

Actors Equity Casting Call
www.actorsequity.org

Casting Networks Los Angeles
www.lacasting.com

Central Casting
www.centralcasting.com

Playbill
www.playbill.com

SAG Indie (independent film opportunities)
www.sagindie.com

Hopefully you'll utilize some of these proven ways of building credits and gaining exposure. Combined with the work of your agent, they will help to get your foot in the door to meet the buyers of talent—casting directors, directors, and producers.

So what can you expect when one of these buyers calls you in to audition? Chapter 13 covers the whole process in detail.

THE POWER OF SOCIAL MEDIA

The fact that we live in the digital age can benefit everyone personally and professionally. For a creative artist like an actor, social media is currency and power. It offers countless opportunities to get the word out about yourself, both artistically and businesswise. Still, you've got to be careful—crafting the right image on social media will help, or hurt, your reputation. You also want to make sure you're dealing with scrupulous people online, and that you target the right potential business associates the right way.

How a Smart Actor Uses Social Media as a Branding Tool

You probably are already familiar with the fun it can be to post news about yourself online, to "like" topics of interest to you, and to catch up with old friends via the web. As an actor marketing your skill set and crafting your professional image, however, your first order of business is to know that *anything* you post is going to follow you forever. Therefore, when you start to think about ways you'll use social media to further your career, you need to understand that every communication you'll make online needs to be strategic. Don't toss off frivolous or critical comments about that bad play you saw the other night—the person who produced it might just be following you on Twitter and see what you wrote. Boom, you've burned a potential bridge.

Instead, your goal is to brand yourself as a capable, likable person and performer who's serious about his/her craft, and leaves an online reader, friend, or follower wanting to know more about you and what you do. You shouldn't make the mistake many people make on social media and share everything about yourself—every thought you have as you have it is interesting only to you, really. Business connections don't want to know what you had for lunch—they do want to know that you're performing in a really interesting web series, and if you frame that information in an interesting way, they may just want to see your work. So leave a little mystery about who you are and what you do personally. Choose the info you share career-wise carefully—make sure everything you post is upbeat and positive. Show your future business contacts that you're hardworking, fun to be around, and bring quality talent to the table, always.

Let's take a look at how this concept translates to different types of social media outlets, specifically.

Facebook

Facebook is a great way to show you've got a vibrant personality, and to quickly spread great news about exciting developments in your career. Mostly likely you already have a personal page. So, now is the time to look, realistically and honestly, at how you are using that page to express who you are to the world. Is your page filled with drunken pictures of you partying, lots of TMI about your personal life, profanity, or anything a casual observer might consider offensive (even if you don't)? Take it down immediately—OK, some people have seen it already and will remember, but so many future business contacts will thankfully be spared what you delete. It's fine to post family and friend photos, and communicate with others on a personal level, but anything that makes you look irresponsible or just plain old gross will turn off potential employers who check you out. (And they will—folks in the industry routinely go to public profiles before making decisions about who to hire these days.)

What should you post on Facebook to boost your like-ability as an actor and person? Flattering photos of yourself from any film or TV show you've recently done. Positive news about upcoming roles. Anything you choose to share should make you seem like someone really interesting, someone who is going places, and someone whom any agent, director, producer, or casting director would want to be in business with, because being in business with you will benefit *them*.

Twitter

Twitter is an excellent way to "sound bite" what you want the world to know about upcoming projects. You can also discuss ideas that matter to you, express your personal philosophy (again, keep it upbeat, honest, and interesting), and very importantly, network with others in the business. Definitely don't be shy about following people of influence who interest you; if you feel it's appropriate to message that director whose work you really admire and would love to work with, do so (but keep things light, and express your genuine admiration shortly and sweetly). Don't hassle or stalk others, though—trying to connect over and over again with business contacts when you aren't getting replies back is a waste of time and makes you look desperate.

Lots of actors build their fan bases with Twitter (more on that later); this can be a terrific idea as you gain a higher profile in the business. (See more on this a bit later in the chapter.) The most important thing to remember when cultivating, and communicating with, your supportive followers is to keep your comments kind and appreciative. Ignoring good will makes for bad karma and bad business.

Youtube and Vine

Many actors are using YouTube to market themselves via audition tapes, as an instructional tool to give acting tips and even seminars, even to create original content that shows off their abilities in a great light. Others are even using Vine to create super-short, punchy skits. All of these ideas can be extremely helpful —if your presentation is good, you'll rack up views and your image will grow accordingly. The key is to make sure any video you post contains quality work and/or information, and that you come off professionally within it. No duck faces; no silliness; don't try to be clever or cute, because that will always come off as cloying. Ask a trusted friend to watch objectively and constructively critique anything you're thinking of putting up on YouTube before you do so.

Instagram

This is another great resource that allows you to be creative in terms of images you choose to present. Post photos that promote a current project, or that authentically show your wonderful essence as a person living life—this will be very attractive to people who might want to collaborate with you. Feel free to express yourself through photography as well—it's great if you can tie photos into the performance work you're currently doing, or hope to do, in some way.

Pinterest

Pinterest is similar to Instagram, in the sense that you can use a Pinterest board to express your creative interests. Here's an excellent place to pay tribute to the films that have helped shape your perspective as an actor, or the performers who have served as your role models—people who are curious about working with you will find these things illuminating.

Linkedin

LinkedIn is an excellent tool for making a professional introduction of yourself to the industry, posting résumé highlights, and of course networking with others you'd like to do business with. Read as many profiles as you can prior to writing your own, so you get a good feel for the style creative professionals use to detail their experience and goals.

Wikipedia

Scores of actors have profiles on Wikipedia, and if you have the credentials to warrant a page by the site's standards, you might consider this as a marketing tool. A few things to keep in mind, though—you can't write your own page! Someone else must do it for you.

Also, once a page has been established about you, know that anyone—that's right, anyone—can edit it however they like. Wikipedia does, of course, keep track of derogatory information as much as it can and notes incomplete or inaccurate research on a subject, but incorrect info gets by—sadly, if you have enemies, malicious info can as well. Understand as well that if there is negative info about you out there that people can dig up—like the time you spent a night in jail for those overdue parking tickets, or your secret ten-day marriage—there's a good chance it will end up in your profile. Weigh the pros and cons of a Wikipedia profile as it might specifically affect you.

Blogs

Writing a blog can be an excellent way to build word-of-mouth about you career, but you want to choose your topics carefully. Focus on the good stuff—causes you feel strongly about, an analysis and appreciation of your favorite screenplay, the story of how a friend or family member inspired you. Avoid ranting about politics, settling personal grudges, or concentrating on anything unpleasant. Again, the point is not to turn off any potential collaborators and business connections.

Message Boards and Forums

Actors often use these to spread the word on jobs, discuss industry trends, and gossip. Definitely take advantage of legitimate info about work (check it out, though—lots of what is discussed on boards and forums is hot air), and learn about industry trends, but don't indulge in gossip about anybody in the industry. Even under an alias/avatar, it's not good for the soul, or your karma.

The Benefits and Pitfalls of Web Self-Promotion

Obviously, the benefits of web self-promotion include broadening your brand and appeal, making the connections we've discussed, and being able to control, to the extent you can, how others in the industry perceive you. The pitfalls? All of the major sticking points involve trust—or rather, the lack of it you should have in *anyone* you meet online until you get proof otherwise. Let's take a look at the main issues you need to identify, and verify, so you don't get scammed.

Knowing How to Identify Web Work Cons

If a potential work situation comes your way in a mass email, it's a con. If a job promises profit-sharing in a production or back end earnings, it's a con. If someone you're talking with isn't willing to answer basic questions about his or her credentials or experience, it's a con. Use the wonderful intuition you've been blessed with—if your gut tells you a job opportunity sounds too good to be true, it's almost always going to be. Don't let your desire to work and succeed cloud your vision.

How Much Personal Info Should You Share Online?

As little as possible! Never tell anyone where you live, what your social security number or mother's maiden name is, when you'll be out of town—your whereabouts are precious nuggets of information. If you meet a criminal posing as an acting coach who asks for your credit card to pay for a nonexistent class, you'll be taken. Also, even lesser-known actors have stalkers, it's a sad fact of life. You have no idea who is looking at what you post anywhere online, so keep sensitive specifics close to the vest.

Weighing Which Web Contacts Will Benefit You

Check out anyone you connect with online and are considering working with the same way this person will check you out.

Google him or her—and go through *every* page that comes up. It's remarkable how much you can learn if you pay attention to small details in a search engine. Go to this person's Facebook and Twitter pages—do you like what you see, in terms of what kind of a person he or she is? Do his/her credits check out when you look into them? Do you *like* interacting with this person? If so, take a meeting in a public place, preferably an office you verify as a legitimate place of business. Feel out the connection in person—that's the best way, ultimately, to evaluate anyone you might invite into your life

Remember: being cautious isn't the same thing as being paranoid. Take care of yourself, and your best interests, at all times!

Industry Interview: Perspective from Ben Whitehair, Actor, on How Social Media Changed My Career Trajectory

In terms of social media, could you talk a bit about your overall philosophy on using it to advance your career (or any actor's career)?

I'm guessing that most of you have heard something to the effect of, "social media is a great way to promote yourself." I often hear it described like a powerful megaphone you can use to inform the masses of your recent Kickstarter campaign, film booking, or how tasty your Philly cheesesteak is. What I have discovered, though, is that the real value of social media is unlocked when you turn the megaphone around and listen. At its best, social media is an acute listening device. Think about it. If you went to the grocery store and someone kept shouting at you, "Buy apples! Buy apples! Buy apples!" you would likely tune out and probably think they were crazy (or at least highly annoying). On the other hand, if that same person immediately asked you how they could support you in cooking an extraordinary meal that evening, I'm willing to bet you would talk to them, buy more groceries, and probably come back to that store. Listen. Learn. Engage. Go on Twitter and follow casting directors, show runners, agents, producers, and everyone involved with your target shows. Find their public Facebook page if they have one. Follow them on Instagram. Pay attention to what they care about, how they think, what affects their day. There is an abundance of information, resources, and opportunity all over social media every day, but you need to turn the megaphone around and listen. Be curious, listen, engage, and add value. Remember that on the other end of that avatar is a human being. Care about "them," and watch your own career skyrocket.

Could you think of any particular and specific examples of using social media to market yourself that you've personally found quite successful?

If you never post a single tweet or Facebook status, social media can still provide tremendous value. Even if you never have a single follower, there is a wealth of knowledge at your fingertips. When I first joined Twitter, all I did was read what industry professionals put out there, and it was the first time I truly felt "part" of the entertainment business. More than that, I gained incredible insight into how the business works, and where to put my focus. Beyond that, I always remember the three keys to social media marketing: listen, engage, add value. I have booked jobs, gotten agents and managers, and made incredible connections via social media with myriad industry professionals. However, all of those came because I developed relationships over time, and was constantly focused on adding value to others. I listened to what the people I was following cared about, I engaged with them like a normal human being, I added value to them, and ultimately found a way to encounter them in person.

In terms of networking, what would your advice be regarding the benefits and pitfalls of making, and utilizing, connections via social media?

The biggest mistake I see people making is asking for something before they have established any kind of relationship. So many people start asking everyone to follow them (stop that, please just stop that), look at their headshots, watch their demo reel, etc. It would be like sitting down to a first date and immediately asking the person if they'll sleep with you. At least see how the meal goes!

It's a gift to have immediate access to so many people who can be beneficial to your career. The key is to take a long-term view and actually build a relationship with these people (on- or off-line). Rather than being so focused on getting a job or an audition right away, focus on establishing a rapport and being someone who engages beyond just being an actor. Industry professionals know you're an actor (it should be right there on your profile with your headshot), they know you want a job, and they know you're always looking for better representation. What they don't know is, why you? What sets you apart? What about you would make them want to support your career for decades? It often has nothing to do with your acting—it's that you're a nice, interesting person who they enjoy engaging with.

Industry Interview: Kyle Walters, Actor, on How Social Media Changed My Career Trajectory

How do you feel social media has helped propel your career forward?

Social media to me can be tricky. You feel like you're getting something done to be on Twitter or Facebook all the time, but unless you're really connecting to fans, to an audience, to casting directors, you might be wasting time. I do suggest actors give social media a shot for sure—it can get you noticed. A few actor friends of mine who went on commercial auditions actually got asked for the names of their Twitter accounts recently, so there can be interest in what you put on Twitter.

I think Instagram can be really great for up-and-coming actors, actually. As performers, we actors are visual artists, and Instagram gives you a chance to be very creative in a visual way. I don't think it's about doing *every* form of social media— you should try out different ways to express yourself, and pick whichever form of social media feels right to you to express yourself through. It's just great to perform and play. I think YouTube is great for this—you can create any kind of content you want. Same goes for Vine, if you happen to be talented at putting together a six-second skit!

My drive and motivation, what is really rewarding to me as an actor, is interacting with the people who support me, the fans I have. Getting closer to them, through what I do on YouTube and through new media, is what I enjoy so much about the work I do. I think too, whether you have 130 Twitter followers or five thousand followers, you always need to treat those people right. Give your best to them, for the support they're giving you!

Could you think of any particular and specific examples of using social media to market yourself that you've personally found quite successful?

It's just about regularity and being on brand (whatever that means)—also about latching onto other social waves and trends. For example, I'm currently working on a web series modern adaptation of *Peter Pan: The New Adventures of Peter Pan and Wendy*. So I live-tweeted during the NBC-TV broadcast of *Peter Pan Live*, as did other members of our cast and crew—we threw a house party and watched and tweeted together. Got a good number of followers and new subscribers for our show.

In terms of networking, what would your advice be regarding the benefits and pitfalls of making, and utilizing, connections an actor can make via social media?

I'm not the best networker, but one benefit of social media connection is research. When you run into someone at a party, you can skip the awfully awkward "What are you working on?" question and go straight to, "I saw your crowdfunding campaign was successful, congrats!" Don't overdo it, though—don't be that guy. Just be yourself, and try to help others instead of yourself—you help others, they'll help you!

Industry Interview: The Last Word from Deanna Meske, Actress, on How Social Media Helps Demonstrate My Commitment

I am constantly on social media. I feel it keeps me out there, people see that I'm pushing and working and they know that if they hire me I will be dedicated and do a great job!

THE AUDITION PROCESS

Your agent calls and tells you that you've got an audition tomorrow. Hurray! You've got your foot in the door! Now it's time to show 'em what you've got!

Taking classes, getting pictures made, and finding an agent were very important steps along the way, but the audition is the most important step in an actor's career. It is the determining factor that gets you the job. Sadly, many new, talented actors mess up their auditions because they are inexperienced at the whole process. It's one thing to be able to deliver a fantastic monologue that you've polished for months, but to give a stunning audition with brand new material definitely requires some practice.

You will need to become a master at it to succeed in this business. Though at first it may be awkward for you, in time, auditioning will become easier and easier. Read on to gain a greater understanding of what you can expect.

The Elements of an Audition

One thing is certain about auditions: No two will be the same. Most of the time, you will read lines with the casting director; however, occasionally you may just meet and never actually go over any material. Of the times you do read, you might be videotaped; other times you won't be. You may chat it up for a few minutes before you read; other times you'll pop in, read, and quickly leave. It really varies a lot, depending on the personality and schedule of the casting director, and the type of part you are auditioning for.

Despite these different situations, there are some common elements you can come to expect at an audition, which I'll try to explain. By being fully prepared and aware of what may transpire, you will have fewer butterflies and more time to focus on doing an excellent job.

The Call from Your Agent. The first aspect of the audition process is receiving a call from your agent. You'll be out and about in L.A., and all of sudden your cell phone rings! You check it and it's your agent! He or she (or the office assistant) most likely has some very important information for you about an audition. You'll be told the time, place, casting director, where or how to get sides (pages of a script that you'll be reading from) if it's a theatrical audition, and details about the part you'll be reading for. It is extremely important that you write down all of this information correctly. Always carry a pen and paper with you, or have them close by so you don't have to keep your agent waiting. (Agents tend to be very busy in the late afternoon and they hate to be placed on hold.) If you have any questions, be sure to ask them, but know that most agents prefer that you first just listen and take notes. If you're caught without a pen and paper, or if you find it cumbersome to carry them around, another option is using your cell phone. Most have a "memo pad" or "scheduler" function that you can use while taking a call.

Usually your audition will be the next day, but be prepared for anything. Sometimes your agent will inform you that you have an audition in two hours! That means you've got to be able to drop whatever your doing and go see a casting director immediately. Smart actors keep a couple of changes of clothes in their car, even grooming supplies, in the event they can't make it home before their unanticipated audition.

After you jot down all the information, if you have a theatrical audition, you'll either have to go pick up your sides, or have them faxed to you. If your audition is for a commercial, you most likely won't have to worry about obtaining sides, unless there is a lot of copy to read. Most of the time, you'll just get them when you arrive.

Spend a lot of time preparing for your audition. (Later in this chapter, tips on how to improve your auditioning will be discussed.) If you have a theatrical audition, go over the sides in-depth. Rehearse them with a friend or coach. Learn as much about your character as you can. If you have a commercial audition, spend time picking out an appropriate wardrobe for the call. With commercials, it's usually better to dress the part, in contrast to theatrical auditions, where only a hint of the costume is necessary. If you aren't sure what to wear, then by all means consult your agent or any more experienced actor you know.

Arriving at Your Audition. Make sure you show up on time! Being late won't necessarily eliminate you from being considered, but it's highly unprofessional, it shows a lack of responsibility, and it only makes you feel more nervous. Therefore, leave an extra half-hour early to compensate for any unexpected delays. If you don't already live in L.A., you will come to know that traffic delays occur frequently here, both on freeways and on connecting passageways like Laurel and Coldwater Canyon.

When you reach your destination, if you have to park on the street, put plenty of money in your meter. Auditions can sometimes run late, and you don't want to worry about whether your meter is about to expire while you're inside the casting director's office. Therefore, it's wise to give yourself at least an hour in the meter to allow for any delays.

You should walk into the casting office at your appointed time—not fifteen minutes early and not fifteen minutes late. Only show up early if you haven't yet seen your audition material. Otherwise, if you arrive early, take a walk around the block a few times or find something peaceful to do. The reason is that many actors tend to get cramped if they sit stationary in a casting lobby for a long time. There's an undercurrent of stress, usually emanating from other waiting actors, that can encroach upon you. It's better to walk into an office at your scheduled time, feeling vibrant and ready to go. So get some fresh air or have a cup of coffee. Do whatever it takes to maintain a sense of calm before you go in.

Signing In. When you finally walk into the office, be pleasant and friendly. Remember that receptionists in casting offices often become casting assistants, who become casting associates, who become casting directors. Most casting people have a welcoming attitude, but if you find someone to be less than cordial, still be nice. Take the high road. Some of these office assistants are stressed out, while a few others are just inherently unfriendly. But try not to let their attitude affect your audition. Remember that if they exhibit an unbalanced state, it probably has nothing to do with you. They probably don't realize how they are behaving, as most rude people don't. So never let a rude casting person, whether it's the assistant or the casting director, throw you off balance.

Next, you should sign in. There will almost always be a sign-in sheet, where you fill in your name, agency, agency phone number, and some information regarding age and ethnicity for a SAG survey. At SAG auditions, sign-in sheets are required. Non-union projects do as they please, though often they will have their own information sheet to fill out.

After signing in, just sit down and wait. If it's a commercial audition, sides or instructions (if there are no lines) will be available near the sign-in sheet. Typically, you'll have at least five or ten minutes to go over them. If it's a theatrical audition, you probably will have obtained the sides the previous day and already studied them with great diligence. Therefore, all you have to do is wait, or review your dialogue a few more times.

The waiting room will most likely have other actors waiting for their auditions also. If you're at a commercial casting facility, there could be four or five commercials being cast in different rooms, with as many as a hundred actors lining the halls and benches, lingering for their turn. If you're at a theatrical audition, the situation will probably be far less chaotic. Maybe a handful of other actors will be waiting to read.

Regardless of the situation, it is best to concentrate on your work rather than chatting it up with other people. But you will definitely be tempted. After a while, you will run into actors you've seen at other auditions. A brief "hello" is always a good thing, and even a few words are fine because conversing with others will probably make you more comfortable. But focusing on your character will afford you the opportunity to collect your thoughts and go into your audition completely ready. Remember, first and foremost, you're out at that audition to book a job.

The Actual Audition. When your turn arrives, your name will be called, possibly along with several others if it's a commercial audition. You will then be led into the audition room. If you have only had a minute or two to look over your sides, then you might politely ask if you can have some more time. Most likely, your request will be granted, and another actor who is ready will go ahead of you.

Inside the audition room, there usually sits a casting director and/or a casting assistant. Also, a video camera might be present, though this usually happens only for commercial auditions and theatrical callbacks. It is important that you greet these people with a warm smile and confidence. Whatever you do, don't be arrogant—just be yourself. If they engage you in small talk, then kindly oblige, but be sure you have more to say than "yup", "nope," or "uh huh." Good topics are current movies, sports, news of the day, tasteful jokes, and odd weather. You probably ought to stay away from how much you adore acting, and when speaking about your acting career, remember that you're not an "aspiring" actor but rather, you are an actor.

After some brief small talk, it becomes time for the audition. The casting director will probably ask you if you have any questions. If you do, then be sure to ask at this time. Casting directors don't mind intelligent questions. They want you to do well. If your audition is being videotaped, you might ask if they want you to look at them or the camera. Most of the time for theatrical auditions (for television and film), the casting directors will serve as scene partners. They will read the lines with you and you will direct your reactions to them. However, at commercial auditions you frequently will direct your attention to the camera, as you often will not have a scene partner. And if you have one, it will likely be another actor, not the casting director. However, it's always a good idea to ask where to direct your reading if you are uncertain about what to do.

If the camera is rolling, you will "slate" by saying your name in a very warm and friendly manner, and then you'll go straight into your reading. When slating, just pretend that you are introducing yourself to someone you've always wanted to meet. Be positive and likeable, but not over the top or phony.

If it's a commercial audition, after your slate you might only have to perform an action, like placing a stick of gum into your mouth or pretending to taste some food. Or else you may have to engage in dialogue, which will be hand-printed on a piece of poster board next to the camera. For theatrical auditions, you will likely do a two-person scene, and you will rely on your sides when delivering your lines.

If you have sides, they should stay in your hands during a theatrical reading. Although you want to impress the casting directors, you don't want them to think you've memorized the lines completely and that you're giving the best performance you could possibly give. (Obviously, your audition would be better with a few more days or weeks of rehearsal.) Casting directors don't expect your audition to be absolutely perfect; they simply want a great reading. So look down at the sides every now and then. However, don't go to the opposite extreme by keeping your eyes stuck to the pages. That certainly won't impress them either. Just try to find a balance between the two situations.

Once you have finished your scene, the casting director might ask you to make some adjustments, such as toning it up or down, etc., depending on your reading. Otherwise, you should thank him or her and then leave promptly. Don't comment too much on your performance and never ask for the casting director's appraisal by asking something like "So, what'd you think?" That is completely unprofessional.

Most likely, the casting director will just thank you. If the casting director wants to have you back to read for the director or producers, either you will be told on the spot or your agent will be called, usually within a day or two. You might be given new material, but usually you will be expected to repeat the same scene. Also, if you were not taped at your first reading, then you probably will be taped during your second or third callback. And be sure to wear the same clothing and hairstyle to your callback. Obviously, it served you well in your initial reading, so don't change it.

The callback process can be challenging to say the least, especially if you are asked to return several times to read for the same role. For example, when you're up for a series regular part on a television show, you might first have to read for the casting director, then go on a callback for the producer, then for the director, then for the studio, and finally for the network. It's tremendous pressure. Anyone who gets through the process and gets the part certainly deserves it.

Auditioning Tips and Suggestions

Every casting director will tell you that it's somewhat difficult to define what makes up a fantastic audition. Usually it's a combination of many things—some that you can control and others that are out of your control. In this section, I'd like to focus on the things that you can control. Following are several universal qualities that should be included in any audition:

Presenting Good Energy. The most common problem with auditions is that they lack energy. Nerves take over, actors retreat inward, and they show only a fraction of their true personality. If you want to be "in the running," then you must display a passion about your work, a commanding self-aware-ness, and an absolute, 100 percent belief in your abilities, all without cockiness or unappealing arrogance. You must also be relaxed and comfortable. Though calmness is an inward state of being that is cultivated from experience, one way to help increase it is by exercising and stretching prior to your audi-tion, both physically and vocally. Go run a few miles and you'll burn off a lot of that nervous energy. Do some deep stretching and you'll enable vibrant energy to circulate through every cell of your being. It really does help.

You have to go into the room and give it everything you've got. Remember that it's *your* audition, and that it's your oppor-tunity to give your interpretation of the material. Nine times out of ten, casting directors are not sure exactly what they are looking for, but they do notice someone who is clear in his or her intention and who feels secure expressing it in a pleasant and meaningful way.

Many casting directors typically make up their mind about you within the first twenty seconds of meeting you. Partly, it has to do with your look, but a lot of it has to do with your energy, so find a way to present yourself uniquely. Do it with commitment. Good energy doesn't necessarily mean bouncing off the walls: If you're playing a depressed mother who's child has died, then you have to commit to that particular energy. And it doesn't mean that every word or line has to be that par-ticular energy. You are trying to create an overall impression. Just be true to your character and make solid choices about the way you want to express yourself.

Casting directors really do want you to be brilliant. Of all the people in the industry, they are on your side. Their job is to find excellent actors for directors and producers, and they are hoping you'll make their job easy and make them look good. In no way is it a "you against them" situation. When you realize this, some of the initial pressure of auditioning will disappear.

Have Strong Objectives. You need to have a clear under-standing of your character before you go in to read. Being wishy-washy won't get you anywhere. You need to define as much as you can and be very specific with your choices before the audition.

One way to obtain information about your character is to ask questions. Be extremely nice to the casting assistant or casting director and ask for any additional information that's not already given in the sides or the Breakdowns. (You should get all of the Breakdown information about your role from your agent.) Don't be afraid to ask for clarification if there is something that you don't understand. You'd be surprised how much additional information you can get just by asking for it.

After you've analyzed your sides, try to determine as many qualities about your character as you can. Really get to know the essence of who he or she is. Try to figure out what the producers or ad agency (if it's a commercial) is looking for. Determine what type of emotions your character must exhibit. For example, are you supposed to be joyful, grateful, loving, satisfied, or a combination of all four? Below are a few questions you should definitely answer before attempting your audition:

- Who am I?
- Who am I talking to?
- Why am I here and why am I talking to this person?
- What is my relation to this person?
- What are my surroundings/environment?
- What is the conflict?
- What are my obstacles?
- How am I attempting to overcome them?
- What do I want?
- What was my previous moment before this scene, both physically and emotionally?

Obviously, the more specific you can be with your answers, the better off you will be. Therefore, read your script or sides carefully and extract as much information as you can. If you can't answer some of these questions based on the script, then fill in the gaps with your imagination. When you are done, you will have a solid definition of your character, and it will inevitably pay off during your audition. If you don't do this homework, most casting directors will notice a shallowness and won't be impressed.

Translate the Words into Pictures and Feelings. It helps greatly to associate pictures and feelings with the text that you are reading. It may sound elementary, but the truth is that many young actors deliver readings that come across as boring because they're just saying the words. When reading for a part, if your character is talking to a best friend, then envision your own best friend. If your character is talking about emotional pain, imagine something from your own past that caused you pain. The point is simply to make associations to your own life, because when you are visualizing and feeling emotions from your own past or present, that's when true passion is generally expressed the most.

Create Transitions. Within every scene, there are usually one or two transitions, often called "beats." These are opportunities where you can bring some real flair to your character. They are places where emotions can change and shifts in thought can occur. By taking advantage of them, you will elevate your reading from boring, flat, and one-sided to exciting and captivating.

You must specifically define these transitions. For instance, notice at a particular point if your character suddenly starts becoming more jealous, playful, angry, or embarrassed. It might translate into a powerful moment of silence, where, perhaps, an ulterior motive is revealed. Take note of when it starts to happen. But be careful not to create beats that don't exist in the script—just look for the ones that do and utilize them to their maximum. You'll add color, life, and variety, and will become much more interesting to watch. If you're not sure about where the transitions lurk, consult a friend or acting coach who can give you insight.

Be a Good Listener. Though you will have defined your character and the scene before your audition, you may discover during your reading that the casting director has an entirely different interpretation. Though yours may be clever, you'll have to listen and adjust to the casting director's viewpoint. After all, good acting involves reacting to another person. So listen closely and flow with the casting director's interpretation by not forcing your preplanned outcome. Allow the scene to go where it goes, from one unanticipated moment to the next, by being flexible and spontaneous. Allow what the moment brings. Think of your preparation as homework for a test, but respond to the test with what it asks for, not your premeditated response.

Display Good Technical Skills. Not all of your auditions will be videotaped; usually just commercial auditions and theatrical callbacks will be taped. But when you do find yourself looking into a camera, you will need to display good technical skills. A lack of technical awareness will tarnish, and often disqualify, an otherwise excellent reading.

The most common problems are too much head movement and too much eye blinking. Frequent bobbing of the head is usually found in younger stage actors not used to the confines of a camera. This can be remedied with practice in a good cold-reading class. Eye blinking, which is usually the by-product of nerves, is remedied by becoming aware of it and then practicing control over it. Its disappearance is proportionate to how comfortable you feel while auditioning.

Another problem is facial or verbal commenting. For some reason, actors tend to be the worst judges of their performances. If you were unsatisfied with your audition, then please don't comment negatively about it to the casting director in any way. That is unprofessional. Just ask if you may do it again. By throwing in your own opinion, facially or verbally, you are not allowing the casting director to make up his or her own mind, and it only works against you in the end. Not only might it influence the casting director, but it also makes you look insecure.

A Few Other Miscellaneous Hints. First, try to stay away from using props in theatrical auditions. Most casting directors hate props, unless they are specifically necessary for the scene to transpire. (For example, all agree that your using your hand as a gun is much better than using a real one.) However, in commercial auditions, you frequently will be given props to work with, so be ready if the moment calls for it.

Second, don't try dialects or accents unless you have mastered them. A mediocre attempt will cast a shadow over your whole audition. It will make you look like a novice.

Finally, make sure that you correctly pronounce any names, places, or foreign expressions that are found in the script. If you mispronounce a word when reading a line, it shows that you didn't take time to learn as much as you could about the material. Very simply, it makes you look less intelligent than the next person who comes in and pronounces it correctly.

After Your Audition

Okay, you're done. You've given the casting director the best you could. Regardless of how it went, you should leave feeling good about yourself. Be happy that you had the courage and initiative to go and seek out an opportunity, thereby placing yourself in a vulnerable situation that most people are too afraid to even consider. If you feel you gave a great reading, then celebrate! Evaluate your performance and catalog it for the future. If you feel you did a poor job, don't beat yourself up. You wouldn't kick and dent a Mercedes if its engine made a peculiar noise, would you? The best thing to do is note what you could have done better, and then work on it. Think about ways you can improve. That's all you can do.

Auditioning is a complex process that requires a lot of practice. It can be very stressful at first, but like anything else, it becomes easier with experience. So audition every chance you get! Think of auditions as opportunities to act, not as opportunities to be judged!

If the casting director wants to have you back for a call-back, you'll know within several days. After that time, you probably can assume you weren't right for that particular part. But you never know where things can lead. The casting director might remember you and call you in for other projects in the future. You just never know. So stay optimistic regardless of whether or not you were called back.

I recommend sending a thank-you card after each audition to casting directors you auditioned for. You should thank them for giving you the opportunity to read, especially because probably less than 5 percent of all actors who were submitted by agents were called. I don't think many actors do this, so you'll definitely stand out by writing. Besides, gratitude is a good thing.

A Few Words about Open Calls

From time to time, you may hear about "open casting calls" for certain roles in a television series or movie. An "open casting call" means that anyone can come without an appointment or audition scheduled. They happen very infrequently in L.A., as compared to a place like New York City, but you should still be aware of them.

If you go to one, then go early! Usually hundreds, if not thousands, show up and wait for hours to be seen. Unfortunately, it seems that in L.A. some of these are publicity stunts and the roles being offered end up going to "name" actors anyway. The goal of such events is really to generate a lot of hoopla about the particular film or television show.

One example is the part of Robin in *Batman Forever*. A major studio held an open call here in L.A. in 1994 looking for a "street-smart, Hispanic" Robin, and auditioned many, many young unknown actors. Chris O'Donnell ended up playing the part, along with an all-star cast. Call me crazy, but was the studio really going to consider an "unknown" for such a blockbuster movie? I think not, but only they know for sure.

Nevertheless, don't be discouraged about open calls. If you think you fit the description for a part, then go anyway. Even if the part goes to a star or the movie never comes to fruition, at least you'll get more auditioning experience, and you might even walk away with a free token. (I once got a baseball cap at an open call for a TV series called *The Untouchables*!) You never know what could happen—you might get the part.

Self-Submissions in the Audition Process

A growing trend among casting directors is to ask actors to read sides on video, and submit for a part. If you find yourself handed this request, don't panic—now that you understand the right way to put together a demo reel (which we covered earlier), you'll be fine. The same principles apply, in terms of background, to asking another actor to read with you, and professional presentation. If you have specific questions about what a casting director is looking for in terms of how to film an audition, call the casting director's office and politely ask the desired requirements to be outlined. Then do exactly that!

Finding Legitimate Casting Work on the Web

The blunt truth: unless you're going through the website of an established casting agency or casting director, or see a notice in a legitimate publication like *Backstage*, don't risk replying to *any* casting notice on the web. Craigslist is notorious for its breadth of casting notices, but no company would risk its reputation putting a notice there.

Any time you are approaching a casting and don't know the people you're dealing with—even if a casting entity does have a legitimate reputation—follow this checklist to ensure you're safe, respected as an actor and person, and not being scammed in any way, shape, or form:

- Don't be bullied. You don't have to do anything in an audition that makes you uncomfortable.
- Don't tolerate sexual harassment. Unfortunately, the casting couch is still alive and well in some segments of the business. Leave immediately if something inappropriate happens.
- Know it's OK to double-check details. If you turn up to audition for a speaking part on a sitcom but suddenly find yourself being checked out for a less-than-savory reality show, ask what's happening. If you don't like the fact that the job has changed (and most likely, any salary to be negotiated would be less than you were led to believe), simply say, "I'll have to call my agent." An unscrupulous casting director/producer won't want you to do that, so then of course, you should leave.
- Don't feel badly if an audition goes wrong. So much of the process can be out of control of even the finest actor. Be proud that you gave it your all, and move on to the next opportunity.

Industry Interview: Kyle Walters, Actor

How have you dealt with bad audition experiences? Pretty much every actor feels like he or she has made a big mistake and not booked a job more than once.

Of course. It's understandable to feel bad when that happens—as actors, we're so close to our emotions. I say, give yourself a set amount of time to feel bad if an audition goes wrong—a day, say. Take the day off, go to a movie, feel as bad as you want—but once that day is over, stop moping and move on. I've found that rough days in the business are easier to handle when I reflect by asking, "What did I learn from this experience?" Also, getting together with a group of actor friends to bitch is a great way to put bad auditions behind you!

Industry Interview: More Perspective from Ben Whitehair, Actor

What's your mindset when it comes to auditions?

The mindset I take for auditions comes out of the mindset I take for my life. I use every factor I can for success—self development is key, whether it's working with coaches, reading motivational books, exercising, getting enough sleep. I make sure I have a happy relationship with my family. So even if I'm nervous in an audition, I'm a happy person as a whole. And if I get rejected? I remember what [casting director] Bonnie Gillespie told me once—getting rejected for a part doesn't mean you can't be an actor. It just means this casting director wants something different for this particular role. A career as an actor is a marathon, not a sprint. I remind myself I've chosen this career, not just a job this week! I'll still be here in five years, doing good work.

Also, I know that if you do a good job at an audition, you still might not book the job for whatever reason, but you could still get work out of that audition later. I've gotten a ton of work because someone I met and auditioned for say, four years before, and really connected with, will suddenly send me an email and say, 'I need an actor now! Are you available?'"

Industry Interview: Advice from Mike Fenton, Casting Director (*E.T.,* *Raiders of the Lost Ark, Back to the Future, Total Recall, Aliens, Getaway, Arachnophobia, Congo,* and hundreds of other films) on Actors and Auditioning

There's a lot of preparation for actors before they walk in your door. Could you tell me about that?

The preparation is to have a picture and résumé that are professional. New actors should find out from other actors, agents, or managers what format their résumé should take. Their photograph should be an 8x10, double-weight matte finish shot—preferably a headshot, for the motion picture business. Photographers couldn't figure out anything better to do, so they decided that people in the motion picture business wanted to see three-quarter photographs. That's nonsense. People in the motion picture business want to see eyes. Therefore, close-ups are better. The photo should be current. A change in hair, facial hair, or weight dictates the necessity of having new pictures.

With any luck at some point, actors will have to devise and put together a videotape, but that's another part of the story.

What do you think distinguishes a really good audition?

I don't see auditions. All we do is interview people, unless we're actually putting people on tape for a particular project. So an audition is nothing more than sitting down and chatting.

Auditions can be very interesting. I'll give you a little story. I went to New York for a film called *Blown Away* and I was looking for a young man to play a particular part. A young man showed up two days before anyone was going to meet the director. He gave me his picture and résumé, and I looked at it. The résumé had been changed. Under special skills and abilities, it said "Long-Distance Runner." Obviously, the agent had told this kid that I'm a long-distance runner. He also put on his résumé that he went to "States in Cross-Country." So I said to this young man, "How did you do in the States?" He told me that he won. I said, "Oh, what was your time?" He said he didn't remember. He was out the door faster than if the door had been revolving.

If you're going to lie on your résumé, you had better have the information and lie accurately. He didn't have a clue what cross-country running was. Not a clue. If you won, you'd know your time for the rest of your life. You'd go to the grave knowing what your time was. It's like any other sport: If you swim the 100-meter butterfly, you will know your times for the rest of your life.

The guy was a liar, and I don't like liars. When I find someone has lied on his résumé, it's the end of the interview.

Could you tell me a little about what really stands out about an actor? Is that hard to define?

There's no way anyone can define what makes a star. I've heard that question for thirty years. You don't know.

When I first met Madeleine Stowe, she came in and sat down, and there was something about her that was just arresting. (Joe Rice sent Madeleine Stowe to meet me. He called and said, "I've got this fascinating young woman you must meet.") I'm not sure whether it was her eyes, her face, or her body. But when you put it all together, she became a package. She became a woman who was attractive, alluring, sensual, and bright, with a very good education. A very smart young woman.

I'm very interested in an actor's formal education. A formal education indicates to me someone who wishes to be a professional. There are a number of people who come to Hollywood and think they are going to fall off the turnip truck, be struck by lightning, and immediately become stars. Therefore, they don't even begin to study. They don't even try to become professionals. I think that a person like that might get lucky and get a job in television, but they will never have a career. Actors who have real careers are usually actors who by and large have formal education and professional coaches with whom they have studied.

Many of our best actors have gone to England. They've gone to the National Theatre. They've become members of the Royal Shakespeare Company. They've studied at lambda [London Academy of Music and Dramatic Art]. They've studied at rada [The Royal Academy of Dramatic Art]. They've studied at Central in London, and they study constantly. And that is really the bottom line. They study and continue to study. Believe me, Al Pacino and Bobby De Niro study when they are home in New York. They study with professional acting teachers. They hone their craft. They are always prepared.

When I look at a résumé, I want to know if someone has studied with an acting teacher who I feel is one of the top professionals in the game. If they have, then all of a sudden it elevates that individual.

Do you have any other suggestions for actors moving out here?
I don't know if this will necessarily help them, but it is imperative in Hollywood for artists to have agents. They cannot succeed without an agent. If they can't get an agent, then they have to get a manager. They need to get someone who can open the door—at least so they can get their foot in. Because

without a foot in the door, or without the door being somewhat ajar, they can never make it. You cannot come out here and send pictures and résumés to casting directors and expect to have a career. It just won't happen.

You probably get many calls every day from agents asking you to see clients. How often do you see those clients?

Well, it depends on how busy we are. Currently, we have a number of pictures starting in the next several months. Right now, we are trying to set the leads, so all of our time is spent working from lists. At the moment, we could care less about the smaller parts. It's a rude thing to say, but you can't make a movie by casting day-players. You make a movie with the people who get the audience to buy the tickets. Therefore, we spend much of our time putting together lists and making offers to entice stars into projects. That is a never-ending task. It goes on constantly.

And once the leads are cast, do you have your assistants bring in actors?

No, Allison, Julie and I cast the movies together. I would not run an operation where I had an assistant do the casting work. In my opinion, that would be unfair to the producer.

Is there anything else you want to say?

Acting is one of the single most thankless professions that a person can attempt. It is heartrending. Actors are so fragile that when they get rejected, they just about blow their brains out. My suggestion is that for any actor, the crux of the matter is that they must love acting.

They can act anywhere in the United States. For them to come to California and vegetate, and not even have the opportunity to have a door open for them, in my mind, is a great waste of time. I think that actors should realize that they can make a living probably anywhere in the United States more easily than they can in southern California. It's important for actors to realize that if they live in Atlanta, New Orleans, or St. Louis, and are making a living as a big fish in a small pond, they are better off staying there and continuing to have a life, rather than uprooting themselves, coming to California, and finding only frustration.

A ton of movies are being shot all over the country. For the smaller parts, the studios don't want us to haul actors from California to New Orleans, for example. They would prefer we use people in New Orleans. Actors have a much better opportunity for really meaningful roles being right where they are, especially if they are the big fish in that pond.

There's one other thing, and this is perhaps very rude. Motion picture stars are attractive people. For the young artist seeking a career, the first thing they have to do is look in the mirror and be very realistic.

Yes, there are exceptions, but for the most part, to really have a career in the motion picture business, one has to be relatively attractive. When we look at the stars of movies, by and large, they are very attractive people. They have some sort of charisma, something that we can't bottle. We can't put our finger on it. If it were possible for an agent, casting director, or talent scout to recognize the magic of an individual and say, "That person will be a star!" and then they emerge as a star, that would be one of the greatest gifts that any human being could have. But I defy you to find somebody who can meet an individual walking into their office and can say in all honesty, "That person will become a star." It's almost impossible to do because we don't make the stars; the people who buy the tickets make the stars. For example, we used Jim Carrey in a movie a number of years ago in Canada. He played a small part and was very good in it. But fifteen years later, all of a sudden he's getting $20 million a movie! What a great business!

Industry Interview: Advice from Mark Teschner, Casting Director for ABC's *General Hospital* and *Port Charles*, on Actors and Auditioning

Mark Teschner has been an independent casting director for seventeen years. He has been described by *Rolling Stone* magazine as "an actor's casting director" and *TV Guide* noted his "unparalleled track record for finding top new talent." Since 1989, Mark has been the casting director for ABC's Emmy Award–winning *General Hospital*. He was the 1996 recipient of the Artios Award for Outstanding Achievement in Soaps Casting and has received eight additional Artios Award nominations. He was also the casting director for ABC's daytime drama *Port Charles*. Additionally, his casting credits range from Broadway to Off-Broadway, regional theater, television, and film.

Could you describe your job and how you spend your days?

I'm responsible for the casting of *General Hospital*. My work is to cast every role that's in the script. I have to cast the contract roles, all the day-players and the recurring actors, as well as oversee the department that is responsible for the under-fives and the extras. So my time is spent reading scripts, coming up with ideas, and auditioning actors for the roles. It's a nonstop process. There's not a week that goes by when I am not in auditions for one role or another. If it's a contract role—a.k.a "series regular"—I'll see anywhere from two hundred to three hundred, even four hundred people for a role, depending on who I feel might be right for it. So most of my audition time is spent casting series regulars. For the day-players, although I will audition people for those roles from time to time, many of the day-players are cast from actors that have read for me for series regular roles and weren't right for them, or else they are actors I've seen on television or in movies. I keep voluminous files, notes, and records, and I also go to a lot of theater.

One of the things I love to do is go and see a play or a showcase and then hire an actor the next day for a part. Many of my day-players or recurring parts are actors I've seen in the theater. So the message to an actor is: You just have to do the work, and if you put it out there hopefully someone will come and see it.

With regard to generals (general interviews with actors), I don't have the time for generals because I'm so busy casting for specific roles, and we literally cast hundreds and hundreds of speaking parts a year. So I have to spend my time reading people that are right for a role, or else going to see things. I'm constantly in auditions or else I'm on the phone with agents and managers. We get voluminous calls. We're constantly being pitched.

It's a very creative job and I love doing it.

When actors say, "I want to work in soaps," what do you tell them?

What I say to actors is: Don't narrow your vision of where you want to work. When an actor says, "I want to work in soaps," my response is, "You just want to act." Don't make it about working in soaps, just like you can't say, "I want to be in films" or "I want to be in theater." An actor is an actor is an actor. And I tell actors, make it about: "I want to work as an actor." There is no such thing as being able to focus on just one area. There are only ten daytime dramas. If they are not casting something you are right for, or you may not even be necessarily right for the medium on certain levels, it's better to just want to act.

We're seeing more crossover in this day and age than ever before, with actors going from daytime to movies to nighttime and coming back. There's just this sense that I've never seen before of actors crossing over from one medium to another. These are not actors that said, "I want to focus in one medium." They are actors who want to act. So I feel very strongly about saying don't ever make it about one medium. Make it about being the best actor you can be, so that wherever the opportunity is, you're ready for it.

When you meet an actor or when you're reading an actor, what qualities do you find most appealing?

The thing that I find most appealing is skill . . . craft . . . talent, because that's what I'm looking for. There are a lot of things that go into the casting of a series regular. For series regulars, we need charisma, presence, sex appeal, and dynamic qualities. We ask, "Is this somebody that the audience is going to want to watch day in and day out?" But all of these elements would mean nothing if we don't hire talented people, because in daytime the demands are very great for an actor. In a typical week, an actor will go through many, many emotional peaks and valleys in their character. We need people who can deliver. Even if we are hiring a young actor that hasn't done much, we are looking for the potential. Because if we don't hire people who can take the stories and bring them to life emotionally, that actor won't be around very long and neither will that story. I can't tell you how many hundreds of actors have a great look on the surface, but when it comes time to do the work they don't make it into a callback situation because they can't back it up.

What things tend to turn you off when it comes to actors and auditioning?

I have very few pet peeves about what turns me off, but my biggest pet peeve is somebody not being prepared. There's no excuse for an actor to come into an audition and not be comfortable enough with the material to make strong, intelligent choices. We always make our material available to actors ahead of time. People sometimes say, "I didn't get a chance to work on it" or "I'm sorry I didn't have much time to prepare." That's immediately a red flag to me because I want to hire an actor who, regardless of how much time they've had with the material, will come in and make choices. An actor is competing with hundreds and hundreds of professionals and they need to treat this as a business. Although there are a handful of people that come out of nowhere with very little training and find success almost instantly, that is a small percentage.

Do you have any interesting stories about casting that you can share?

You know, it's funny. One of the questions I often get asked is, "Do you have any interesting or unusual stories?" and I guess to illustrate my earlier point, the answer is, "No." I've been a casting director for seventeen years, and I have virtually no interesting stories in terms of how an actor got in to see me or a bizarre situation where I met someone walking their dog and they turned out to be the next series regular. I guess the point is that casting is really about the actor and the material and the magic that happens in that room.

It's one of those things where the actor has to be tenacious in terms of their intention to get the opportunity, and then they have to be able to back it up with talent. I have surprisingly few stories that differ from the process of how it happens. We could turn on the television right now and watch *General Hospital* and everybody you'd see on screen that I cast is someone that came in through these doors, read the material, and had some kind of magic happen. It's the truth.

So there's no discovering people sitting in ice cream shops . . .

There have been times I've been out and saw somebody who was innately right for something I was casting and I asked if they were an actor, and if they were, they've gotten the opportunity to read. I can't say that I've actually ever ended up casting anybody from that type of situation, but that's not to say it won't happen tomorrow. The truth is—and I hate to take away the mystique—that it happens through a lot of hard work, timing, and a lot of luck in terms of getting the chance to show what you can do.

If you had friends or relatives who were coming out to Hollywood and they knew nothing about the business, what would you tell them?

The best advice I could offer anyone is that the only reason to come out here is because you love the craft of acting. You can't make it about wanting to "make it," or to be a star, or to get on a series. One has very little control over all of those things, because there are so many outside factors. The only control you have is your work . . . your craft. And if that's why you are in this business—because you love doing it—then it becomes about acting, not about "making it." I see a lot of people who come here who don't have a craft; they only want to "make it." But that's somebody who doesn't have a center. That's somebody who doesn't know who they are, or what they are about.

The "star" thing either happens or it doesn't. I think the statistic is that only about 5 percent of Screen Actors Guild members make over $11,000 a year. Well, if you look at the statistics, you have to be an actor for all the right reasons. And that will guide you through the tough times, of which there are many. It can be a very "up and down" business. It can be very tough. And it *is* a business. You have to be both an artist and a businessperson, in that you are responsible for your career as well. It's a very complex, difficult business. The highs are probably the greatest highs one can get and the lows are probably the lowest lows one can get.

It's like a roller coaster at times . . .

It is, and sometimes not necessarily a roller coaster, because many people don't even get the highs. It can be very tough. I have a lot of friends who are actors and I see it firsthand. I respect and admire actors, but I certainly don't envy them because they've chosen, I think, the most difficult profession one could enter.

Industry Interview: Advice from Sheila Manning, Commercial Casting Director, on Acting in Commercials

Sheila Manning has cast thousands and thousands of television commercials, and her casting office is one of the busiest in Los Angeles. Having launched the careers of many actors, she is considered by many in Hollywood to be the Queen of Commercial Casting.

Could you tell us about a day in the life of a busy commercial casting director? You seem to be the busiest casting director in town...

Well, we work at it. Some say that at Sheila Manning Casting we never close!

On a typical day, I get here around nine o'clock in the morning. At this office, we start the day by checking to see that the actors we've booked conform to all the legalities. We check to see that they are members of the Screen Actors Guild in good standing. We then look to see that all of our casting sessions for the day are filled in. We generally cast from 10:00 a.m. until 6:30 p.m. We check to see if we have the shipping straightened out—the addresses to where we're going to send out the tapes to the directors and producers. Usually the ad agency gets one and the production company gets one. I also speak throughout the day to clients, who are either calling in to book talent, put talent "avail," change a spec, or give me a job.

If they give me a new job, we call Breakdown Services and we put it out on the Commercial Breakdowns. We also put it out on The Link, which is their computer network. I love using the computer. We also put it out on the Theatrical Breakdowns. We put it out to every agent in town, and sometimes we send it out to the print agents.

During the day, we also open packages and sort pictures into stacks, so that I can more easily look at what they are. Then we set up sessions. No picture comes into this office that I do not look at personally with these two eyes, unless, of course, the job is cancelled for some reason. And we are not an office that throws away the smaller agents' pictures. If they spend the money and the time to get us the submissions, then I look at them. I book a lot of people from smaller agents. That's why we stay so busy. We take great pride in finding new faces who can act.

What advice do you have for actors who say, "I want to work in commercials"?

I suggest taking acting classes. Learn how to act, which is a really good thing to learn. You can also take a commercial class. Commercial classes will knock six or eight months off your lack of knowledge. They will teach you what to expect when you go out on your auditions, but that's all they do. They don't teach you how to act. And when taking classes, know from whom you are taking classes. I saw an ad in *Backstage West* recently where this person was teaching a class, and I don't think she has ever even booked a job. She even had testimonials in the ad—one was from her ex-husband. So be careful: Know from whom you are taking classes.

Then once you've got some training, the practicalities are to call the Screen Actors Guild and get a list of all the agents. Then send out one nice headshot to every agent.

What impresses you about an actor during an audition?

Reality. The ability to project who they really are in the situation. When you are being who you really are, then you're barely acting, you're just reacting.

What don't you like?

Being plastic. I don't like people who try to get you to believe who they are. Generally, if you have a really strong need to impress upon me that this is the "box" you fit in, then you generally don't fit in that box. This is because "who you are" will show itself to me immediately. I can tell within the first few seconds whether or not someone is a person I want to get to know, and so can every human being in the world. Think about it. How many times have you met a person and before you finish shaking their hand, you're thinking, "I really would like to get away from this person," or "Gosh, I wish I could get to know this person really well"? And this happens before you've even exchanged a sentence.

Do you have any advice on pictures?

Actors should try to get a nice, straightforward picture from the shoulders up. You are the product, and your face is what I want to see. When I am buying you, I am looking at your face. If you are heavy or skinny and feel you have to show your body, you should know that I can tell your size from the headshot. And if I can't, I probably shouldn't be doing this.

Just get a good headshot that really looks like you. It should have living eyes, preferably with some amusement in them or some emotion in them, so that I feel that there's a real person inside there. Some people used to say, take a blank piece of paper and cover your face except for the eyes, and see if the eyes are alive. For example, look at this picture on my desk. There's much more about this girl in this picture than I need to know about her. I only need to know what her face looks like, not her whole body.

And don't wear any jewelry, and only wear light make-up. Don't wear anything that distracts. Don't wear anything that will make me say, "Oh, I wonder wear she got that blouse?" or "Oh, I wonder where she got that necklace?"

And there's been this thing lately where agents are telling actors that if you print your headshot horizontally, then when the casting person is going through the stack of pictures they will have to stop and pay attention and turn the picture around. But the truth is that we don't. We just don't bother to look. I don't bother because I find that to be annoying.

So you end up just seeing the picture sideways?

Yes. So maybe you have a 70 percent chance of me seeing your picture, instead of a 100 percent chance of me seeing it.

There's this impression that commercial casting directors want three-quarter shots . . .

That's wrong. We don't want anything other than a good headshot. And we all want résumés attached to those headshots. We want to know that a person can act. There's this idea some have of, "Well, it's only a commercial. We don't need to include a résumé." Guess what? It's harder to act in commercials. You have twenty-eight seconds to develop your character, give me the story line, and then get out of it, instead of twenty-eight minutes or even four minutes.

If you're good at characterization, that's great, but the acting changes in different mediums. You wouldn't do the same acting for a sitcom, as you would for a commercial. You wouldn't do your music center performance if you were auditioning for *Will & Grace*, which happens to be my favorite show.

So you need to be a trained and versatile actor who knows that a commercial is different from a sitcom or a movie or musical theater.

What's your advice on slating?

The best way to slate is to say your name as if you are meeting somebody. If you were at a party and somebody walked up to you and said in an over-the-top, over-friendly, or crazy kind of way, "Hi, I'm so-and-so!!!!" you'd say, "Bye!" And that what's some actors do; they don't know how to be themselves. Just remember that slating is your introduction. Believe it or not, many directors do not watch actors beyond their slate. The person who says, "Hi!!!!" in an unnatural or weird way gets fast-forwarded without the director ever watching their audition. It might be the best performance they've ever done, but it will not be seen. Just a real simple, "Hi, my name is so-and-so" will do.

What about crashing auditions—where actors sneak in on an audition even though they weren't given an appointment?

If an actor crashes an audition at our office, they'll never walk in our door again. The reason is that I get paid to bring in people who are right for the job. That's the only reason they pay me. That's why they need me. You might be wrong for the part and you don't even know it. You have no idea what they've asked me for. Maybe you look like everybody else in the waiting room, but maybe everybody else in the waiting room is a former smoker. So when you come into the audition and we say, "So what brand did you smoke?" and you say, "Oh, I never smoked," then I look like the jerk. I look like I didn't pay attention to what my producer told me to bring in. And I lose the job. And believe me, if I lose the job, the actor who crashed the audition loses the chance of ever working for me again. We keep pictures of everyone who has ever crashed an audition. And we also have great memories.

What would you say to new actors in town about their job?

Well, I love actors and I say this to them every time: "The job of an actor is to go on interviews." That is the job. Then if we really like what you do, we reward you by letting you come to the set and play with us, and we give you money for it. But that's the reward for doing the job. The job is going to the interviews, and then if you are lucky, then you get to play. The majority of people who become successful are great actors, men and women who have put in their time. At the Emmy's, Holland Taylor said, "Overnight!" when she held up her Emmy. The truth is that she's a brilliant and talented actress who's been working hard for many, many years.

GETTING THE PART

Hopefully, after you learn the ropes of auditioning and you practice at it, you'll go out into the real world, audition your heart out, and soon be hired as an actor here in Los Angeles! Someone might want your services for just a day, maybe a week, possibly a month, or even in a starring capacity in a motion picture or television series. Whatever it ends up being, be happy about it. Any credit, big or small, will help to advance your acting career.

As a new actor, there are a few things you should know about being hired. These include understanding your contract, how it's negotiated, how you should be prepared for your job, and how you can publicize it afterwards. This chapter aims to cover all of these important details.

Your Contract and How It's Negotiated

As mentioned in chapter 10, your agent will be negotiating your contract for you. Fortunately, this is not something that will be drawn up from scratch or that requires a tremendous amount of work. Remember the helpful union, SAG-AFTRA, which was established to protect actors? Well, every few years a union negotiating committee renegotiates a standard agreement with all motion picture/television producers and the networks. The agreement applies whenever an actor is hired, and it covers significant things like minimum wages, overtime, per diems, and a wide variety of regulations governing working conditions.

For example, the agreement clearly spells out the minimum wages (called "scale") that a union actor is to be paid when working in television or in theatrical films. Day performers earned a minimum of $880 per day in 2014-15. Weekly performers earned $3,053 per week. As mentioned in chapter 5, these minimums are subject to change, so check with SAG-AFTRA about their current rates. There are also other salary provisions for stand-ins, extras, stunt coordinators, and residual payments.

The parts of the contract that will actually have to be negotiated are few. These include your actual salary (which will either be scale or above), your credit or billing (where your name appears), and a per diem (a daily allowance, if you are shooting out of town). When it comes to negotiating salary, your agent will not have much leverage if you are totally unknown as an actor. Many new actors or relatively new actors receive "scale plus ten," which means SAG-AFTRA minimum wage plus an additional 10 percent to cover the agent's fee. Even some established actors, but not stars, are sometimes forced to accept scale wages if they want to work at all.

Over the years, production companies have been paying less and less to day-player and featured performers as they shell out larger and larger sums for the stars. In other words, in some productions there are one or two actors making several million dollars, and most of the others are earning scale.

One positive for actors, however, is that new networks and channels are being created every year, which ultimately leads to more products being produced. That means there are more acting jobs out there!

Understanding How Deals Are Made

Deal making can be very simple and also very complex. As I mentioned, for most acting jobs, the negotiation of the contract is very quick. The only time it can get complex is when you are a star or you are up for a major role. Star-level talent agencies, with the assistance of entertainment lawyers on staff, will ask for as much as they can get for their clients who regularly earn millions of dollars. In addition to sky-high salaries, they negotiate things like special living quarters, special meals, percentages of profit, and even things like having a golf or batting cage on the set. These things are not relevant to newcomers, so for now, I'll explain how deals are made for most actors in the business.

As a newcomer, in the beginning you typically will be hired for smaller parts that require only one day to perhaps a week or two of work. When a director or production company is interested in you for a particular project, your agent will be contacted. Usually the casting director will call and say that you are wanted for a role (usually the one you auditioned for, but not always). They will also specify the number of days for which you are needed.

Determining Your Salary

Many times the casting director will tell your agent how much the production company is willing to pay, if it hasn't already been disclosed in the Breakdowns. For example, at the top of a Breakdown casting notice for a particular project, it might say "Salary: Scale + 10 percent." That lets agents know right from the start what the production company is willing to pay. Therefore, there won't be any negotiating and agents won't submit actors who only work for amounts higher than what is offered. This opens the door to newcomers who almost always work for scale.

Other times, the casting director will ask your agent for your day-quote—your daily working rate—before disclosing how much money the production company might be willing to offer. As a new actor, you probably won't have a day-quote, because a day-quote is established by working on projects where you've made more than scale. Your agent will either tell them that you have no quote or give them your quote if you have one, and then the casting director will present it to the producers of the project who will then put together an offer.

Whenever an offer is presented, a good agent will usually try to get more money than proposed. Agents will say, "Listen, she worked on *Movie XYZ* and got *X* amount of dollars, so she should at least get that now." The casting director will then try to verify that previous salary. However, that still might prove to be pointless. If the production company is only willing to pay a certain salary, the job will go to another actor if your agent won't accept the offer. That means you might lose the job because you and your agent tried to get you more money! Bargaining is part of the business, but in today's world where competition is fierce, most actors are willing to take lower-paying jobs than they are used to (as long as the casting director won't tell anyone that they were paid less than their day-quote). If you need food on the table, you take what you can get.

Some new actors think it's unfair that stars and celebrities make so much money, and they—struggling actors—often only make scale. Here is the reasoning behind those huge salaries: Big stars are not paid $20 million because of their tremendous acting ability. They are paid large sums because they have an ability to attract an audience that will pay millions of dollars to come see a movie. An "unknown" actor has no power at the box office. An unknown can't draw in the masses to see a movie. Therefore, that actor is usually paid scale, or slightly above, for his or her acting services only, not for any box office power. Can you understand the rationale?

What About Billing?

Where and how your name appears—billing—helps to give you name recognition and also greatly satisfies you and your relatives who might be watching you. Since most newcomers are hired for small parts, billing is usually not a big issue. It's usually left to the producer's discretion as to where your name will appear. In film, featured players with speaking lines are listed in the ending credits, along with crewmembers, soundtrack credits, and other miscellaneous credits. However, if you have a nice supporting role or you are co-starring on television, your agent might want to discuss billing. If you've landed a really big part, your agent will also have to discuss where, how, and if, your name will appear in advertising. But for most roles that newcomers get, billing is very straightforward and not even necessary to negotiate.

A Per Diem

One other element that might need to be negotiated is your per diem, which is an additional daily allowance. If the movie is shot outside of Los Angeles—and more and more are these days—you will receive a per diem to cover additional meals and living expenses. This is not usually a debated issue, although some agents have been able to negotiate high per diems for their actors, sometimes hundreds of dollars a day or more. That's a lot of pocket change! But, like billing, it's usually not necessary to negotiate it when it involves a relatively new actor who's only hired for a few days.

Getting Ready for Your Job

After your contract is negotiated and you are officially hired, there are still a few more details that need to be attended to before you start work. They are:

Getting a Script. You'll need to get a copy of the script. One will either be delivered to you, or you will pick one up before your first day(s) of work. If the part is tiny, you might actually just get to see the script the day you show up. For example, if you yell out only one word in one scene, getting a complete script in your hands is not of the utmost urgency. On the contrary, if you've got twenty lines, plans will definitely be made for you to get a script immediately.

Getting Dressed. You'll also have to work out wardrobe details. Sometimes the production company will provide your attire, especially if you're working on a period piece. Other times they might want you to bring in your own clothes, especially if you have a very small role, in an effort to save money on costume rentals. This is all cleared up with a simple phone call to wardrobe. Depending on how important you are and how important your role is, you will either have to make the call yourself or you will get a call from wardrobe. The discussion will probably take only a few minutes, and will cover things like shirt sizes and wardrobe colors. So be attentive and make sure you know your measurements.

Once these details are straightened out, you just have to work on the acting aspect. Make sure you learn your lines. Constantly forgetting or stumbling over your lines on the set is something you won't want to do. Therefore, practice, practice, practice. Try to foresee all possible circumstances—though if you could do that you might not be in this business! Prepare different ways you can deliver your lines in the event that the director says, "I want you to try it differently." Also be aware that your lines may be changed overnight. Yes, that's right. The writers might change, add, delete, or swap any of your lines and not even tell you until you show up. You'll arrive ready to go with your scene only to find out that a new one has been written. So plan for this possibility, though it's more likely that it won't happen. Developing an ability to pick up new material, learn it fast, and deliver it well on cue will only help you.

The Day You Go to Work

Make sure you set a couple of alarms to wake you up the day of your job. Can you think of anything worse than oversleeping for something you've worked so hard to get?

Next, go over your lines as you get ready. Get warmed up! Stretch, exercise, eat right, and practice. But don't drive yourself crazy—you have to make this business fun! When you get ready to leave, another good idea is to have the production office's phone number with you, in the event you have any unexpected delays. And as with auditioning, make sure you leave for your destination early.

If you are shooting on a studio lot, your name will be on a list at the front gate, and you'll be allowed to enter. You'll also be given directions to the stage where you are shooting. If you are working on location, you could be shooting anywhere from downtown L.A. to Long Beach. So keep a map handy!

When you finally get to the set, the first person you'll probably be looking for is the second assistant director (the second A.D.) not anyone else. He or she will have your contract, in addition to some brief tax forms for you to fill out. You'll have to sign these papers sometime during the day. Be sure to look over your contract to see that everything is stated correctly. Check for your name, your ID numbers (telephone, social security, address), your salary, per diem, billing, and anything else that might have been negotiated by your agent. Otherwise, everything on it should be okay. Remember, it's a standard SAG contract, so you won't have to worry about the fine print.

Next, you'll probably be directed by the second A.D. to one of several places. Most likely, you'll go to your trailer or dressing room, but if they need you soon, you might be ushered off to wardrobe or make-up. You'll notice that big stars generally have bigger dressing rooms or trailers. If you are only working for a day or two, you might only get a fourth of a trailer! The general rule is the bigger the part, the bigger the trailer. That's just the way it goes. However, when it comes to make-up, everybody usually shares the same make-up room.

The second A.D., or one of his or her assistants, will keep tabs on you throughout the day. It's the assistant's job to know where everyone is at all times. To avoid any unnecessary all-out searches for you, it's best to stay just in your designated area. Of course, you should feel free to visit "craft service," the food area, for some munchies. (A sidenote: You can always tell the budget of a film by the expansiveness of the craft service set-up. A major feature film production will have money budgeted for all kinds of goodies: cereals, fruits, veggies, snacks, cookies, drinks, and even vitamins. A small budget movie might only have cheese balls. Yikes!)

Working on Television Is Different from Film

While all of the above information applies to both television and film, you should know that there are some differences when working in each medium. On movies, you generally will show up for your part, wait in your trailer for a few hours or even most of the day, and come out when they need you. You'll probably have only a brief rehearsal if it's a small part, maybe a couple of run-throughs of your scene and then you'll shoot. Obviously, this is for small parts. If your part is larger, it will be a little different. You will get to know the cast and crew, and feel much more at home on the set.

For sitcoms, you typically are hired for the week if you have a co-starring role, and sometimes three days for smaller parts. Most rehearse for four days, and shoot on the fifth. That gives you the opportunity to become more familiar with everyone on the set. Dramatic serials shoot more like movies, filming different scenes on different days of the week. Thus, you'll be called when they need you, without four days of rehearsal. Soap operas shoot a full episode every day, which is the toughest job of all. This is why everyone says that soap work is the hardest. Most soaps rehearse the full episode in the morning and tape in the afternoon, with usually only two or three takes per scene. So make sure you know your lines! (Soaps do use cue cards though, because it can be very difficult for cast members to perfectly memorize pages and pages of script every day.)

You're On!

Depending on which director you work with and in which medium, you may get a lot of assistance or virtually none. Film directors seem more apt to discuss your work with you, offering suggestions and guidance as they can shoot one scene for days. Television directors seem more intent on getting the show finished on time in an acceptable state. But it really depends on the director. There are plenty of exceptions in both mediums.

If you are on a movie, you will have to shoot the scene several times from several different angles. Then it will all be edited together. You'll start with a master shot that opens the scene with all actors in it, and then proceed to shoot close-ups of each actor. Most television serials, such as medical or legal dramas, shoot this way also. Sitcoms and soap operas shoot with four differently located video cameras that tape the dialogue simultaneously. This is why their shooting schedule is much more rapid.

Even if you don't feel like a professional when you show up for your first job, you must act like one. That means many things. First and foremost, you should do what you're told. Don't pretend that you know better than anyone, even though you truthfully might. Just listen and follow directions. Don't make suggestions unless someone asks you for your opinion. On any production, everyone has clearly defined responsibilities. So if something doesn't seem right—your hair, your make-up, your wardrobe—it will be someone else's fault and not your own. However, if you start making changes to any of these things and the director doesn't like it, it will become your fault.

Another important part of being professional is delivering your lines and staying in character until someone says "cut." Even if you think you've delivered a line poorly, you have to keep going until somebody says "cut." It's not up to you to decide whether or not you did a good job. (Obviously, if you totally goof up a line, you will have to cut. But I'm talking about people who unnecessarily censor themselves repeatedly.)

And never criticize another actor. Just be concerned with what you can do to make your performance as good as possible, and follow directions. You might feel like you're "brown-nosing" a bit, and the truth is that you are. But know this: It's far better for your career to be an agreeable, flexible, and pleasant actor, than to be known as someone who is difficult, stubborn, and a "know-it-all."

That's a Wrap!

Okay, you've given an Academy Award–winning performance and now you're done, or "wrapped" as they say. You'll be thanked and then all you have to do is sign out with the second A.D. They will have your call-time for the following day if you are scheduled to come back. Go home and revel in your experience.

Publicizing Your Success

Publicizing your job is important, but overly celebrating it is not only a little tacky but also like "counting your chickens before they hatch." You can only definitively celebrate your moment in the spotlight once that film or television show airs and you're still in it. If you had a sizable role, you will probably still be included. Smaller roles, especially in films, can occasionally end up on the cutting room floor if the scene wasn't crucial and footage had to be cut. Think positive, but be prepared for that possibility. Hopefully that won't happen to you.

In the meantime, it's nice to casually inform any industry people you meet that you just finished working on this movie or that television show! Work breeds work. Directors, producers, and casting directors love to hear actors say that they are working. It gives more power to those actors because it shows that someone was interested in hiring them.

But before you contact anyone about going to see you or watching you on television, make sure that you are definitely still going to be seen and that your performance warrants watching. If you only have a line or two, then be up-front about it. (No one but your mother and your agent will be overjoyed to see you pop on screen, say "Madam, here is your drink," and then disappear for good. It's a nice credit to put on your résumé, but realistically no one will remember it as a stunning performance.) On the other hand, if you have a meaty role, make some phone calls, send out some flyers, or even take out small ads in the trade papers.

Most television shows don't cut footage very much, so a part on TV will probably stay in the final product. Motion pictures, however, tend to cut out a lot. Therefore, contact the production company or go to the premiere first to make sure you are still in before you do any mass publicity. I know stars of movies who have gone to sneak previews and were absolutely stunned at how many scenes were cut. The moral of the story is that your true achievement comes when you are still in the final product.

If you really want to do some major publicity and you have the money, then hire a publicist. They specialize in promoting actors and artists to the public, and can create campaigns for actors at all different levels of their careers. They range from mailings to all-out media blitzes, and can cost you anywhere from $500 to thousands and thousands of dollars a month.

The Snowball Effect

Booking your first job in L.A. is a nice feeling. For some, it takes a few weeks; for others, several years. No one can decisively say when it will happen but, with persistence, your efforts will eventually pay off.

You will find that after you book your first job, it may be slightly easier to book your second, and third, and so on. I call this the "snowball effect." It happens partly because your confidence level goes up. It radiates through your entire aura. Another reason is that casting people take you a tiny bit more seriously. After you've worked for someone else they respect, especially if your role was in a critically acclaimed project, it will become easier to get into their offices for auditions and general interviews. They won't necessarily be begging to hire you. They'll just give you more acknowledgment. Some will give you an opportunity to read for bigger and better roles that otherwise would have been offered to someone else. Of course, getting the job will usually still depend on your audition.

The snowballing of your career is a gradual process, with many turns in the road. Some actors book five or six jobs in one year, and then don't work at all in the next. So working isn't always a guarantee of future employment. But, in truth, it can be said that the more work you do, the more you will be respected and appreciated, which usually will create more opportunities for you in the long run.

Industry Interview: Ben Whitehair, Actor, on Motivation to Get Booked

What's been very helpful for me is studying the early careers of actors I admire. I'll go on IMDb and look at an actor's history—so many of them spent at least a year before their first credit working at a fast food joint.

Even for the biggest actors, most of the time, it's about getting jobs. A celebrity who does one film a year is probably only on set acting for three months; the rest of the time, he or she is looking for work, making connections to get a job, doing press junkets to stay in everyone's minds and get more jobs. And the biggest actors in the business *all* manage their careers like CEOs—if you have your own series, or you're a movie star, that's just part of what you do. You can be a brilliant actor at any level, but you can't treat your career like a hobby.

REALITY TELEVISION: A RECENT TREND

Okay, so that's how it works when it comes to being cast as an actor for TV or film. But what about "Reality Television"? We've all seen these shows, and we've all become addicted to one (or more!) of them. Those reality TV shows seem to haven taken over the tube. From *Dancing with the Stars* to *The Bachelor,* and countless others have caught the public's attention. In the last few years, they've become more and more outrageous, and honestly they can sometimes be quite fun to watch. A guilty pleasure, of sorts. And just when you think you've seen the craziest show ever, yet another one comes along with an even greater twist. It started with *The Real World* on MTV in the 1990s, and now we've seen stranded islanders, would-be brides being duped into thinking their potential husband is a multimillionaire, to even a "fake" reality show where everyone except for one contestant was in on the charade. (I should also mention rich girls who have never had a job, trying unsuccessfully to maintain a menial job for just a few hours. How hard can that be?)

There is good news and bad news for actors with regard to this new trend. I was recently looking at the latest SAG-AFTRA newsletter and was shocked to see so many listings for casting director contacts for upcoming reality TV shows. What's more, some casting directors are almost exclusively seeking reality show performers. Actors can use this trend to their advantage if they act wisely.

The Good News

The trend is great for people who are new to Hollywood. If you are just starting out, then these shows provide plenty of great opportunities for you to get into television, though the competition is still pretty stiff. The nice aspect is that for reality shows, the casting directors don't want seasoned actors with long résumés. They mostly want "interesting" people with strong and unique personalities. Good looks are always a plus, too.

When you watch some of these shows, you'll often see a contestant's name followed by their hometown, but in truth, it doesn't necessarily mean that the person currently lives there. A lot of casting for these programs takes place in Los Angeles, and I would guess that at least 50 percent or more of the contestants you see are aspiring actors living in L.A. who have other professions on the side. On the other hand, it's also true that some of these shows do have talent scouts traveling around the country to both find new talent and to promote an upcoming show as well (*American Idol*, for example). But I bet most of the would-be champions you see on many reality shows are already in L.A.

Why does this happen? It all comes down to one thing: money. For most shows, there is no need to spend tens, if not hundreds, of thousands of dollars traveling around the country looking for people when there are plenty of exciting personalities already in L.A.

And speaking of money, one of the reasons the reality show phenomenon has developed into a solid presence in Hollywood lately is because they are fairly inexpensive to produce, compared to, say, a sitcom or drama. When a sitcom or drama becomes highly rated, everyone in the project wants more money. The writers, directors, actors, and everyone else involved seeks a bigger piece of the pie. So after a successful run of a couple of years, a show runs into the dilemma of how to stay profitable. For instance, when popular actors want $1 million per episode, it becomes difficult for the network to make tons of money on that product. With reality TV, producers can pay contestants a nominal fee to appear, and then simply offer a prize of $500,000 or $1 million to one lucky person at the end of the season. And though there are writers (or as they say in reality television, "story editors") and producers who still need to be paid, it's still far less expensive than having a team of talented and expensive writers, actors, and producers who must consistently be paid to create a brand new refreshing episode every week.

Some actors have indeed sprung from the reality show scene to stardom. The best example of this is Jennifer Hudson, who started out in the public eye grappling with Simon Cowell on *American Idol* before going on to win the 2006 Best Supporting Actress Oscar for *Dreamgirls*. Jacinda Barrett has established herself as a successful film and TV presence after her turn on *The Real World: London*. Wise performers like Hudson and Barrett knew how to take the notoriety they initially gained on reality TV and use it to get their feet in the door for legitimate auditions, rather than fall into the trap many "reality stars" make once they become instantly famous; appearing in *another*, almost-always cheesier reality show (which turns out to be the nail in their career coffin).

So who are the major players behind the scenes in reality TV? The smartest way to learn who's who is to check out the websites of the reality shows you might be interested in applying to be on. Here are five entities that are undisputed kings of the biz to kick off your education:

Ryan Seacrest Productions. Not only is he America's top DJ and *American Idol*'s enduring host, Seacrest produces E! Entertainment Television's top-rated reality roster (and brought the Kardashians to the world's attention). (www.ryanseacrest.com)

One Three Media. Mark Burnett, creator of *Survivor* and one of the "fathers" of reality TV, presides over this company, which is constantly developing new show ideas in multiple forms of media. (www.hearstintegratedmedia.com)

Bunim-Murray Productions. The producers of numerous adventure-styled reality productions, including the *The Real World*. (www.bunim-murray.com)

495 Productions. This company presides over the hugely successful *Real Housewives* franchise. (www.495productions.com)

Syco. Simon Cowell's reality empire is run by this multi-tasking entity—Syco produces everything these days from reality shows and hit songs to musical stage plays. (www.simoncowellonline.com)

The Bad News

So many "stars" on reality TV are really, to be frank, former celebs whose careers have seen better days (often decades ago). Reality TV most often serves as a boost for these performers, refreshing them in viewers' minds very briefly before they slink back into obscurity. Casting old talent means slots on reality TV shows fill up instantaneously—slots that perhaps, in a different creative landscape, might go to deserving up-and-comers instead.

Many people want their fifteen minutes of fame, so as long as you are here in Hollywood, you may as well try out for some of these shows, and there are some easy ways to apply.

The Reality TV Application Process

Start by going to your targeted reality show's website—often casting notices are posted there directly. A few other good resources for casting info to check out:

- Backstage (www.backstage.com)
- Reality Wanted (www.realitywanted.com)
- Project Casting (www.projectcasting.com)
- The Learning Channel (TLC) website: www.tlc.com

One way to get into reality TV is to target your favorite show. The best way to learn how to apply is to visit the Web site for that show. There is always a link on a TV network web-site that will tell you how to apply for that show's next season. But understand, some of these shows get tens of thousands of applications, sometimes 50,000 or more. I will guarantee this: applying is sort of like playing the lottery. I know a casting director for one of the top-rated reality shows, and she told me that they never get the chance to look at all of the appli-cations. For example, if there is a staff of perhaps five or six associate casting directors, and they have three weeks to cast a show, and they receive 45,000 packages in the mail, not to mention many other video applications taped at promotional events, then they would have to look at 15,000 videos per week. That's more than 2,000 tapes a day! If you do the math, even if an office has five casting people, there is no way each casting person could watch 400 three-minute audition tapes in a single day.

The parts of the application process are as follows: Typically you will have to create a three- to five-minute video of yourself showing your personality and explain why you would be great for the show. In order to stand out, you have to be vibrant, a bit unusual, opinionated, and still very like-able, even if you have less-than-desirable traits. There is no perfect way to audition—you just have to project personal-ity, as is the case for any audition whether it's for a com-mercial, movie, or TV role. Also realize that casting directors usually have particular personalities in mind to round out a show, which may include different ethnicities, ages, levels of education, professions, socio-economic backgrounds, etc. If they see your tape and they like it, then most likely it will go into one of several different categories of people that they are looking for.

In addition to the video, you will have to submit a seven- to ten-page survey that asks all kinds of probing questions about your interests, your opinions, and sometimes bizarre questions, and then you are asked to sign away your life. (Just kidding . . . but I've seen a couple of those forms, and the fine print seems to look like that.) Then you send in your package and cross your fingers.

Once that happens, packages arrive and the casting directors whittle down the piles of applicants. Once a hundred or so finalists have been selected, those people go through phone interviews, several meetings with producers, and ultimately through background investigations. Pretty much all of the reality shows hire specialists to thoroughly investigate every part of your background, including any criminal offenses, medical history, financial background, family and friends, etc.

Then if you make the cut, you may be on TV every week for a season and have a one-in-ten, or one-in-sixteen chance for a million dollars! Not too bad.

But from everything I have heard, reality TV isn't always what it's cracked up to be. In other words, it's not always "reality." Producers have a desire to make the shows provocative. They always need a "villain" type of person on the show. They need conflict, which makes each show better. Thus, producers have been known to instigate conflict amongst contestants, and some contestants have complained about being "pigeonholed" into a particular character role, such "the Bitch" or "the Buddy" or "the Lazy Person." So even though in one sense you are on a reality show, you can bet you might be portrayed as a semi-fictional character of yourself.

Other Ways to Get on Reality Television

In addition to applying for your favorite show, there are numerous upcoming shows that are always looking to cast people. The way to find out about these shows is to do an online search for such shows. There are numerous websites that keep track of upcoming casting calls, but these sites come and go. The best way to find out about new shows is to simply do a search for "Reality TV Casting" on any popular search engine. You'll probably find a dozen or so sites that contain many links. My suggestion is that if you are interested in these types of shows, only respond to shows that are being developed by major networks or well-known cable networks. Don't send an application to a production company if you have never heard of it.

Reality Shows Are Here to Stay

For established actors, work in television has definitely declined because of reality television. As I mentioned, there used to be dozens of sitcoms and dramas in the 1990s, and now there are far fewer such programs. America gets a kick out of *The Apprentice, The Biggest Loser,* and other makeover shows. Because show business is a business, that seems to be the one way for now that many networks prefer to make a significant portion of their money.

Some say the reality TV bubble is about to burst, but that's something I've been hearing for years. I think the reason for its success is, in part, due to the fact that many of us like to see everyday people on TV in peculiar situations. We begin to root for someone on a show, much like we root for a favorite sports team. It also gives us a chance to look at our lives and say, "Hmm, I can totally relate to that," or else "Hmmm, my life isn't so bad after all!" We feel an affinity with some of these everyday people, perhaps sometimes even a much stronger bond than with actors and stars that we see in movies, simply because we know that the people we are watching are like neighbors or friends. Yes, their image may be only somewhat "real" in terms of their portrayal by producers of these shows, but it's still more real than most things we often see in Hollywood.

So go for it! I hope to see you on a reality TV show someday soon!

Industry Interview: Deanna Meske, Experienced Reality Host/ Performer, on My Reality Ride

I know you've done hosting work and some reality TV appearances; how would you say that reality TV can help an actor's career?

I think reality TV is great, personally. I think you get paid, which is good, and if it's a nice role, you can clip it into your demo reel and use it on Actors Access. If it's not a great role, just don't promote it. I think you get experience with improv. [Reality TV] makes you work harder because [the producers and directors] don't treat you like a star a lot of the time. That makes you want to really up your game. But hey, it's on TV and gets you exposure, so I don't think reality TV is bad unless it's a trashy show. Then that can cause you some unwanted attention, and block you off for certain productions.

PERTAINING TO THE WALLET

Unfortunately, living in L.A. as an actor isn't as simple as showing up at the set, playing your part, and then relaxing in the California sunshine until your next booking. Yes, L.A. is the real world, which means you'll have to take care of, among other things, the financial matters of your life. This includes preparing your taxes, living within your means, understanding unemployment (if you should ever need it), and saving money in whatever ways you can. When you become rich and famous, you'll have plenty of people to take care of all these affairs for you, but for now you should know how to manage them yourself.

Handling Your Taxes

No one likes taxes. In fact, the thought of preparing a tax return makes most people cringe. As an actor, you'll have to start keeping good records and saving receipts, since you'll be able to take many legitimate deductions by having them. I strongly advise that you hire an accountant, preferably one well-acquainted with actors and entertainers, to prepare your tax return for you. Not only will it save you time, especially if you have somewhat complicated taxes, but it will protect you from a tremendous headache and probably save you more money than if you did it yourself. The typical $200 to $300 fee is well worth it.

In order to maximize your deductions, you will need organized receipts of acting expenses and mileage records. Deductible expenses include accounting fees, admissions and tickets to movies and plays, agency and manager commissions, business gifts, copying/typesetting fees for résumés, acting lessons/coaching, hairstyling, make-up/cosmetics, cell phones, voicemail, photography, picture-duplication costs, postage, union dues, theater company dues, publicity, trade magazines and books, wardrobe cleaning expenses, and any other expenses that are solely related to acting that cannot be attributed to personal use.

You should also keep receipts of auto expenses, such as gas and repairs, as well as a mileage log for business miles driven. Your accountant will tell you that to derive a total figure for auto expenses, you can either take the total business miles driven during the year and multiply that by a standard per-mile figure, or you can total up all your auto expenses and then multiply that by the percentage of business miles driven out of the total miles driven during the year. Whichever comes to a higher dollar amount will be used as a deduction.

Thus, it's so important to keep good records. Get a file cabinet or a special drawer so that you keep all your receipts in one place. The more organized you start out, the easier it will be next April when you are scrambling to do your taxes.

The VITA Program

Once you are a member of SAG-AFTRA, you'll be able to receive free tax assistance if you want it. Volunteer members of the guild who have been trained by the IRS help other members prepare their tax returns. You can register to attend a small class held at the Guild in the months prior to every April 15 filing deadline. The program is called VITA (Volunteer Income Tax Assistance) Committee. For more information contact the Screen Actors Guild at (323) 954-1600.

Protecting Yourself from Identity Theft

In recent years, we've all heard about the growing problem of identity theft. Someone assumes your identity, gets credit cards in your name, charges them up, and then you are left with the bill. How does this happen?

For starters, these people who steal identities are not necessarily the hardened criminals you might imagine. They don't use guns, ski-masks, or have a team of cohorts waiting in a getaway car. They simply ask for your Social Security number. Do not give that information until you are officially hired by a legitimate production company. It will be used for tax purposes. In the 1990s, it was very common to sign in for an audition using your name and Social Security number. Then, SAG made it a little safer—you could sign in using your SAG membership number instead. This is now the common practice.

According to the Federal Trade Commission, American consumers lost over $1.6 billion due to fraud in 2013; identity theft was the leading deceptive practice that caused financial loss. If you are unfortunate enough to become a victim of identity theft, the impact to your life can be catastrophic—your bank accounts may be emptied, your credit may be ruined, and correcting erroneous information may take you months to years.

According to former California State Senator Debra Bowen, "In 2001, California became the first state in the nation to impose sweeping restrictions on how Social Security numbers could be used by preventing businesses from using them as membership, account or identification numbers and on any materials put in the mail. That means health plans can't put your Social Security number on your medical ID card, credit unions can't have your Social Security number double as your checking account number, health clubs can't use your Social Security number as your membership number, and much more. California expanded that law to cover government agencies, meaning public schools and colleges will have to take Social Security numbers off student identification cards and stop posting grades by Social Security number."

So the lesson is this: Don't ever give that information away at auditions, or even on the most basic of things, such as checks. Some friends of mine from small towns back East still have that information pre-printed on their checks. There is no need for that. It only puts you at risk.

Also, according to California State Senator Bowen, "One of the cruel ironies is your good credit history actually helps the thief who ripped off your identity. That's because when some-one "becomes" you on paper, they can walk into a bank or car dealership and the lender will pull your credit report to approve the loan or new line of credit. To prevent that from happening, California now lets you freeze access to your credit reports main-tained by the three major credit bureaus: Experian, Equifax, and Trans Union. Should a thief rip off your identity, the freeze will probably prevent them from establishing new credit in your name because few lenders will issue a loan or a credit card to someone without being able to check their credit report."

To find out more about what you can do to protect your identity, visit the California Office of Privacy Protection (*www. privacy.ca.gov*) or the Federal Trade Commission (*www.ftc.gov*).

Living Within Your Means

It sounds like common sense, but you'd be surprised how many actors seem to lack time- and money-management skills. Many actors start to slowly spend more than they earn, resulting in serious financial worries down the road.

This over-spending encompasses all aspects of life. For example, some people live in an apartment that they really can't afford. Some people come out to L.A. and rent a one-bedroom apartment starting at $1,000 a month. That's okay if you have a constant income, but a lot of actors don't. Living in a cheaper place that's perhaps $500 to $600 a month could save you several thousand dollars a year (and you could easily achieve this by splitting costs with a roommate, too).

Another bad habit that some actors develop is that they eat out too much. The money you spend on an average restaurant for one meal can buy food at a grocery store that could last several days. It's nice to go out to eat, but you should also learn to cook if you are on a limited budget. Think grains, salads, and fruit. Not only will you save money, you'll start looking healthier too.

The same goes for socializing. In L.A., not only will you spend at least $5 and up to $20 just to get into most clubs, but you could easily spend another $10 to $20 on drinks. (And if you have a date, it could be double.) So be smart. While it's fun and can also be important to socialize and make contacts, just be aware of how much you're spending.

Finally, watch your credit cards. Charging a little here and little there won't add up to much at the end of the week, but at the end of the year, you could easily accrue an extra debt of $5,000 to $10,000. Charge cards are convenient, but don't let them get too convenient. Try to survive just by using the cash in your wallet. In other words, if you really don't need something, then don't buy it.

Learn to develop a practical way of thinking when it comes to money. You'll have plenty to spend when you're starring on television or in features, so for now just lead a simpler life.

Unemployment

Many actors have sought assistance from unemployment when times were just too lean to handle. There is mixed sentiment about actors using this program. Some actors feel they shouldn't have to take jobs outside of their chosen profession. Others say you should take any job you can get when you have to pay bills. For your sake, I've gathered the appropriate information on unemployment and you can decide for yourself.

The Unemployment Insurance Program is administered by the State Employment Development Department for citizens of California. If you file a claim and qualify for unemployment, you will be awarded weekly assistance based on previous earnings during a prior twelve-month period. This assistance will be for up to twenty-six weeks during a benefit year of fifty-two weeks.

Your payments will be modified on a weekly basis if you have any reported earnings during that week. Also, in order to qualify, you have to fill out a form every week that reports any work you have performed and lists all attempts at seeking employment. (They want to make sure you're trying to find work.)

Unemployment has saved many actors from destitution. However, it's also encouraged some to be a little less tenacious in their quest for success. But if you need help, call your local Employment Development Department office for assistance.

Saving Money in L.A.

As an actor who might be living on a limited income, you'll want to save money any way you can. This applies to nearly every aspect of your life, from food to résumés to clothing.

Below are a few money-saving tips that I've learned or that have been passed on to me by fellow actors.

Résumés and Other Stationery Supplies. Get your résumés copied at Staples, where you can get them sometimes for as low as two or three cents apiece, in quantities of one hundred or more. It's much cheaper than using major copy chains, which typically charge seven cents or more per copy. You end up with exactly the same product!

When in need of envelopes, staples, paper, rubber cement, or any other supplies for your mailings, head to Staples again, or one of the major club warehouses, like Costco or Sam's Club. You'll find items in bulk quantities at all of these stores, which saves money. And as an actor, you will definitely go through one hundred or more envelopes in no time, so buying in bulk is definitely the way to go.

Raid the 99-Cent Store! Do you need trash bags, soap, toilet paper, or batteries? No problem. The "99-Cent Stores," a chain of stores in L.A., have just about anything you could possibly need—and never need. Many items are day-to-day disposables you would normally buy at a supermarket or drugstore; other items are much less functional—like tacky painted figurines or cheap plastic picture frames. Nonetheless, if you've never tried it, cruising the aisles of a large 99-Cent Store can be a highly entertaining experience!

Hopefully, money will be one of your lesser concerns while you pursue your acting career. If it gets to be a major problem, then take time out to resolve it. It's not a crime to get a temporary day-job for a month to pay your bills, if you have to. Granted, your acting career will be on hold, but you need to take time to straighten out your financial situation when it needs attention.

Industry Input: Financial Mistakes Aren't the End of the World! Advice from Ben Whitehair, Actor

Every problem is the opportunity for creative solution. You can think, "I did this wrong; this financial deal did not work"—but you have to ask, "What did I just learn?" As an actor, you have to remind yourself you're not curing cancer —you're telling stories. If I make a mistake, what I know is, I'm going to learn from it — the sooner I do it, the sooner I get to the next lesson. If a contract goes bad and I lose a thousand bucks, that sucks, but it's a lesson I needed to learn. Embrace mistakes!

Finally, now that you understand the nuts and bolts of the business, let's focus on one of the most important things to create during your first year in Hollywood: a positive existence.

CREATING A POSITIVE EXISTENCE

Having covered the basic steps you should take during your first year, it's now time to talk about how you can create an existence that will be conducive to success.

When contemplating your reality, are you going to look at your glass as half empty or half full? Are you going to focus on your problems or on finding solutions to them? It's so easy to sit back, complain, and proclaim to the world that you are a "victim." It's so easy to blame someone or something for why your life isn't working out. Such negative thinking never really gets you anywhere, except into a deeper depression.

The acting business will probably challenge you like nothing else, and for you to succeed you'll need great strength—physically, mentally, emotionally, and spiritually. Let's take a look at what I mean specifically.

A Healthy Physical Body

You will be challenged physically a great deal as an actor. The challenge is not so much the acting, but rather it's the juggling of one or more jobs, running to auditions on a moment's notice, going to acting classes, going to see your agent, networking, and taking care of everything else in life simultaneously. If you don't eat right, exercise, and stretch, in time you will probably start to look exhausted and worn-down. You may start to develop any one of the following unappealing conditions: big dark circles under your eyes, an unhealthy complexion, droopy cheeks, an expanded mid-section, muscle twitches, and/or an overall wounded and depleted-looking aura. If you are a character actor and that's the look you want, then great! But I have a feeling that's probably not the look most people will want to be projecting.

Therefore, try to take care of yourself! I'm not suggesting that you try to look like a supermodel. Just treat your body like it's priceless—which it is. Nourish yourself with plenty of healthy raw foods, like fruits and vegetables, and try to stay away from processed, fatty foods or fast food that ultimately doesn't supply your body with much useful energy.

We all have cravings for unhealthy things from time to time, but moderation is the key. Some actors tend to drink heavily, so if you drink, keep it under control. And drugs? Don't even think about it. Getting involved with drugs is the surest way to get you off your path as an actor, not to mention ruin your life in the process.

With regard to exercise, it can take any form. You don't have to join a gym, which is a very "L.A. thing" to do. Instead, you could go hiking in the Santa Monica Mountains. (Will Rogers State Park, Coldwater Canyon Park, and Topanga State Park are all great places.) What about dancing around your apartment to your favorite tunes for fifteen minutes every day? Have you tried kundalini yoga or power yoga? (Power yoga is a great overall workout for the body, mind, and spirit.) Do whatever you enjoy and understand that exercise will revitalize your body in the long run, not make it more tired. It will also give you a cheerful disposition because it causes endorphins to circulate throughout your body.

A Balanced and Focused Mind

Because of the hectic schedule that most actors lead, it's easy for the mind to get distracted, agitated, and bent out of shape. Worrying about finances, worrying about how well you did at your audition, worrying about whether your agent really likes you, worrying about that funny noise in your car, and worrying about when you're going to be a star are just a handful of concerns many actors have from time to time.

One of the keys to living an easier life is to practice watching your mind when it starts to race out of control. You actually *do* have the power to bring it back to a peaceful state. It just takes a lot of practice. Developing an even and balanced mind, which is commonly referred to as "meditation," is just like lifting weights. For example, if you want to develop a muscular physique, then you have to train every day. Similarly, if you want to develop an ongoing state of peace in your mind, you have to practice stillness of mind every day. So practice! Don't let your mind drag you around like a dog on a leash—try to become the master of your mind. Focusing on remaining calm, finding solutions to your problems, and taking decisive action are much more practical uses of your time and energy.

Many people, especially actors, tend to worry about things that are out of their control. For example, this is a common situation many actors fall into: After leaving an audition, actors will replay the audition over and over in their head until they have a splitting headache, as if it's going to change their reading. It's in the casting director's hands once you walk out of the room. All you can do is evaluate your audition and contemplate how you can improve future ones. Therefore, don't go home and nervously run the whole scenario through your head a hundred times. Just intelligently evaluate it and then try to let go.

Practice watching your mind, not only after auditions, but in every situation in life. When you notice your mind heading into high gear—getting frantic, upset, or angry about something—ask yourself to calm down. Try to look at the current situation from another perspective. Perhaps it's a blessing in disguise. Nothing in life is worth getting terribly upset over for an extended period of time. The result is only that your negative thoughts bombard your body like invisible missiles that deplete your energy.

Negative thoughts are most noticeable in moments of extreme anger or hurt, but be aware too that negative thoughts are also common in the subconscious and unconscious. For instance, many people hold onto thoughts like "I'm not good enough," "I'm not attractive enough," "I'm not smart enough." or even "I'm not tall enough." Try to become aware of any critical comments that you might be telling yourself over and over again. Then begin to replace them with positive ones. An old pattern that's been repeated thousands and thousands of times won't disappear overnight, but if you consciously work at reprogramming it, you'll begin to see inner changes that ultimately will be reflected outwardly in your life.

With regard to focus, when you've got a job to do, then just do it. As an actor, don't try to memorize lines with the radio on, the television blasting, or with a beer in your hand. Focus on whatever you have to do and eliminate as many distractions as possible. If you have a major audition tomorrow, then don't worry about something three days in the future. Give 100 percent to the task at hand. A little focus goes a long way.

A Healthy Emotional State

As I've said, acting can be a very challenging business and many actors are prone to depression. The thought of, "Am I ever going to make it? It's taking so long!" runs rampant among actors. If you focus on that thought long enough, consciously or unconsciously, it can lead to a profound sadness in your being.

At some point, or on several occasions during your adventure into show business, you will have to sit down and reevaluate whether this is the career for you. You'll have to be honest with yourself. You may find that you really hate almost every part of it and that you'd probably be happier doing something else. And you know what? That's okay! It's far better to do something you enjoy rather than something you dread. Or you may decide that you have some kind of indefinable drive and passion that compels you to continue onward. No matter how hard it gets, you just know that you have to continue. Regardless of what you decide, coming to some kind of resolution is what will allow your emotions to find some solitude on this common issue. You probably won't have found all the answers, but just having a clear sense of direction will bring a renewed sense of peace.

A different source of emotional conflict for many people, actors included, pertains to regrets about past events. People often contemplate what might have happened if they had only done something differently. The only way to heal such pain is to look at every incident in your life as a learning experience, something that you can grow from. For example, getting back to auditions, you can learn and grow from an unpleasant audition and become a better actor because of it. A bad audition is not the end of the world. Likewise, in life, you can grow from any experience from which you still feel hurt or pain. Ask yourself what you can learn from that experience. How are you a better person because of it? Look at every unpleasant experience as an opportunity for growth instead of just a bad thing that happened to you. If you really contemplate the value and lessons of any past situation, you will find some healing answers.

Understanding and realizing that everything in life can be a learning experience will bring great ease to you. Remember that it's not about *pretending* that an apparently bad thing is a good thing, but rather truly discovering how you can consciously grow and become a wiser, more empowered person from *every* unfolding in your life.

Another important thing to do for your emotional well-being is to set aside time for the little things that make you happy. Do you enjoy going to the movies, taking a walk on the beach, playing a sport, or going on a long drive? What about reading, painting, or spending time with friends? You have to set aside time for these important things. They nourish the soul. If you are unhappy, you will only become unhappier sitting around thinking about your unhappiness. So go out and do something good for yourself.

And don't forget to laugh. Probably the best way to thrust your life into instant joy is to get someone to tickle you for five minutes. Laughter is healing. If that's too much to handle, then try going to a comedy club or watching stand-up on television. Some cancer patients have claimed that a healthy dose of laughter every day helped to heal them! Some might question that, but no one can dispute that laughter makes you feel good. So laugh your heart out at how funny life can be!

Finally, remember to try to find something to appreciate in every moment. It can be done! Not only will you be happier, but other people will find you to be a much more appealing and attractive person. You will light up a whole room if you sincerely develop an enthusiastic love affair with life.

A Spiritual Self

I think it's important to recognize yourself as a spiritual being. I don't necessarily mean you have to visit a church, temple, or other spiritual center once a week. I mean that you have to know that you are meaningful and that you have a purpose in this world. It's true that going to places of worship once a week can help to cultivate this feeling, but I've been amazed at how many people seem to lose their spirituality when they are not sitting in a pew.

I believe that there are infinite spiritual paths to fulfillment, so I'm not about to recommend any particular one for you. I think that everyone's spirituality is unique, so you have to practice whatever brings you the most love and joy, and whatever allows you to spread the most love and joy out to the world.

Try to be a positive contribution to the planet. Try to be gentle, loving, and forgiving, even when your ego would rather hold a grudge or place blame. Your life in Los Angeles, or any city, will be much more peaceful if you recognize that everyone is a spiritual being just as important as you, from the stranger at the street corner to the casting director in front of you.

Also, if you develop a helpful attitude toward everyone in your reality, it will help make this a much better place for everyone. And think about the fact that you, as an actor, want people to help you to become successful. Can you honestly expect others in the entertainment industry to assist you, if you yourself are not a helping person by nature? Food for thought.

You Are Here to Have Fun!

Wherever you find yourself in life, whether in Los Angeles, your hometown, or another part of the world, try to make it a habit to find enjoyment with whatever you are doing and with whomever you're with. That's my bottom line. Why waste precious time being unhappy? In any moment, you do have the power to change your attitude, albeit in some moments it can be quite a challenge. One of my friends frequently says, "Happiness is a choice." (I know it's not that simple . . . but it's definitely something to contemplate.)

When you are on your deathbed, you won't be thinking about the movies you starred in, the business empire you built, the house you lived in, or the great screenplay you wrote. You'll be thinking about the loved ones in your life and the joyful moments you shared with them. Those are the things that really seem to matter the most in life. Worldly possessions and large sums of money won't have any value anymore. Therefore, nurture friendships and relationships, and try to have fun. Your life will feel much more rewarding.

So when you turn your thoughts to work, do as Ben Whitehair wisely suggests: "Release expectation. I'm an eternal optimist, so I keep my mind on getting better—that brings luck. The Chinese symbol for luck means hard work and opportunity!"

ADVICE FROM ESTABLISHED FILM ACTORS

And now comes advice that's worth its weight in gold—our final three chapters are packed with sage wisdom from some of the most respected pros ever to grace the business. The enduring advice these actors, writers/producers, and publishers impart stand the test of time, and will be as relevant years from now as it is today.

There is a tremendous wealth of information to be had from talking to actors who are very established in the business. Not only do they have practical knowledge, but more importantly, they have collected experiential wisdom over the years that can help new actors stay balanced and be prepared as they pursue an acting career.

This chapter contains interviews with three successful actors: Mariette Hartley, William McNamara, and Michael Harris. They are all very different, in terms of age, background, and the types of roles they play, but all are honest, sincere, and passionate, and have worked many times in a "starring" capacity in both film and television.

Mariette Hartley is an Emmy Award winner and six-time Emmy nominee. As a stage, screen, and television actress for more than forty years, she has starred in a myriad of films, including *Ride the High Country* and *Encino Man*; television series, such as *Peyton Place*, *The Incredible Hulk*, and *WIOU*; and acclaimed television movies, including *M.A.D.D.: Mothers Against Drunk Drivers* and *Silence of the Heart*. William McNamara is an accomplished young film actor, having starred in a number of features, including *Stealing Home, Texasville, Copycat,* and many others, as well as several major television projects, including Showtime's *Beggars and Choosers.* Some of Michael Harris's credits include *Sleep Stalker: The Sandman's Last Rights, Bar Girls, He Said She Said,* and many other film and guest-starring television roles.

Industry Interview: Advice from Mariette Hartley, Actress

You've had a long career. Could you tell me some of the things you've learned about the business, and some things that you feel new actors need to know?

As an actor, what you really need to know is that this is what you want to do more than anything else in world. But also listen to the truth about yourself. I never surrounded myself with "yes men." I always wanted to know as much as they could tell me. What was the truth? If I was trying to sing, I wanted to know that I wasn't making a total ass of myself. I knew that I had people around me, including a husband and a manager, who were very honest with me.

Another thing I had to learn is who I was, because in this town they try to make you into anything that you aren't. To find your center in the midst of this town in today's world— and I'm a mother with children in the midst of this town—is very, very hard.

You do have to have a deep spiritual base. Wherever you can find a deep spiritual base, make use of it. This is the kind of advice that nobody ever gave me, because nobody knew to. You have to have that. Find a church. Find something other than this business, because my discovery is that you can't act unless you have a life, and you can't have a life (supporting yourself by acting) unless you act!

I did this for myself and I would also recommend this to anybody: Get busy writing if you can. Do whatever you can to shore up your own talent. If you can't support yourself writing or acting then get another job. Don't be too proud to get another job. I did. When I was starting out, I went to I. Magnin and worked in budget dresses and found that I could sell. I then went back to acting and came back in a totally renewed way.

Get into a theater group. Start doing scene work. Also, you don't have to just be a good actor. You also have to have an incredible sense of publicity and commercialism. It's very important. You have to do that too. In the beginning, you're your own one-man band. It is a business.

Most people know you from television, movies, and those Polaroid commercials. What's your feeling about the commercials—did they help you?

In those days commercials were not hip to do. But as much as I resisted them, it was the commercials that put me on the map.

Today they are very hip, and I would recommend to anybody to get a commercial agent for narrations, voiceovers, and so on. (It takes a long time to get into voiceovers, because there's a small group of people who only do those.)

How did your strong theater background and training prepare you for film and television?

My feeling is that if the break happens, you've got to be ready for it. So I never stopped working and training. I never stopped toning my instrument. I was always in a group. I was always taking singing lessons and I always did scene work.

I think there are tremendous advantages to having a theater background. There's a style that happens. You learn to work on the arc of the whole story. In films you sometimes do the last scene first, and you've rarely had a chance to rehearse it. That's what makes it so fake. How can you get there from here unless you've really rehearsed? When I did *Silence of the Heart*, I insisted on two weeks of rehearsal, and we had two weeks, and it turned out to be a wonderful movie, because I knew where I was going to go. I could get there. I had done all the work.

The thing I love the most about acting is the process of rehearsal. It's so exciting. It's when the birth happens. It's when the excitement of trying things is really alive. It's so exciting when something evolves.

There's a disadvantage to theater, too. When I was a kid, you got going for a result in theater. In movies, your acting is a much more internal journey. It really is in your eyes. Carroll O'Connor taught me that when I did *The Last Hurrah*. And I keep learning that. And you don't learn that on stage.

The balance of the two mediums is so exciting!

What important things should actors keep in mind as they proceed?

My commitment as an actor is to stay as available to my feelings as I possibly can. I don't know how you portray feelings unless you allow them to become available to yourself—unless you know what the feelings are.

I came from a community where nobody talked about feelings. We worshiped secrets, and that was how we got along. But in 1963 after my dad died—from suicide—I surrendered to therapy and it was the beginning of my life. I deeply needed it.

There are all kinds of therapy for struggling actors, because we crash and burn. It's a very hard business to be in and to stay in with hope. You're dashed to the rocks constantly. You are constantly open to rejection. Where do you go, unless you drink? I can't do that and work, but there are a lot of actors who do drink and take drugs. Where do you go to keep filling yourself up and nourishing yourself? Where do you go so you can go back and nourish your children? Go where you can get help. I have no qualms about saying "How do you do this?" or "Could you help me and teach me how to do this?"

I used to have an enormous kind of pride, which was "I'll do this myself!" That way is such a lonely journey. You don't get to meet people. You don't get to learn things. You're continually embracing only yourself. It doesn't work.

I've been a member of a church since 1963, that's gone through many changes. It's so exciting now. I also found friends in other support groups. The baseline is you cannot do it yourself.

In addition to the arts, you're also involved in charities, for instance, the Foundation for Suicide Prevention . . .

And that happened by accident. That happened through my life. That happened because I did this movie-of-the-week called *Silence of the Heart,* which is about a child's suicide. After being a survivor of my father's suicide for twenty years, I was introduced to the fact that there were many other people this had happened to. I had no idea. Now I meet thousands and thousands of survivors all over the country. They forced me to start talking about it because I was visible. I was a celebrity and I could finally bring a highly visible public spotlight on the topic of suicide. And we've been bringing in thousands and thousands of dollars for research.

I think it's something very important to touch upon in the book, because actors do have a tendency to get depressed. Creative people do. There's a whole study coming out now about creativity and suicide. That's when priorities have to get straight. If I found out that I could never act again, I'd better have another choice somewhere along the line. Whether life will show me or whatever. But to have acting be the be-all and end-all, saying "If I'm not a star, then I'll die!" is not good. When you're on your deathbed, from what I've heard, you do not remember your last job; you remember the last time you held your child's hand. So take time to smell the roses.

When I wake up in the morning, the first thoughts that come into my head are "Thank you. No matter what happens today, if I appear to not be grateful for it, please forgive me because I don't see the whole picture yet." It really helps me a lot. And then I get down on my knees. That's the beginning of the day. It's an amazing journey.

What I would pray is that there is a balance between expectation and fantasy and reality. A lot of actors have a lot of trouble with that. People need to know that building a career takes time, no matter what other people say to them. It's one thing to come here hoping to become a star and being willing to work, but I think people have to know the statistics. There are about 3 percent of actors who make over $25,000 a year. The rest of the people make, literally, $7,000 a year or less. Poverty wages. But if I was new in town and knew that, I don't think I would get scared because I would know my mission was acting. Everybody has his or her own journey, and that's the exciting thing about life and about being a human being. Actors are going to fall down, they are going to dust themselves off, and they are going to start all over again, if they really want to do this.

Industry Interview: Advice from William McNamara, Actor

Could you tell me a little about your background?

I lived in New York City. I went to boarding school since I was twelve, so I was never really around any drama or theater. Theater wasn't very cool—guys dressed up in girls' clothing wasn't very cool.

I always wanted to be an actor when I was really young, but I didn't really know how to go about it. My mom wanted me to go through high school and finish college first. After that, she said I could do whatever I wanted, but I had to complete college. So I ended up at Columbia University in New York, which made my mother happy, and also gave me access to New York City, which had so many teachers, photographers, agents, and commercials.

At Columbia, I took enough classes to get by, the minimum requirement, and meanwhile I started studying acting. Ben Stiller was in my class. We were both terrible. Now he's a big actor/director. I got an agent, J. Michael Bloom, and I started going on commercial auditions. I started booking commercial after commercial. My first year I did ten commercials. So I made about a hundred grand! I was nineteen or twenty years old.

Soon after that, I'd heard about a place called Williamstown, a theater festival—summer stock—so I auditioned for that and got in for the whole summer. My agent said "Oh my God! This is when all the commercials are happening!" But I didn't care. I wanted to go to Williamstown to try it.

What Williamstown did for me was amazing. It was three months of doing Shakespeare, Chekhov, and something different every week. I got to watch Christopher Walken every night in *A Streetcar Named Desire*, because in the daytime I worked, but at night I had to serve refreshments in front of the theater. Like an apprentice.

So I did that, and came back to Columbia. Three weeks into my second year at Columbia, I booked an acting job, which was a movie called *The Beat*. It was only a four-week-long shoot, so I decided I would go to Columbia and explain that I would take four weeks off. I actually rigged it so that I'd get credit for what I was doing. On-the-job credit. I had to keep a diary.

So I did the movie, but then I never went back to school, and I don't really regret it. Maybe it's because I didn't have very good teachers at Columbia. I had pretty bad freshman teachers, which I guess are bad at any university. But you'd think Columbia would be better.

Then I got a mini-series that shot in Morocco and Rome for about five months. That was more of an education to me than anything else, and I made a lot of money. In *The Beat* I made nothing, but when I went to Morocco and Rome I was getting paid a weekly salary that was humongous. I was twenty or twenty-one years old.

Then I did another Italian movie when I was over there, which screwed everything up for me, because I was offered the brother's role in *Bright Lights, Big City* but couldn't do it. I had already committed and shot film on this cheesy Italian thriller. But I met a really good friend of mine, a really wonderful actor, who taught me a lot about Shakespeare. He was a very great English actor named Ian Charleson. He's dead now—he died of

AIDS. Died of AIDS doing *Hamlet* in London. He was the guy in *Chariots of Fire*—the priest who wouldn't run on Sunday. He was a very, very well-known English stage actor.

So I lost *Bright Lights, Big City* because of it. Then I came back to New York. Then I booked a movie called *Stealing Home* with Jodie Foster and that was a big studio movie, so that was a big break. Then after that, I did an after-school special, and some TV movies.

The first time I came to L.A., after *Stealing Home*, I had signed with CAA (Creative Artists Agency). I had done one or two movies with them, small roles that they had put me in, and then I got a movie called *Texasville* that Peter Bogdonovich had directed. It's a sequel to the *Last Picture Show*. I played Jeff Bridges's son.

At the same time I got that, CAA packaged a terrible television series called *Island Son* with Richard Chamberlain. It was his comeback to episodic television, and I played his son. It shot in Hawaii for a year, so that basically screwed me up for a long time.

When I came back to L.A., that series was canceled. I couldn't even get an audition for a feature film or anything. It was pretty terrible. I think I moved back to New York City, and got serious. I got in a really good acting class. I was a professional observer at the Actors Studio.

Then I came out here to L.A. once in a while because the business is so shut down in New York; there's probably hardly anything going on now. As far as making a living, it's really hard in New York. So I'd come out here for a week at a time, and that's how I booked those TV movies.

Then I moved back out here after those movies. I made enough publicity from them and enough money, that I thought I'd take another shot at Hollywood.

How did you support yourself early on, before your commercials?

Well, I worked at a nightclub in New York City called Area, down in Tribeca. I worked on the weekends, because you make a lot of money on tips. I was a bar back—that means you carry all the dirty glasses from the bar to the kitchen, and then you bring all the clean glasses back. In a popular club, you're back and forth. It's just straight nonstop work all night. And I worked at a little restaurant called the Bank Café, and made tips there as a waiter. That sucked.

Prior to becoming an actor, every summer I spent working for Twentieth Century Fox as a production assistant. So I worked on movies. When I came out to L.A., I worked at the Fox studio, so I kind of got the other side of the business. I knew what to expect. I knew how actors were treated.

In fact, the last movie I worked on, I worked in the casting process too, with Marcia Shulman who cast *The Beat*. So I already knew her and I knew how the whole process worked.

You can't take anything personally. And the casting process really is insane. People really are not cast because they're too thin, too fat, have too big of a smile, don't have enough of a smile, their lips are too thin, their lips are too fat. It really boils down to that sometimes.

What other important things should actors keep in mind, emotionally, physically, spiritually? What should they be prepared for?

Well, L.A. can be such a scary place. Whenever I found that I was losing ground or not gaining any ground, I immediately left. In my opinion, it's a really bad place to be when you're not having any sort of success. I'd rather go wait on tables and be anonymous in New York City.

I think it's important for an actor who wants to be a serious actor to get started in New York. At least you can afford a ticket or stand in the back for a Broadway show. You can pay for standing room for about $6 or $12, or be an usher and see the show for free, just to be around that.

So you think theater is really important?

Seeing it is so important. That's what's so inspirational. Every time I see something on TV—like last night there was a thing on HBO about all the black comedians who've made it and they showed Whoopi Goldberg's first thing she did on Broadway with all those characters that she played—and I'm like, "I saw that. I was sitting out in the audience." It's funny. And that was one of Whoopi Goldberg's first big breaks.

I saw so many great plays. I saw *Burn This* with Malkovich four times in a row. I thought he was so awesome. I saw this incredible play called *Breaking the Code*. I saw a play called *As Is*, which is like the original play about AIDS.

New York City is so much more inspirational than Los Angeles. With L.A., you come out here just to get an episodic or to get on a soap, or whatever. And I think that it sort of narrows the scope of things.

Also, the competition out here in Los Angeles is so tough, because everybody from the United States and from Europe is now here. Now all the European actors are coming to L.A. This is the only place where the film business is doing so well. It's like the number two or three business in America—the entertainment industry.

So what would you tell a friend in a nutshell, about what to expect in L.A.?

I think the most important thing is to be prepared, or trained. If you're going to do community college, do an extra two years of community theater. Do it for as long as you can before you go insane. It's almost like telling an Olympic swimmer that you don't need to train until you're at the Olympics. These guys train for four years prior to their one swimming race, or whatever race they have. It's the same kind of attitude and mental commitment you have to have here, because L.A. is like the Olympics of the entertainment business. It's so competitive. You've got all these people from all over the world trying to get work.

The best thing to do is not be so eager to get here. Put all your eagerness and that energy into that training prior to getting here. Sometimes an agent will take you on, and send you out on three auditions and then call the casting director and say, "What's the deal? Give me the bottom line. I just got this guy. Should I keep him?" And if the casting director says, "You know what? He wasn't prepared, he never brought his head up from the pages, he was nervous, and blah, blah, blah" then that agent is going to drop you. So the best thing to do is put all your energy into training before getting to Los Angeles. If that means making the circuitous route, and that means going to Chicago, New York, even Dallas, then fine.

If you're coming from some small town, it would be much more important to do some kind of summer stock or theater all over the United States. There are places to go.

And if you have nothing to write down on your résumé, then you're definitely not going to get an agent—forget about getting an audition. But if you've done twenty-five plays, even if it's regional theater, you're much more likely to get an agent.

Another suggestion is to go to a really good college with a great theater background—NYU, SMU in Dallas, and a lot of other great places. Then, you fulfill your parents' wishes and have them pay for your preparation.

And learning how to audition?

Yeah, in New York City before I ever even went on a commercial audition, I studied for five months. I booked the first commercial I ever auditioned for. I was trained so well. It's all about the preparation. That's what it's all about.

What do think makes good actors really good actors? What qualities make them stand out?

A lot of the actors that I admire are the ones who, when they are working on film or TV, you don't see the acting. It's totally invisible. The better actor isn't necessarily the guy who can recreate what it's like to be coming down off heroin. It's more or less the guy who can come into the room and say to the secretary, "Do I have any phone calls?" and you believe him. That is so much harder to do than a technical exercise of what it is to come down off heroin.

So I like actors like Steve McQueen, who was brilliant at doing absolutely nothing, underplaying everything. He was so real and so attuned to the details of what reality is. I love actors that pay attention to the details.

Also, I love actors who make what they do really interesting. They've always got something else going on. Take the actor who comes into the room asking for messages: At the same time he'll look over at the candy tray thinking about if he wants a piece of candy or not. Always thinking about really making it real—always having another objective, instead of coming into the room acting, saying "Do I have any messages?" and then looking at the phone.

Another actor I've always loved is Don Knotts, on *The Andy Griffith Show*, one of my favorite television shows of all time. Everybody was so real on that show; it's mind-blowing. But the great thing about Don Knotts is that he is so committed to what he is doing, however ridiculous or absurd it is in a scene. He was so committed to that absurdity that you totally bought it. You totally got sucked into his energy. Also, he had a sense of humor about everything. He didn't mind looking ridiculous.

Industry Interview: Advice from Michael Harris, Actor

When you were starting out, what were some of the obstacles you faced?

Part of the problem in starting out as young actor is that nobody knows who you are. The other part of the problem is that you don't know who you are either. You are in your early twenties and you're full of talent and energy and self-righteous indignation, and you've obviously got a really healthy ego or you wouldn't even think of attempting a career like acting. But the question is, "What have you done?" not as an actor, but "What have you done in your life?"

You don't really know who you are until later on. Some people do, and sometimes that makes a big difference in how people perceive you. If you don't really know who you are and you haven't really established a persona with yourself, it's really hard for anyone else to see you. For me, I had a lot of ideas about who I was, but I was in such a state of change. I was not a young leading man on the inside. (I don't know if I looked like that on the outside.) But on the inside, I was never a young leading man, so I was never right for the parts I was right for—because I wasn't right on the inside for them. So I was at a loss. I wanted to play parts of guys who were in their forties, wild character roles.

So that was one obstacle that I came up against: I didn't yet know who I was.

How do successful actors become successful?

I think there are two ways that that happens. It either happens right away and you're hurled into success and stardom in a film that happens to gross $300 million, and you happen to be the person that Rob Reiner or Steven Spielberg points to and says "You!" Or you're on the TV series of Aaron Spelling or Norman Lear, and you're like "Boom!" You made it, you were here for three weeks and you got the gig and now you're famous and rich! This may be the end of your career too. But nonetheless it happens right away.

The other side to that is the people who come and they stay and they don't leave. They continue to work and not work, work and not work, for some extended period of time, between two years and thirty years. Eventually at some point they become a cumulative success.

And that's actually the majority . . .

The majority of people who make a living as an actor are in that category. Of the SAG membership, I think under 5 percent make a living as an actor. And under a quarter of 1 percent become wealthy.

So I guess those are important odds to keep in mind. Not that you should discourage people if they have a passion . . .

Oh, I think you should always discourage people! [laugh]

I met some executive at Universal when I was seventeen, when my hair was down to the middle of my back. I was wearing a lot of jewelry and I said, "I want to be an actor, yeah!" and the guy said, "Well, if there's anything else you'd like to do as much as acting, then go do that."

The only people who are going to make it here or even survive are the people who don't have another choice of what to do. Even with those people, no matter who they are and no matter how special they are, there are going to be at least a hundred thousand other people exactly like them who are just as good as they are. So if they don't really love it and really want to get involved in the process of trying to become an actor, they should forget it because the odds are huge.

And just because you're talented doesn't mean anything. Everybody's talented. Nobody's out here who's not talented, except for some few successful people that we all know. Some people's talent is just who they are. That's their talent. It's something about what they give or how people see them. That's their talent. Their charisma is their talent and that's just as valid as being Robert De Niro or anybody who is a highly skilled, inspired actor.

If you had friends or relatives coming out here to work on a career, and they needed to know how Hollywood works, in a nutshell, what would you tell them? What key things should they keep in mind?

I would tell them, go home! Go back to the incredibly nice life they had before they got the stupid idea to come to Hollywood to start an acting career!

The most important thing to know about Hollywood is that it doesn't matter who you know or how good you are, and it doesn't matter what you know. None of that matters. You could know everybody and still have things not work out. You could be at all the parties and still not be able to survive as an actor.

Hollywood is like Las Vegas. It's just like Las Vegas. It's built on the same premise of chance, for actors. It's not built on hard work.

So if you're a gambling type of person, it's the place to be . . .

And if you like the game, and don't mind losing more than you win in the hopes that you might hit the jackpot, then that's okay. If you don't like that game, and you're not into that process of losing more than you're winning and just trying to manage the losses because you might get lucky eventually, then rethink it.

ADVICE FROM A WRITER/PRODUCER AND A PUBLICIST

Often new actors learn about the business from other actors, which is very helpful and practical, though sometimes it can be limiting. For that reason, throughout the book, I've included interviews with agents, casting directors, teachers, and others to help broaden your perspective on the industry. Now it's time to take a step further and hear from a highly respected writer/producer, Earl Hamner, and a prominent publicist, Michael Levine. Publicists and producers are very important people in Hollywood; every actor should get to know them.

Industry Interview: Advice from Earl Hamner, Writer/Producer (*The Waltons, Falcon Crest*)

What would you tell new actors moving to this town? In other words, what should they expect emotionally, financially, and psychologically while living in Los Angeles and the whole Hollywood environment?

To an actor coming into town, I would say that the preparation should start long before you get here. Ideally, the best thing would be to be born into a very rich family! That way you have financial stability. That seems to be one of the problems that most people that I know face when they come here: how to make a living. I would come with some kind of substantial nest egg, something that would mean that I wasn't desperate, so I didn't go to auditions with the feeling that this is "all or nothing."

Failing a rich mother and father, I would be prepared to find some kind of job. There's no stigma in coming to town and taking a job as a valet or a waiter or waitress, or any kind of so-called menial job.

The other day I was at lunch at Warner Commissary and I asked the waiter, "Are you an actor?" He said, "No, I'm just out here to look around." I thought "Well, this is the most astonishing thing in the world! Here is a waiter who is *not* an actor or an aspiring actor!"

I would also tell newcomers to remember that acting is a business and to prepare for it as you would for any profession. Going on an audition, be as professional as possible with the preparation of the material. Try to give it your best shot the first time you read it. Don't say "If that wasn't right, I'll read it for you again." That shows some self-doubt. It is best to give it everything you've got in the one reading. If the casting agent, director, or producers suggest that you read it again, then of course you would, and take any guidance they will give you. But don't offer to do it again because it might diminish what you gave them in your first reading.

It sounds calculated and self-serving, but I would also, in preparation for the audition, learn everything I could about the people for whom I'll be auditioning. When you get there, a director would love to hear, "I saw your work last week. That was very interesting what you did." We are all human and a quick, sincere compliment to any one of the people participating in the audition can be quite meaningful.

At the same time, those people who are auditioning you are very busy, and one of the worst things you can do is to come in and start a conversation on your own. If the director, producer, or casting agent initiates something or a friendly kind of overture, then by all means respond. But, at the same time, remember that these are busy people and don't overdo it. One of the worst auditions I think I've ever been in is where we couldn't get the person to read. This person kept talking and talking and talking, and finally the director said, "Would you kindly read?"

Just keep in mind how busy these people are. They are professionals and they have been there over and over again, and chances are that their judgment is going to be very professional. If you get the job, it's because you've done a good job and because it's what they are looking for.

Also it's a very good idea not to take it personally if you don't get the job. It's not that you were rejected. It's simply that you didn't meet the requirements. A lot of people get all broken up over the fact that they didn't get the job. It has nothing to do with your interpretation of the role. Maybe the age is wrong or the look isn't right, or maybe the director took an instant dislike to you. There's no reason to take things personally.

Another thing that I've learned from going to auditions and from casting many people is "Don't do anything bizarre." I remember one role I was casting: It was for a young fundamentalist minister. The actor strode around the room as he read the lines. He jumped up on the table. He shouted and he gesticulated, and he scared the hell out of everyone else in the room! Of course, he didn't get the part.

Also, I've found that—this may just be a personal preference—people who dress for the role in an exaggerated way frequently are wrong for the role. If a girl comes in who's going to be a tart and she's got on a short leather skirt and a low cut bra, I think she didn't need to dress the part. If a man comes in and he's trying out for the part of a cowboy, and he's got on a plaid shirt, chaps, and boots, it's just ridiculous. It's much more business-like not to try tricks.

I've done a lot of casting and I've been in some casting sessions that were absolutely thrilling. When I was doing *Falcon Crest*, the actress Ana Alicia came in and was so terrific that she held us all spellbound. It was rather a sexy scene, and Ana did it with such finesse and with such good taste. A scene of that kind could have gone overboard. It could have been embarrassing to her and to us, but it was so perfectly done. When she left the room we all looked at each other, and the director said, "I want to work with her!" I said, "That's the role I had in mind!" Ana is a consummate actress.

I had that same experience with the actress Ronnie Claire Edwards, who plays the role of Corabeth on *The Waltons*. She plays the storekeeper's wife. She was so perfectly right for the role. She understood the role. She did it short, sweet, in, out, and left us speechless with admiration and pleasure. It was just wonderful. It is just so thrilling when an actor comes in and gives you a character right away.

So how could you sum up what you look for in an actor during an audition?

A direct approach to the role. Nothing tricky. Nothing bizarre. Just a very honest appraisal of the role, and then fitting into it, sort of loosely. Don't define it rigidly because the director wants his interpretation, but just like a loosely fitting garment, if that makes sense.

You are the classic story of someone who grew up in a small town—you're from a small town in Virginia—and you eventually found yourself out here in Hollywood as a successful writer and producer. Could you explain what inspired you to be a writer and how you got from there to here?

I have no idea of why I became a writer, except that it was the only thing I ever wanted to do. I think I would have failed miserably at any other thing that I might have tried.

I've wanted to write from the time that I could hold a pencil. I always kept a journal, and whether a writer, or actor, or producer, or whatever we become in this business, I think that keeping a journal is invaluable. For a lark, I once took a course in acting and the textbook was *Six Lessons in Acting* by Stanislavski. One of the lessons is called "Memory of Emotion," in which he tells you that you don't have to murder somebody to play a murderer. Perhaps once inadvertently you killed something—say you ran over a raccoon on the highway—but if you can remember the feelings of having killed a living thing, then you can draw on that memory to play someone.

So the journal I think helps you to look back over your own experiences and when you need that experience in acting, you can draw on your memory.

But, yes. I've been wondering about how I've got from the hills of Virginia to New York. It was a passion to write and it drove me to overcome a good many obstacles, such as being quite poor with no hope of ever going to college, with no hope of really getting beyond those mountains in Nelson County, Virginia. But I had a passion to write and I had a passion to see things and go places, and I did. I went from the University of Richmond to the army, and was fortunate that I was stationed overseas in England and in Paris. Then after the war, I went to the University of Cincinnati. I graduated there and I started writing professionally as a radio writer in 1948. At the same time, I began writing novels and one of those became a bestseller. In 1954, I married Jane, who was an editor at *Harper's Bazaar*. We lived in New York for ten years and then moved to L.A. in 1961. I freelanced for a year and then I was fortunate enough to sell *The Waltons*, which was on CBS for ten years. Then I produced *Falcon Crest* for ten years and now, all these years later, I'm seventy-two years old and I have twenty minutes to live, and I'm a very happy old man!

How would say that Hollywood has changed since you first came here?

I came here in 1961. It was a fairly innocent time. There were shows like *Mayberry RFD* and *Green Acres*—a lot of family shows. It was a kinder, gentler world. As I watched from 1961 to 1995, it became more restricted because it became more of a hard-edged business. People became less interested in quality and more interested in mass appeal, which, of course, means a lowering of standards. I'm not shocked and I'm not surprised, and I'm not even dismayed to see the progress of more frankness in language and in displays of nudity. That happened along with the whole society, as it has become freer and more relaxed.

I always promised myself that when I became a senior citizen, I would be tolerant of young people. I wouldn't say, "This terrible younger generation!" I wouldn't be judgmental and I'd try to stay young with the young people. But I find that now I go into the networks (because I still pitch ideas—I'm still producing a show in Australia and I'm developing another *Waltons* special—we just did one last year), and I feel ancient. I look at the young people who are in positions of authority and they seem younger than my children. And they are! I find a reluctance on their part and I understand it, but I don't forgive it. Because they look at me as if I am their father, and, of course, they don't want their father coming in and telling them how to run things. And it disappoints me.

I have a concrete example: When I first came to Hollywood, Rod Serling was a friend and I sold some *Twilight Zone* scripts to Rod. He liked what I did, and I did a good many of them. Years later, I ran into another person who was a story editor on the new *Twilight Zone*. I said, "I hear you're on the *Twilight Zone*. I know a nice old writer who would love to write episodes for you." He said he would get back to me. A few days later he came back and said, "They don't want any of the old guys." I thought, "Well, that's foolish. But that's all right. I'm still happy doing what I do."

Other changes in Hollywood are that all of the big studios have sold off their back lots. To my great dismay, Warner Bros. is turning the area that used to be the *Waltons* set into a parking lot. They are not destroying the house; they are saving the framework and they are going to move it over to the ranch. When we do revivals or specials, it will be available to us. But we have to move it to leave the original locale. I feel great affection for that area. Will Geer, who's dead, lives there. He's there. You can feel his spirit. I have such memories associated with that area from that time. I can see Richard Thomas when we were just starting out in 1972. I can see all those actors, like Kami Cotler, who was six when we started the series. She is now a grown woman teaching school in Virginia.

Is there any one thing during your career that you've learned, either about yourself or about other people in this town or about show business, that might be helpful to pass on to a new person?

Yes, and I can illustrate it with a story. There's a moral, which is to be arrogant. This is a town where hundreds of actors get off of airplanes, trains, and buses every day. The town is flooded with actors and would-be actors. The competition is incredible, as you know. For every role there are probably fifty people who could fill that role. But because of your agent, your talent, or some past showpiece you've done, you are there to try out for a part.

It's a town where you have to shout to be heard. You have to make your presence known. And when I say to be arrogant, it goes back to a willingness to display what your talent is. When I was in New York right after World War II, I had been writing radio scripts. Then television came, and I would go to see television producers. I found there was a prejudice against radio writers. They would say, "You have been writing for the ear. You can't write for the eye *and* the ear."

So after some rejections I went to see a friend named Mark Smith, a story editor. That was in the Golden Years of television. There was a show called The Theatre Guild on the Air and it was sponsored by United States Steel. I went to Mark and said, "I'm not getting jobs. I've written books and I've written for radio, but I can't get a job in television." Mark said, "Well, what do you want me to do?" I said, "I'd like to show you what I can do. Give me the same assignment that you give your very best writer and for no money I will take the same assignment and I will write it better than your best writer. I simply want to show you what I can do." He said, "Well, if you are that arrogant you must be good. I won't take you up on your offer, but I will give you an assignment." So I've always found that a certain amount of arrogance, if you have the talent to back it up, can help.

There's one other thing I would say to actors: If you don't make it here, there's no disgrace in going home and using your talent there. Sometimes, I think it's probably better for actors to not come directly to Hollywood, but to go to Philadelphia, Cincinnati, New Orleans, or San Francisco and work in theater while you're honing your talents. At the same time, if you're a young person and you have the youth and the looks and the energy, it seems a shame not to use them. But if you're getting along in your years and you aren't making it, don't be ashamed to go back to Cincinnati and open an acting school or take up ice skating, or get married, or have two and a half children, or God forbid, become a normal person.

Industry Interview: Advice from Michael Levine, Publicist, Owner of Levine Communications Office, Inc. (www.LCOonline.com)

Could you tell me how you got started in this business and how you've come to be where you are today?

I was born in New York City and moved here in 1977. I always felt very pulled and called to L.A. and to Hollywood. It's not something I really understand fully, except that underneath my vocational dream was to, in some way, participate in the entertainment industry or in Hollywood. So for me, Hollywood was not a vocation, but an avocation—like a calling to the priesthood. So I came here, and then in 1983 I started a P.R. firm.

Could you explain to the readers of this book the importance of having a publicist?

Well, public relations is kind of like gift-wrapping. I tell people that if I give someone a gift and I give it to them in a Tiffany box, the gift has a higher perceived value in their mind than if I gave it to them in no box, or a box of less prestige.

And so that's what we do as publicists—we gift-wrap things. In the culture in which we live, we gift-wrap our movies and TV stars, our politicians, and our corporate heads, and even, to some extent, our toilet paper. We gift-wrap everything and gift-wrapping is very important.

Then it's another extension of the whole advertising process, I guess?

The difference between advertising and public relations is in advertising you pay for it, and in public relations you pray for it.

You work with a lot of different people in show business— actors, writers, directors, producers. In your opinion, what distinguishes the successful people you know?

Well, I've studied this quite a bit and I do work with some fabulously talented and successful people. The truth is that people who fail in life both personally and professionally have two roots: Most people fail because of fear and most people fail because of irresponsibility.

First we'll talk about fear. Either consciously or subconsciously, people who fail are often scared or frightened. This isn't always a conscious thing; it's often subconscious, and their fear holds them back significantly. They're afraid. They're terrified. Again, it's not always a conscious thing; often it's subconscious.

The other thing is that irresponsibility is a big reason for failure. And the truth is, many people—most people as a matter of fact—to a greater or lesser degree, are flaky. Now that doesn't mean people are all equally flaky. Some people are terribly, terribly flaky—they kind of fall into the "four-square not-very-functional" category, and some people are mildly flaky. One of the things about flakiness, though, that is hard to diagnose is that nobody thinks of themselves as flaky. The most flaky people think they are not flaky.

So fear and irresponsibility are the two things that hold back most people from becoming successful.

What do you recommend to new actors in the business, who have few credits or maybe limited training, who are trying to develop a solid career in the business?

Well, I think that even this book is helpful. I think that information in the beginning is very useful. I think that we need maps. Without information, it's kind of like building a house without a hammer and nails. Now it's possible to build a house without a hammer and nails. I just am not sure it's the most efficient way.

It's possible, of course, to stumble across the right combination of things, but I think that in the beginning the first responsibility is to get a map together. Through the accumulation of information, it's possible to draw a map. That's why I think a book like this can be useful.

So I guess that includes talking to as many people as possible?

Yes, but I have to guide people in this area. I think that talking to people can be useful, but it depends on who you talk to. If you're seeking information about mental health, and you stumble upon Charles Manson and you ask him some questions, I think it's probably not a good idea to talk to him. On the other hand, if you were walking down the road, and you were to stumble upon M. Scott Peck, the author of *The Road Less Travelled*, I think it would probably be a good idea.

It depends on who you talk to. My observation is that often people in Hollywood talk to too many people. Particularly creative people, or actors, talk to too many other actors. I think that one of the biggest problems that actors have is that they don't know any business people. And business people don't know any actors. I think this is a tragedy and a real problem.

What insights can you give about the nature of Hollywood and how it works?

Well, I think that the entertainment industry, which is generally referred to as "Show Business," has an interesting title. It's two words: "Show" and "Business." It's not called "Show Art," it's called "Show Business." I think it's overwhelmingly a business; I know it's overwhelmingly a business! I think that, to the extent that creative people can come to make peace with that, unfortunately despite their very best efforts, it has as much to do, if not more, with who you know as what you know. And that's a painful realization for people. I think those are some possible insights on how to get through this unusual obstacle.

If friends of yours, or your brothers or sisters, were coming to this town to begin an acting career, what words of wisdom would you give them?

The first thing I would remind them of is that all journeys begin as internal journeys, and that they need to have a serious understanding of their real calling in life, and what it is they want to do. If there is anything else they can do besides act, I'd recommend they do it because it's a very difficult life. On the other hand, if they are convinced that this is the only direction God is calling them in, then I would pursue it.

There's a saying that we should "both pray and row to shore," and I think that we should both pray and row to shore. Not only check out what's going on with the spiritual part of yourself and what you're being called to, but prepare yourself. "Rowing to shore" means working actively on making sure that you get to your destination. One of the best ways is by getting information.

MORE ADVICE FROM WORKING ACTORS

Your success will come from the knowledge you acquire and how you apply it with determination and a strong work ethic. This chapter has interviews with four working actors—Max Alexander, Jimmy Wlcek, Veanne Cox, and Brad Greenquist—whose personal stories and situations are shared by many, and whose successes are inspiring because they show the great reward of perseverance.

Max Alexander is one of the funniest people I know. A well-known and very talented comedian, Max has an extensive list of television and film credits. He also regularly performs in Las Vegas and has had great success in television commercials.

Jimmy Wlcek has starred in three different soap operas, *Ryan's Hope*, *One Life to Live*, and *As the World Turns*; numerous television commercials; and has been seen in *Steel Magnolias*, *Walker, Texas Ranger*, and *Sons of Thunder*. His first major "break" in the business demonstrated how the audition process can be like a roller coaster.

Veanne Cox starred in the 1987 Broadway production of *Smile* and in the 1995 Broadway revival of *Company*, for which she received a Tony Award nomination. She has also had supporting roles in several films, including *Erin Brockovich* and *You've Got Mail*, and numerous guest-starring roles on television shows, such as *Seinfeld*, *The Norm Show*, *Caroline in the City*, *Love & War*, *Hope & Gloria*, *Joan of Arcadia*, *Judging Amy*, *Law & Order: Criminal Intent*, and many others. She is the epitome of a hard-working actress, someone every new actor should emulate.

Finally, Brad Greenquist has starred in several features, including *The Bedroom Window, Pet Sematary,* and in many other made-for-TV movies. He has also had numerous guest-starring roles on television series, including *Charmed, Star Trek: Deep Space Nine, Law & Order, CSI: NY, The Practice,* and many others. He offers practical, sensible, and helpful insights for every new person in Hollywood.

Interview with Max Alexander, Comedian and Actor

What are some of the obstacles that you faced when you were first starting out as a comic?

First, there was my ego. When you are first starting out as a comic, you think you are better than you really are. You say, "Oh, I can do that!" You look at other people's careers and other comics and say, "Hey, I'm better than them. I can do that." So in the beginning, my ego got in the way.

Also, the obstacles you meet in the beginning are the same obstacles you are going to face when you get further into your career. You are going to face the obstacles of others saying you are too old, too young, too fat, too skinny. Those obstacles include having casting directors and agents think you aren't funny and you think they are funny.

Also, agents will not see you until you are in SAG; that is a definite, so don't even try to do a mailing when you first get here. The first obstacle is that you have to get into the union. How do you do it? Do extra work—beg, steal, borrow. Try to get into the union as fast as possible.

Not having tape in the very beginning is also an obstacle. People want to see tape. Your 8×10 used to be the calling card, now it's tape. They want to see tape of you. So, if you are not in the union, the way to get tape is to do a student film. Do anything that will give you something on video so they have something to see.

When you were starting out, how did you support yourself?

Well, I was lucky. Before show business, I was in the garment line and I had saved some money. But during my first week, I got a FedEx commercial and eventually became the voice of FedEx. And then two weeks later Sidney Lumet put me in a movie called *Garbo Talks*. I was very lucky.

I also took every comedy job out there. If I had a day off, even if a job didn't offer the money I wanted to make, I worked. I just made the money and saved it, because you just don't know when the work might disappear. I did every comedy job I could, from $15 to $50 a night. I took whatever work I could.

What about "Open Mic" nights?

You have to do the "Open Mic" nights. You have to go on stage as much as possible, and not only do the material that you know works. Also, when you are first starting out, you have to add a minute of new material every week. If you do that, at the end of the year you'll have about fifty minutes of new material. So always do open mike nights. You have to get on stage.

Tell me about your first audition.

My first audition was for a FedEx commercial during my first week. I didn't know how to audition. A comedian, Ron Darion, who's now a producer on Frasier, showed me exactly what to do. He told me how to slate. I didn't even know what "slate" meant. And he told me how to look into the camera.

I went to the audition, and I didn't hear back after two days so I forgot about it and I shaved off my mustache. The next day, they called me back in. I showed up not realizing that I did something wrong. As soon as I walked in they said, "Where's your mustache?" I said, "What mustache?" They said, "You auditioned with a mustache." I said, "Oh." They said, "How fast can you grow one?" I said, "When do you need it?" They said, "Tomorrow." I said, "I'll have it!" So, without panicking, I got the job. I quickly went out to a wig maker who made me a paste-on mustache with some of my real hair and I did the commercial the next day. Do whatever it takes to get the job, and after you go to your auditions, don't change your look before callbacks!

How would you describe how Hollywood works?

There are no rules and a lot of it is luck. You just have to accept that. But you have to develop your talent, train, get better. Get as good as possible because when the luck hits, you have to have the talent to back it up. You have to have the talent.

There are a lot of good people out there and they will never become successful. I don't want to sound like a downer, but that's the way this town works. But if you work at it and persevere, you will get somewhere. Unfortunately, a lot of people quit before their luck hits.

If a young comedian came to you, what would your advice be?

Get on every "Open Mic" night you can in L.A., except for the big clubs. Don't go to the Improv, the Comedy Store, or the Laugh Factory, because you don't want them to know that you are a new comedian. First, get "good" outside of the big clubs, or else they will always think of you as an "Open Mic-er." You have to become famous and really good before you go into these clubs; otherwise it's very hard to grow from there. You actually do lose some steps.

Also, always write. A lot of people say you have to find a point of view. My theory is: Be funny. If you want to be dirty or crass, that's up to you. And, you know, when I first started out, people told me to be clean. They said, "You've got to be TV clean." Meanwhile, Sam Kinison became famous, Andrew Dice Clay became famous, and a lot of others. Just try to be different. It's not so much "point of view," it's about being different, because you'll stick out.

When casting people go to comedy clubs to look for new talent, they are not very creative. They are not going to go in there and say, "Oh, he might be a good actor, let's let him do this part." They want to see on stage an idea from which to make a TV show. So you have to be different. You have to be a precise character. Don't try to imitate somebody. Just be different. You'll stick out.

And, of course, be funny. It's very easy to say, "Be funny," but the truth is you've got to be funny. Don't be sarcastic, just funny. There's a difference between being sarcastic and being funny. Some people will laugh at sarcasm, but it doesn't last long. You've got to be funny.

Also, practically speaking, if you are going to come out to L.A., you have to come out with a good car. I'm not talking about an expensive fancy car. You just have to come out with transportation. You can't rely on public transportation. If you don't have a specific job lined up, you should come out with $10,000 to kind of make it easy so that you don't freak out. I'm not saying you have to. Some people come out with $2 in their pocket and live on a friend's couch. That's just as good. But if you want to make it easy, come out with a car and $10,000 and you can last for six months to a year without panicking.

And then when you first get here, don't worry about an agent or your 8x10s. First, get a job. Get a job that will free you up during the day if you want to be an actor, or during the night if you want to be a comic. And don't worry about not being creative when you work. You are sometimes more creative when you have work, because it keeps you on some kind of schedule.

Finally, tell me about one of your strangest work-related experiences.

Here's a story about the theory of saying "yes" to everything. I went out on an audition for a print job for *National Lampoon*, which was doing a take-off of the *National Enquirer*. They were doing a spoof of the Virginia Slims ads that say, "You've come a long way, Baby." They wanted to have pictures of a guy who eventually ends up in drag. That was the humor for "You've come a long way, Baby." So I went in there and, in the end, it was between me and another guy.

I told them that I already had the outfit, which I didn't, and they said, "All right, you got the gig!" So I went home, and my mom—I thought she would be mad—she was so excited! Being a heavy person also, she took all her dresses out and wigs and everything, and she dressed me up and it really looked great. Then there was a knock on the front door. I looked out the window and it was my brother with his fiancée, who I had never met before. So I said, "I've got to answer the door like this." My mother said, "Sure." My mother was very funny. So I opened up the door and my brother looks at me. And I said, "How are you doing, Mark?" And he said, "Good." Then he turned to his fiancée and said, "This is my brother," and just walked in like nothing was wrong. She looked at me and went, "Oh. Okay."

The other funny thing about getting ready for that job was buying the shoes. (I had to buy the shoes because my mom had small feet.) I was embarrassed. I went outside of a shoe store for like an hour, and just stood there afraid to go in. And when I finally went inside the lady said, "Would you like to go into the back? We help your kind all the time." So, that was that. Don't ever say "yes" unless, of course, you want the job.

Interview with Jimmy Wlcek, Actor

Could you tell me a little bit about your background?

I got my first agent in 1984 in New York and I didn't get my first gig until 1986, which was a *Tales from the Dark Side* episode. That gave me some confidence. In the meantime, I was always auditioning for commercials—never got one.

In 1987, I auditioned for a part on *All My Children*. When I met the casting director, she didn't think that I had a womanizing quality. She told my agent, but my agent convinced her to let me read for the part, and she liked it. Then I read for the producers and they liked it. Then I screen-tested, and all the feedback was "You did it! You hit the mark!" I was excited. And I thought I got it.

In the end, I didn't get it because I wasn't old enough. I was devastated. I went to Texas to visit my mom and sisters, and I figured I wouldn't bother with acting any more because I was never going to get that close. When I came back, I got a phone call saying they sent my tape over to *Ryan's Hope*, and then they just gave me the role. And that's how I got *Ryan's Hope*.

So, for instance, if you're auditioning for *Days of Our Lives*, and they don't take you because you're too young, too old, too blonde, too short, but they liked you and they know somebody in their network is looking to fill a certain role, they'll submit that tape over to that show. So that's how I got *Ryan's Hope*. It was pretty easy. I just went in there, and they pretty much wanted to give it to me.

At the time, I was working for Keebler Cookies in New Jersey in a warehouse loading trucks—mostly graveyard shift. It took me three months to get adjusted to my new job on television and feel like I belonged and deserved getting paid for it. I just felt that I should still be loading trucks.

In the beginning, I just wasn't that good. My confidence was nowhere. Then I got adjusted very well. I loved the show, and it's been my favorite experience ever since.

After the show was canceled, *One Life to Live* created a role for me. I wasn't too happy with *One Life to Live*. In nine months, I asked to be let go because I was up for a series called *True Blue*, which was canceled after thirteen weeks. Grant Show got my role. I had to ask to be let go before they would screen-test me.

Then I did a play Off-Off-Off-Off-Broadway. Eight months later I got *As the World Turns*, and I did that for two years. Then a whole year after that, I came out here to L.A. for pilot season. I've had the chance to do several really good commercials.

If you had a little brother who wanted to start an acting career, what would you tell him about Hollywood?

Well, first I think you've got to give it at least three years. They say if you can get one pilot in three years, you're lucky.

You have to study too. They say that New York actors are usually better actors—more serious—but I find that untrue, because in any class that I've audited or been in out here, the actors are phenomenal and hard-working. So you really have to be in a class, and reading plays, and doing scenes, and working on your craft very hard.

And don't ever take any rejection personally. You have to be tenacious. You can't let people sidetrack you. There are a lot of people who want to mess your head up and try to discourage you. I had one experience when I was starting out where somebody in an office said, "Why do you want to be an actor? Do you really want to be an actor?" He really wanted to see how much confidence I had with that question. And I think I gave it to him. I didn't back away saying, "Well, gees, maybe I shouldn't be an actor." You've got to know that you want to do this and that you're willing to give what it takes.

Tenacity is the key word. Time and hard work. You can't think that you are going to come out here and be a star. Think craft. Think, "I just want to be a good actor. How can I grow as an actor?" Take each thing as a steppingstone—an episode here, a commercial here, a soap, whether an under-five or day-player. That all comes with the territory. You can't think, "When am I going to get my big movie and be on Jay Leno?" Those are few and far between.

The only thing that's really different about Hollywood from New York is the amount of actors. It's just overpopulated with actors in L.A. But I heard someone say recently, "There's not a lot of competition out here, just a lot of people."

At auditions, you see a lot of faces and a lot of guys better-looking than you or taller than you, and you think, "They're gonna kick my ass." But really they are some of the worst actors or the most unprepared.

So whenever you're at an audition, don't ever get discouraged by somebody seemingly better—better-looking than you, more character-y, taller, or someone trying to psyche you out. Don't let that throw you. It doesn't mean squat.

The big thing is just the amount of people. There are probably six times as many actors out here for your part as there are in New York. But this is where you've got to be. With the economy affecting our business so much, they don't fly out to New York looking for actors as much anymore, because they know they have such an abundance of actors here. There's no need for the extra expense of money and time. Today, New York is basically theater, soaps, and commercials. That's why I think actors are all flocking here to L.A.

Do you see any difference between New York agents and California agents?

In New York, if you have soap opera experience, they love that. That's a strong point. Here, they don't care about your soap work. It doesn't mean squat.

Also, at first, you don't want to be represented by too big of an agency that you'll get lost in. You want someone who's going to be a hard worker. I have five years of soap experience on three different soaps, and out here it didn't mean anything. I was shocked. I thought it would be no problem to get an agent. In New York, I got any agent I wanted basically. Out here, they want episodic work. They want nighttime series experience and film.

Jimmy Wlcek Interview with Veanne Cox, Actress

Can you tell me a little about your background and your studies?

I spent ten years in New York. The first two and a half were spent never saying "no." I never said "no" to anything. I said "yes" to everything. I did more Off-Off-Off-Broadway shows in dingy little no-budget, no-money productions. I was rehearsing at one in the morning. Rehearsing another show in the afternoon, and performing another one at nighttime. And it was a great training ground. Basically, I went to the School of Hard Knocks. Actually, I went to the school of

Doing-Is-Learning. Sitting at home saying I wanted to be an actress was not the way I did it. I went out there and I did it over and over and over again.

And then I finally got my Equity card by having balls—no fear—by sneaking into an Equity audition for the musical *Smile*. It was at the end of the day. They came out and said, "We're not seeing anybody else. I'll take your pictures and résumés." There were still ten girls in front of me. And while the woman was taking the pictures and résumés from all the other girls, I snuck in the door behind her, closed the door, went in, and said, "You have to see me. I'll sing sixteen bars, I'll sing eight bars. I'll sing one note." And they said, "Okay." They were all getting packed up to go, but they thought, well, nothing is going to stop this girl. So I did it. I had five callbacks, and I then made it on Broadway!

So you can't be afraid, because if you don't try, you won't ever know. And that was my philosophy, and I got a lot of jobs being fearless like that.

How did you support yourself when you first started out?

Well, I paid the bills by being a foot model. I was a size six, and in *Backstage*, there was a little ad saying "Five/Six Shoe Models Needed for Shoe Shows." And that's how I got into it. I went to a modeling agency and they said, "You've got the perfect foot, we'll send you out on this." (After twelve years as a ballerina, I don't know how it happened!) So I did foot modeling, but basically I really committed to acting.

I lived very cheaply, without a lot of extravagance. Actually, no extravagance. And I committed myself to my art, and I basically suffered for it.

My ten years in New York were full and wonderful, and great, and I've been in L.A. for two years now. And I had a name in New York. People knew who I was in New York, and when I came out to L.A. nobody knew who I was. There were maybe a handful of people who might have seen one of the shows I did in New York. So I basically started from scratch all over again.

Basically, I don't ever say "no." I don't know if that's the best philosophy, but I do know that work breeds work. And when you're working, the energy that you have and the confidence and the exposure is great. You never know who is going to see you, and you never know when that person will come around again. It also keeps your muscles up.

What are some of the things that help to keep you in-tune as an actor?

Well, I can highly recommend a couple of things. Studying. I believe in keeping your instrument in-tune, even when you're not working. Voice classes, acting classes, Shakespeare, everything. I don't have an accredited diploma, but I deserve about ten of them with the amount of studying that I've done!

Also, yoga is a wonderful mind, body, spirit connecting experience. Doing something physical or exercising is a great habit for any artistic person, because I think it clears out the blocks and everything else. Eating right is really important too because all of this running around can really take its toll on you.

I also do a morning diary. That's been a real wonderful thing.

Also, try to have friends who are creative and energetic toward their own artistic advancement. Getting together with them, and not being afraid to say something like, "Hey, let's read a play," is important. Even playing charades is an incredibly creative artistic experience. It exercises a muscle that is totally applicable for whenever you walk into an audition.

Also, watching television is very important if you're going to try to get on television. Because having a knowledge of what's on there and the genres, and what you *can* do, is very important. You need to get a sense of the trends.

Let's say you know some people moving out here. What advice would you give them? How should they set their goals?

There are a lot of people in this business. So first of all, you have to want to do it more than anything else. You have to be willing to sacrifice. You have to be willing to struggle and commit, and dedicate yourself to it. If there is any chance that you want to do anything else, then do it. The competition out here is fiercely fierce.

I would tell them to be prepared to take risks. As I said before, don't ever say "no." Go with your instincts. If your instinct says to go up to someone and say, "Hi, I'm so and so, here's a picture and résumé. I want to work for you," then do it. You've got nothing to lose and everything to gain.

Getting out there and being seen is incredibly important, which means working and doing plays. Getting on stage is important. People will come and see your work. It's much better than going into their office and saying "I'm really good!" Unless you're exquisitely beautiful and you have a great instrument, it's not going to be as good as someone coming to see your work.

Also, you have to have a knowledge of how much money you're going to need. You should have another job as a back-up at any given time to pay bills. Be prepared for long periods of time between jobs. There's a lot of work out there, but there are a lot of people trying to get it.

My biggest piece of advice would be don't be afraid to do something different. You have to just go for it. Do something wildly creative or commit to something wildly creative. Be different. You have to strike something extra-normal, something extraordinary. You have to believe that there is something inside of you, and use it and let it flow. There are just too many people not to do that.

What can you say about pictures and résumés?

It's important to have a picture where you look the best you can. If you're not stunningly beautiful, you need a picture that shows everything that you possibly have to offer, that really shows who you are. It needs to be 3-D, even though it's a two-dimensional picture. And if you are attractive, you need to make it as beautiful as you possibly can be, while still looking like you. In Hollywood, there is an attraction to aesthetics, which is beauty. It's never going to hurt to look the best you can possibly look. Your picture is very important because that's what's going to get you in the door.

When I first went to New York, I lied on my résumé. When I say I lied, I mean that I stretched the truth. I put down things that I had done in my acting class, plays and stuff like that. I'm not advocating it, but if you've got nothing and you want to be an actor, you can't hand somebody a blank piece of paper! You never know what the right thing to do is.

If you stretch the truth and someone calls you on the table, you have to be prepared to say, "You know what, I worked on that play in my acting class really hard, and I did a great job, and it was wonderful. I needed to put something on my résumé." You have to be honest. You just have to be prepared if you lie. And if the person is a real jerk about it, say, "Hey, you got me!"

Interview with Brad Greenquist, Actor

When you were first starting out in the business, what are some of the common obstacles you faced? In your opinion, what obstacles do most new actors in the business face?

Well, complete anonymity is one. You come to a place (in my case New York before Los Angeles) and you don't know anybody in the business. You may not have many friends, which is difficult too. And to succeed you have to let people know who you are.

That first year, I tried to just get settled into the city and become self-sustaining. I learned my way around. It was a step-by-step process of getting settled and getting into a good acting class. I eventually started taking acting classes, which got me out of the college thing and into the real world.

The acting class that I was in eventually led to putting up a one-person production, which, in turn, led to my agent. I had courted the agent for a year. After having seen my one-person show, he signed me. Soon I started booking jobs. I wasn't expecting any sort of quick success, but actually, in a way, that's what happened. (If you can call two years of anonymity a quick success.)

During that first year I had new headshots taken. After another year, I got another set of headshots made. My own personality had changed a great deal in one year, having come from Virginia to New York, which has a way of slamming you around. You grow up very fast! I had changed a great deal as a person in that time, and that was reflected in the second set of pictures. The first pictures were just "average guy" pictures. I look at them now, and I see a hayseed from Virginia! But with the second set, I took some chances with the way I presented myself. I knew how I wanted to present myself. I knew the kinds of actors whose footsteps I felt I could realistically follow in.

Defining who you are and what you can play, rather than thinking you can play everything, is important too. You have to figure out what roles you're going to be marketable in. This is a real problem with a lot of actors, a very valid problem of defining what kinds of roles are going to be most suited to you. It takes asking a lot of people—people you know as well as people you don't know.

Playing any and every role isn't going to happen unless you are a star. When you're starting out, it's better to have a niche. A certain type of role that you could get known for. I had stumbled on it, basically. The roles I found myself getting were invariably bad guys.

Very often in colleges and universities, they still teach the theater repertory system, where you are hired for several seasons in theater and you play everything. With television and film, you've got to find your niche that's going to get you in the door—something that identifies you with a type of role. A lot of actors resent this, but it's just the way it is. Once you've got your foot in the door, then you can try and expand your realm, or (more likely) your agent will try and expand your realm.

It's hard to define what roles you can play because most actors are fairly regular people. It's hard to know exactly where you fit in. It takes years to figure that out and it's really difficult, but it's something you have to do. Often it's figured out for you. In my case, I was fortunate in that the roles I started getting were generally bad guys and other extreme roles. After the fact, I found out that I was quite comfortable playing them and that I enjoyed playing them. But at the beginning I never would have imagined it. Not at all.

So that's what the first year was all about, basically. I've known many actors who in their first year, were just so anxious and impatient and wanted everything to happen all at once. It rarely does, though occasionally that happens. Impatience is good, but you also need persistence.

What are the important things to remember along the way, as you pursue acting?

I think one important thing that is highly underrated among actors and other artists is to find some form of financial stability. You need to find a job that can pay your bills that also doesn't crush you. It should be something you can enjoy that also brings in enough money to sustain you. You're not going to live high off survival jobs, but you need money for expenses like pictures, résumés, mailings, food, rent, and all that stuff.

My first survival job was as a theater usher and I was fired after one day! It was an awful job. I had to sit and take tickets, and I couldn't talk to anybody. It was terribly boring. As it happened, I was scheduled to work on a night when Olivier's *King Lear* was on television, and this was before VCRs were in vogue, or at least before I could afford one. I told my supervisor that I had a conflict that night, so she fired me! Thank God!

Good friends are very important too, both actors with whom you can talk about the business as well as people who are not in the business who can give you a sense of reality about the whole thing. They'll help you realize that not only actors can be downtrodden at times. The things that happen with actors—unemployment, competition, etc.—are not unique to the acting profession. They are everywhere. Actors are just very vocal about it.

Keeping a good sense of self-confidence about yourself is also important, and that can be done through acting classes. Some teachers like to rip people down, and a lot of actors like being ripped down, but I think it's a waste of energy. It's important to find a good teacher, someone you trust, and someone who encourages you. You have to shop around. Every teacher has a different style. It's a very personal thing.

Let's say you know some people coming out to L.A. to start careers as actors and they don't know anything about the business or the way Hollywood works. Based on your observations, what would you tell them about the way Hollywood works?

My image of Hollywood (and Los Angeles, in general) is that the industry works behind closed doors. Every door has a big bright smile on it and everybody is very happy. Very few people say, "Get lost!" They'll say, "Oh, nice to meet you," and then they don't remember your name.

It's a huge network of who-knows-who. This can be very difficult to get into. Some people have success at doing the party thing—meeting people and schmoozing up to them, which is great if you have that ability. There's going to come a time when you'll have to schmooze, as with any business. It's something to be learned.

Another important quality about Los Angeles is that it's an industry, an entertainment industry, unlike New York. That's a big difference I've found between New York and Los Angeles. In New York, you always have the feeling that you are pursuing something as an artist and that the quality of your art is something important, something to be proud of. In Los Angeles, however, it's an industry. The actor is basically a cog in a machine. As an actor, you are at the low end of the totem pole and you don't have much power, unless you're a star. So you've got to learn to behave like a businessperson. If some art creeps into your work, great, but that seems secondary somehow. That's what you do once you have the job and you're on the set.

You've got to learn how to write letters, how to call people, how to keep up relations, how to advertise yourself, and how to make a lot of noise. It doesn't really matter what kind of noise you make, just some kind of noise. Get people to notice you, because there are thousands and thousands of actors out here. You've got to develop a business mind-set. I think actors tend to be more on the artistic side, and often don't want to deal with that stuff.

And in high school or college, there's usually not even one class that talks about the business side of the acting profession.

Where I went to school, nobody knew how to teach any of that. You just have to jump in and figure your way through it. A lot of it depends on luck too. Sometimes you're unlucky. Sometimes you're lucky. Actors often beat themselves up because they feel they are not doing enough, or they're not good enough, when it often just comes down to pure luck.

Sometimes it comes down to, "This actor is with this agency, that actor is with that agency, and we owe that agency a favor." Sometimes it comes down to what they had for breakfast. There's nothing you can do about those things.

One person may say, "That was a terrible audition," and another person may say, "That was a great audition!" It's all very subjective. So you have to satisfy yourself. Don't try to move the auditors; move yourself. Because there is no way you can know what they want. You can guess at what's necessary from the scene and the script. But you don't know what they want, unless they tell you. If they do, you make an adjustment. Otherwise, you have to make yourself happy. They'll know what they want when they see it. Sometimes it's you and sometimes it's not.

What helps to keep your creative juices flowing?

I think acting classes help. Putting together your own show is good too. If you do that, then be sure to get a director. Don't imagine that you're Woody Allen. Get a director.

Also, with audition preparation, it's good to have somebody you trust that can read through the scene with you and help you work on it. It could be another actor, a teacher, a director, or somebody who has nothing to do with the business but who has a good sense of what's necessary. It doesn't have to be an actor. Actually, I've found that when I work on a scene with another actor, he'll generally tell me to act more, and that's exactly what you don't want to do.

If you have the urge to do something creative, it's going to come out somehow. You can't keep it locked up.

What can you say about demo reels?

Here in Los Angeles it's important to have a good reel of scenes. The only problem is: you can only get one by working. In New York, it's not as important to have a reel. But in Los Angeles, it seems to be necessary to have a reel.

I would discourage anybody from filming an acting class scene or a theater piece unless you have a very good photographer. What happens is that, though your acting might be brilliant, if the lighting, photography, and editing aren't excellent, it's not going to impress anybody. And the point of the reel is to impress people and entertain people. You are going to want to put together a reel that people will enjoy watching, not something boring or painful. You want it to be entertaining, like an eight-minute TV show or movie preview! You want to leave them wanting to see more.

Put on little clips in an order that is entertaining. But don't put on something that you've filmed yourself with a little video camera. It will hurt more than help. You've got to put yourself in the mind-set of these people who are hiring you—casting directors, directors, producers. They don't know you, and so you don't want to present yourself as some cheap product. You want to present yourself professionally. After all, this is your career, your profession.

Whatever you do, whether it's getting pictures or résumés, auditioning, putting up your own show, performing a scene before cameras, always present yourself professionally. Strive for a certain level of quality.

A lot of actors will opt for cheap pictures because they may not have the money for good pictures. I think it's better to wait until you can afford really good pictures. I've known many actors who every year get a new picture done, the cheapest thing possible, and every year it's a lousy picture. Whereas if they had just waited a while and saved up some money, then hired a good photographer, they probably would get much better pictures.

The same quality and professionalism goes for résumés, the letters you write, and how you conduct yourself, whether on the phone or in person. If you put up your own show, make sure you have enough money to do it in a professional manner. Don't throw things together, because it only reflects badly on you. It looks like you're a used-car salesman, and you want to behave as if you are selling a Mercedes. You are the Mercedes. I think it's very important that you have a sense of quality about everything. A lot of actors seem to throw things together at the last minute. That's no good. It reflects badly on them.

Of course, it means that there is a financial consideration, which means that you've got to save up the money. If you put up your own show, don't do it unless you have money to advertise it. And advertise it well. Don't just scribble out some flyer, like so many showcase productions do. Why would anyone want to go see a show represented by a less-than-professional flyer? Get a little money together and have somebody help you design something that's really nice. It doesn't have to be tremendously expensive, but it takes a lot of thought, consideration, and asking for a lot of advice.

What about taking risks?

There's a lot of talk in acting classes about taking risks, and of course that's part of your job as an actor. In the craft of acting as well as in business, you do have to take risks. However, a lot of actors really go overboard with this, and behave totally inappropriately in certain situations. Of course, you hear anecdotes of people who are now stars, who say, "When I was starting out, I did this and this outrageous thing." A lot of people emulate these anecdotes, but generally they don't work. There's a level of appropriateness.

Take risks, but within a certain context. If you're doing a Shakespeare play, you're not going to start in a style of Sam Shepard. Take risks, but don't make yourself look really foolish.

APPENDIX A
SAG-AFTRA Franchised Agents

When researching any agent, always consult SAG-AFTRA to make sure any agent you approached is signatory to the union, is currently in business, and to get current website, phone, and email info for that agent. Go to the following links and do a search (it's very easy):

For SAG-franchisees:
www.sagaftra.org/professional-representation/
sag-franchised-agents

For AFTRA franchisees:
www.sagaftra.org/professional-representatives/
aftra-franchised-agents

Great help is also available from the union if you have questions or concerns about seeking representation—go to the following link:
www.sagafra.org/professional-representatives/
agency-representative-faqs

APPENDIX B
Soap Opera Contacts

Casting directors for soap operas are willing to consider new or relatively new actors, so you should send your picture to each soap. Often they need very specific physical types, usually very beautiful people, and that beauty can sometimes be more important than experience.

Along with your picture, attach a brief note explaining that you'd like to be considered for principal work, U/5's (under-five's—parts with five lines or less), and/or extra work. Also, it's nice to briefly introduce yourself. A short paragraph will do. Letters more than a page long usually don't get read. Hopefully you'll get a call sometime within a few weeks.

The Bold and the Beautiful
All Casting Submissions to:
Christy Dooley
c/o CBS
7800 Beverly Blvd. #3371
Los Angeles, CA 90036
(323) 575-4138
(No phone calls. Please include AFTRA membership number, if you have one, on your picture and résumé.)

Days of Our Lives
Principal and Under-Fives Casting Submissions to:
Fran Bascom
Corday Productions
The Pinnacle
3400 West Olive Ave., #315
Burbank, CA 91505
(818) 295-2831

Background Actor Casting and Five Lines or Less to:
Linda Poindexter
Corday Productions
The Pinnacle
3400 West Olive Ave., #315
Burbank, CA 91505
(818) 295-2832
(*Atmosphere Call-In Line is (818) 295-2830. Once your picture is on file, you may call it once a week to leave your availability.*)

General Hospital

Principal Casting:
Mark Teschner
ABC Prospect Ave.
4151 Prospect Ave.,
Los Angeles, CA 90027

Extras Casting and U/5's (Under Five Lines):
Gwen Hillier (same address as above)
Casting Call-In Line is (310) 520-CAST. If you have already worked the show before, then you may call this number to leave your availability.

The Young and the Restless
Principal Casting and Five Lines or Less:
Marnie Saitta
c/o CBS
7800 Beverly Blvd., #3305
Los Angeles, CA 90036
(323) 575-2532
No Phone Calls.

Background Actors Casting:
Susanne Robins (same address as above)
(Include your AFTRA membership number on your picture and résumé.)

APPENDIX C
SAG-AFTRA Contract Specifics

The union offers up-to-the-minute (and updated continually as warranted) contract information at: www.sag-aftra.org/contracts.

Here you'll find sample contracts and contract summaries, plus extremely helpful contact info for departments/point persons in case you have questions or concerns about any contract details or procedure.

For a detailed booklet on the union's most recent actors' agreement (which took effect in July 2014) go to the following link:

www.sagaftra.org/files/sag/documents/sag-aftra_2014_tv_theatrical_contracts_referendum_booklet.pdf

APPENDIX D
Game Show Contacts

If you have some free time, you might consider trying out for one of the many game shows taped in Los Angeles. Not only could you have a lot of fun, but you might also win some cool prizes, a date, or even a whole lot of money! (I know of a guy from college who won $100,000 on *Jeopardy*!) To become a participant on most shows, you typically have to pass several rounds of interviews, from which the best players are selected. It gets to be pretty competitive with written tests and mock game-playing.

Listed below are a few of the standard long-running programs and their contact information. However, many new shows pop-up every year on cable television, and they all offer their contact information on a website or at the end of show. If you see something that intrigues you, then go for it and try out!

Jeopardy
Quadra Productions
10202 Washington Blvd.
Culver City, CA 90230
(310) 244-8855
(Tapes at Sony Studios, Stage 10)

The Price Is Right
2700 Colorado Ave., #450
Santa Monica, CA 90404
(310) 255-4700
(Tapes at CBS-Television City)

Wheel of Fortune
Quadra Productions, Inc.
10202 W. Washington Blvd.
Culver City, CA 90232
(310) 244-1234
(Tapes at Sony Pictures Entertainment)

Family Feud
Email: casting@familytryouts.com
(323)-762-8467
(Tapes at Burbank)

APPENDIX E
Studio Locations and Contact Numbers

ABC - Prospect
4151 Prospect Ave.
Los Angeles, CA 90027
(310) 557-7777

ABC - Burbank
2300 Riverside Drive
Burbank, CA 91521
(818) 460-1000

CBS Studio Center
4024 Radford Ave.
Studio City, CA 91604
(818) 655-5000

CBS Television City
7800 Beverly Blvd.
Los Angeles, CA 90036
(323) 575-2345

Culver Studios
9336 W. Washington Blvd.
Culver City, CA 90230
(310) 836-5537

Disney Studios (Touchstone)
500 S. Buena Vista St.
Burbank, CA 91521
(818) 560-1000

Empire Studios
1845 Empire Ave.
Burbank, CA 91504
(818) 840-1400

Fox Broadcasting Company
10210 West Pico Blvd.
Los Angeles, CA 90035
(310) 369-1000

Hollywood Center Studios
1040 N. Las Palmas
Los Angeles, CA 90038
(323) 469-5000

Jim Henson Studios
1416 N. La Brea Avenue
Hollywood, CA
323-802-1500

KCAL TV - Channel 9
5515 Melrose Ave.
Los Angeles, CA 90038
(323) 467-5459

KCBS - Local CBS -
Channel 2
6121 Sunset Blvd.
Hollywood, CA 90028
(323) 460-3000

KCOP - UPN - Channel 13
915 N. La Brea
Los Angeles, CA 90038
(323) 851-1000

KTLA - Channel 5
5842 Sunset Blvd., Bldg. #1
Hollywood, CA 90028
(323) 460-5500

KNBC - Burbank Studios -
Channel 4
3000 W. Alameda Ave.
Burbank, CA 91523
(818) 840-4444

The Lot (formerly Warner
Hollywood Studios)
7200 Santa Monica Blvd.
West Hollywood, CA 90046
(323) 850-2500

NBC - Hollywood,
Sunset-Gower Studios
1420 N. Beachwood Ave.
Hollywood, CA 90028
(323) 617-0153

NBC Television
3000 W. Alameda Ave.
Burbank, CA 91523
(818) 840-4444

Oakridge TV Studios
(formerly Glendale Studios)
1239 Glendale Ave.
Glendale, CA 91205
(818) 502-5500

Paramount Pictures
5555 Melrose Ave.
Los Angeles, CA 90038
(323) 956-5000

Production Group
1330 N. Vine St.
Hollywood, CA 90028
(323) 469-8111

Raleigh Studios
5300 Melrose Ave.
Hollywood, CA 90038
(323) 466-3111
also at:
650 N. Bronson Ave.
Los Angeles, CA 90004
(323) 466-3111

Ren-Mar Studios
846 N. Cahuenga Blvd.
Hollywood, CA 90038
(323) 463-0808

Sony Pictures Entertainment
10202 W. Washington Blvd.
Culver City, CA 90232
(310) 244-4000

Sunset-Gower Studios
1438 N. Gower St.
Hollywood, CA 90028
(323) 467-1001

Warner Bros. Studios
4000 Warner Blvd.
Burbank, CA 91522
(818) 954-3000

20th Century Fox
10201 W. Pico Blvd.
Los Angeles, CA 90067
(310) 369-1000

Universal Studios
100 Universal City Plaza
Universal City, CA 91608
(818) 777-1000

Valley Production Center
6633 Van Nuys Blvd.
Van Nuys, CA 91401
(818) 988-6601

GLOSSARY

action: a director's cue to begin filming.

A.D.: an assistant director. While a hierarchy of A.D.s exists (i.e., first assistant director, second assistant director, second second assistant director), their duties generally include helping to set up shots, coordinating and writing call sheets, and directing and corralling extras.

AFTRA: The American Federation of Television & Radio Artists, which governs programs that are shot on video tape (not film). These include sitcoms and soap operas, as well as voice-overs for radio and television.

agent: an individual representing actors. They submit actors for parts, negotiate contracts, and support and guide their careers.

atmosphere: another term for "extras" or "background artists."

audition: when you try out for a role in a production.

back to one: going back to your starting, or first, positions when a scene is being shot take after take.

background: another term for extras or atmosphere.

bit part: a small part, usually consisting of a few lines.

boom: the overhead microphone used to record actors' voices.

bump: a pay adjustment or increase for performing a special activity in a scene (pertains to extras).

callback: when you're called in to audition for a part a second, third, or fourth time.

call sheet: the daily sheet for a production that lists all the scenes to be shot that day as well as actor and crew arrival times.

call time: the time you are supposed to report to the set.

calling service: for extras, a company that helps to book them on extra jobs.

camera right: when looking into the camera, your left.

camera left: when looking into the camera, your right.

casting director: the person who is hired to find the most appropriate actors for each role in a production.

continuity: the concept that all shots in a scene should match in terms of props, dialogue, and extras.

craft service: the food table on a set, or refers to the person(s) who handle the food.

crew: everyone on the set who is contributing to the production, in addition to the cast.

CU: a close-up shot.

cut: the director's cue to stop filming.

day-player: someone who is hired at SAG scale (minimum) for the day.

D.P.: Director of Photography. The person in charge of designing and lighting the shot. They have tremendous influence on the overall style of the film.

first team: the actual cast members who are being used in a given scene.

golden time: refers to overtime paid after working sixteen hours straight, equal to one's daily rate every hour.

grip: someone who handles, carries, moves, and stores lighting, electrical, and other equipment on the set.

headshot: an 8x10 photograph of an actor.

holding area: place where extras are kept on a set or location.

honey wagon: the trailer on a set that has mini-bathrooms.

(on) location: place other than a studio lot where filming is done.

looping: when actors re-record their voices after filming has been completed, usually to replace or repair unclear dialogue.

marks: exact locations of an actor's feet on the floor during sequences of a shot.

meal penalty: a small payment actors receive when not being served a full meal after every six hours of continuous work.

must join: a non-union actor who must join SAG because they have already worked union once before under the Taft-Hartley law.

omnies: sounds or exclamations extras make as a group.

P.A.: a production assistant. A coordinator on a set, who usually gophers and manages the extras.

pantomime: being silent, yet appearing to talk.

photo double: an actor, usually an extra, used in place of a principal actor who is either unavailable or only seen partially. Never any speaking lines.

pick-up shot: small parts of a scene that are re-shot, usually because all angles were not captured satisfactorily during the first shooting.

P.O.V.: the point of view that is filmed, usually referring to that of one of the actors.

principal player: an actor with lines, paid at least SAG scale.

print: director's cue that the shot was good enough to "print" or use.

reel or tape: an actor's video compilation tape of his or her best work.

residuals: payments an actor receives each time a commercial or program airs.

rolling: cameras have been turned on and film is rolling.

rush call: when actors, usually extras, are rushed to a set on a moment's notice.

SAG: the Screen Actors Guild, a union which protects actor's rights and guarantees certain wages.

SAG-eligible: a non-union actor who is eligible to join SAG by being cast in a principal role, being a member of an affiliated union and having had a principal role under that union's jurisdiction, or performing three days of union extra work. Also known as a "must join."

SAG-franchised: status of an agent or agency that has signed papers with SAG and agrees to operate within SAG guidelines.

scale: minimum SAG daily wage for principal actors.

second team: group of stand-ins who replace principals before each shot on a set.

sides: partial script pages used for an audition.

silent bit: when an actor or extra performs a noticeable or required action in a scene (no lines).

slate: at an audition, stating your name and sometimes your agency for the camera.

speed: exclamation that indicates the film and the audio tape are running simultaneously at the correct speed.

stand-in: person who stands in place for a principal actor when shots are being set up. Usually similar in height, weight, and appearance.

strike: remove something from a set, or tear it down.

Taft-Hartley Law: law that allows non-union actors to work under a union contract for their first role. After that, they must join the union.

U/5 (Under Five): five lines or less, on AFTRA shows. This category has a specific pay-rate, less than day-player.

upgrade: a pay-rate increase, usually from "extra" status to "principal" status.

voice-over: when an actor has lines but is not seen, often for a radio or T.V. commercial.

wrapped: finished, done for the day.

INDEX

Books from Allworth Press

Allworth Press is an imprint of Skyhorse Publishing, Inc. Selected titles are listed below.

A Life in Acting: The Actor's Guide to Creative and Career Longevity
by Lisa Mulcahy (paperback, 6 x 9, 192 pages, $16.95)

Actor Training the Laban Way: An Integrated Approach to Voice, Speech, and Movement
by Barbara Adrian (paperback, 7 ⅜ x 9 ¼, 208 pages, $27.95)

Building the Successful Theater Company
by Lisa Mulcahy (paperback, 6 x 9, 240 pages, $19.95)

Business and Legal Forms for Theater, Second Edition
by Charles Grippo (paperback, 8 ½ x 11, 240 pages, $28.95)

Creating Your Own Monologue
by Glenn Alterman (paperback, 6 x 9, 208 pages, $14.95)

The Health & Safety Guide for Film, TV & Theater
by Monona Rossol (paperback, 6 x 9, 256 pages, $19.95)

The Lucid Body: A Guide for the Physical Actor
by Fay Simpson (paperback, 6 x 9, 224 pages, $24.95)

Mastering Monologues and Acting Sides: How to Audition Successfully for Both Traditional and New Media
by Janet Wilcox (paperback, 6 x 9, 256 pages, $29.95)

Promoting Your Acting Career
by Glenn Alterman (paperback, 6 x 9, 240 pages, $18.95)

Starting Your Career as an Actor
by Jason Pugatch (paperback, 6 x 9, 320 pages, $19.95)

Starting Your Career in Voice-Overs
by Talon Beeson (paperback, 6 x 9, 208 pages, $16.95)

Voiceovers: Techniques and Tactics for Success, Second Edition
by Janet Wilcox (paperback, 6 x 9, 208 pages, $19.95)

VO: Tales and Techniques of a Voice-Over Actor, Second Edition
by Harlan Hogan (paperback, 6 x 9, 256 pages, $19.95)

To see our complete catalog or to order online, please visit *www.allworth.com*.